GCSE for AQA

Busin Studies

Second Edition

Jonathan Sutherland &
Diane Canwell

United Kingdom: Folens Publishers, Waterslade House,
Thame Road, Haddenham, Buckinghamshire HP17 8NT
Email: folens@folens.com

Ireland: Folens Publishers, Greenhills Road, Tallaght, Dublin 24
Email: info@folens.ie

**Consulting Editor: Ann Bennett,
Subject Leader Business Studies,
Icknield High School, Luton**

Project development: Rick Jackman (Jackman Publishing Solutions Ltd)
    and Adrian Moss (Instructional Design Ltd)
Editor: Yvonne Percival
Design and layout: Patricia Briggs
Index: Indexing Specialists (UK) Ltd
Cover design: EMC Design
Cover image: The Physicist/Fotolia

First published 2007 by Folens Limited
This edition first published 2009

British Library Cataloguing in Publication Data. A catalogue record
for this publication is available from the British Library.

ISBN 978-1-85008-455-6
Product code FD4556

Contents

Introduction: Studying and the exam

What is the unit about?

Unit 1 provides an idea of what it is like to set up and run a small business. It looks at the kind of activities a business gets involved in, and why some are a success and others a failure. The unit is split into five parts, each of which focuses on a different aspect of setting up a business:

- Starting a business
- Marketing
- Finance
- People in business
- Operations management

The unit headings, and the amplification (additional information and required coverage) exactly match the specification. Throughout, business terminology is kept to a minimum. Remember that Unit 1 is the foundation unit; the concepts, techniques and ideas that you will go on to study all build on this unit.

Why is it important?

Small businesses are of considerable importance to Britain. They provide a vast range of products and services to tens of millions of people, and they provide employment, taxes and income for the country through the sale of their products and services around the world.

Unit 1 looks at the process of setting up a new business, where ideas come from and how they are developed, what type of people want to start their own businesses and many of the basic worries and concerns they may have when they start out. The unit also provides the basic information that you will need to study Unit 3: Investigating Businesses. Unit 3 does not have an exam, as it is a controlled assessment, but it is based entirely on the content of Unit 1. So, to master Unit 1 is to master 65% of the full GCSE.

What is the assessment like?

The assessment for Unit 1 is a 1-hour written examination paper, worth 40% of the entire GCSE mark. There will be 60 marks available on the paper, equivalent to one mark per minute on average. All the questions in this book are based on that formula; in other words, if a question is worth 4 marks you should spend no more than 4 minutes on it, otherwise you will find that you will not have enough time to answer other questions that may be worth more marks. Timing is only one consideration, however. The quality of the answer is also very important.

ASSESSMENT OBJECTIVE	WHAT IT SAYS	HOW IMPORTANT IS IT?
A01	Recall, select and communicate knowledge and understanding of concepts, issues and terminology.	12% of the marks for this unit and 30% of the overall GCSE.
A02	Apply skills, knowledge and understanding in a variety of contexts and in planning and carrying out investigations and tasks.	14% of the marks for this unit and 35% of the overall GCSE.
A03	Analyse and evaluate evidence, make reasoned judgements and make appropriate conclusions.	14% of the marks for this unit and 35% of the overall GCSE.

How do I get a good grade?

Examiners use a uniform marking system, which means that you will need 36 marks out of 60 (60%) to achieve a grade C, or 54 marks (90%) to achieve an A*. However, it is important to remember that whatever your mark for this paper, your final GCSE mark is gained across the three units.

Examiners are particularly interested in the *quality* of your answer. They have set three assessment objectives, as shown in the table above.

So we can see that Unit 1 is worth 40% of the GCSE. The examiners will also be interested in ensuring that you produce good-quality written English:

- Writing needs to be legible.
- Words must be spelt correctly.
- Punctuation and grammar should be accurate.

- Your meaning should be clear.
- You should use a style of writing that is appropriate.
- You should organise your information clearly, and use specialist words when needed.

Wherever you see this logo: ⏩ you will find a section of text specifically designed to help you extend your understanding of a particular aspect of the specification. These sections will help you analyse and evaluate information in a manner required by the examiner for the assessment objective AO3.

Each of the double-page spreads has a set of questions on the right-hand side, all of which follow the mark-a-minute system. You should pay attention to the marks offered for each question. For example, if a question asks you for 'three advantages' but

offers six marks, you know that it is not looking for a three-word answer, but requires a little more depth. Similarly, it is important to provide explanations when required, or to show your working out when doing a calculation.

At the end of each section there is a revision guide with a set of integrated questions. The sections build up to this final spread, which takes questions from a broad area of the specification – not simply what you have just read. The deeper you get into the unit, the more likely you are to come across questions that require you to apply knowledge gained from other parts of the unit, just as you would in the exam. This is excellent practice for the exam, and it is a very good idea to get into the habit of answering all the questions you come across in the book.

UNIT 1 SETTING UP A BUSINESS

What is a business?

What is a business?

A business is an organisation that sells products and services to **customers**, other organisations and government.

Most businesses have the main objective of making money (a **profit**). To do this, they may have to take risks. However, not all businesses operate just to make money. Some are owned by a large number of people called **shareholders**. Some businesses put the majority of their profits back into the business. Others are run like charities to provide services to people for free, or at a reduced cost.

There are several different types of business. In this unit we will look at sole traders, partnerships and private limited companies. Once you understand what these are, you will recognise plenty of examples in your local area.

Sole traders tend to be quite small, often only one or two people working together, with one of them as the owner or boss of the organisation.

Partnerships can be bigger groups of people (between two and 20 partners). The partners share the responsibility of running the business, own a part of the business and, as we will see, have unlimited liability. This means that if the business fails, they may have to sell off their own belongings to pay the debts of the business. The profits are shared by the partners.

Private limited companies are more complicated. They are owned by shareholders. Shareholders simply own a part – or a share – of the business. The more shares they own, the greater their level of ownership. The managers of the business are normally shareholders. They probably get a wage or a salary, but they also get extra money (known as a 'dividend') if the business is doing well. Many shareholders do not work for the business at all, but are simply investors.

A business can operate in almost any area of work. For example, manufacturers make things like cars or washing machines. Plumbers and decorators provide a service. Retailers run shops, and **distributors** supply the shops. Agricultural businesses grow crops or raise animals. Financial businesses offer banking, insurance and mortgages. Utility businesses provide us with gas, water and electricity and deal with sewerage. Transportation businesses deliver goods up and down the country, or run buses and trains. Some businesses are small; others are huge, with shops or offices around the world.

In this unit we will look at small new businesses, how they are set up and what is in store for them. They need to get it right to have the best chance of survival. Just opening a shop because you want to, and hoping that people will walk through the door and buy things does not usually work. We will see how businesses make their ideas work and why it is important not to leave anything to chance.

2

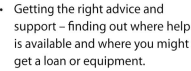

Why are businesses set up?

Lots of people dream of setting up and running their own business. If someone has a great idea and lots of ambition, they will almost certainly consider it. It might mean having to put in long hours, but with hard work and commitment the business can succeed.

People set up businesses because they like the idea of being independent and not working for someone else. And they get to keep the profits they make – after they have paid tax, of course.

People can have a sense of achievement and pride in setting up their own business. They need to be positive, committed and willing to work hard to succeed. Lack of experience can often be a big problem. Greater independence means more responsibility; there is no-one else to take the decisions.

A lack of skills, qualifications and training can slow things down, and many people do not know the first thing about managing a business. It can be difficult to attract finance and to convince customers that you know what you are talking about. The owner of a new business needs to prove himself or herself – fast.

There are legal issues too – rules and regulations that determine what you can and cannot do and what is expected of you. But finding the finance you need to start up a new business is often the most challenging part. There is plenty of help and advice available, but the business owner needs to plan properly, get advice, and research the market to see if there really are customers out there and how many other businesses are offering the same product or service.

Someone looking to start a new business needs to think about:

- Being fully committed to it – it is going to be hard and there will be plenty to do. Just being enthusiastic will not be enough. You may have to sacrifice a lot to make it work.
- Being fully prepared – the business needs to be planned in advance before the start-up. If the planning is in place, people will take you more seriously, including banks and others who might help out with the finance.
- Getting the right advice and support – finding out where help is available and where you might get a loan or equipment.
- Thinking things through – choosing the right time to start up is crucial. Is it the right time for you? Is it the right time for every other reason?
- Having a market – are there customers who will be interested in buying your products and services?
- Being able to compete – does the business have something special to set it apart from the competition?

We begin by looking at starting a business enterprise, why people do it and what they have to think about.

3

K E Y   T E R M S

Customers ▶ people and organisations who buy products and services.

Profit ▶ the difference between a business's income and its expenditure.

Shareholders ▶ people and organisations that own a part (or a share) of a business.

Distributor ▶ a business involved in handling products or transporting them.

Sources of business ideas

Where do people get their ideas from?

People look for opportunities. They may not necessarily have any specialised knowledge, but they try to make more use of what they see and hear, and then identify an opportunity. Opportunities exist where individuals want a particular product or service that is not yet available. in short supply. better quality, or cheaper.

In looking at whether an opportunity has the potential to become more than just a good idea, a number of questions need to be asked:

- Is it a real business opportunity?
- Is there a market for it?
- Is there a gap in the market that the business is aiming to fill?
- What will the competition be?
- How long will the opportunity be likely to last?
- Has the opportunity been correctly identified?
- Is there sufficient and accurate information about the opportunity?
- Is it possible to come up with a product or service to meet the opportunity?
- What are the most likely risks that will be faced?
- Is the opportunity worth the potential risks?
- Will the potential rewards outweigh the risks?

For example Wensleydale Foods

In 2005, Elizabeth Guy, the mother of three children, spotted a gap in the market and created Wensleydale Foods. She created a range of potato-topped pies without additives or preservatives that provide nutritious, home-cooked-style food for young children. She now has a successful line of food products stocked by Waitrose and Budgens.

Many existing businesses use research and development to come up with new ideas. Ideas can come from a variety of different internal sources, such as suggestions from employees or brainstorming sessions. Some businesses have their own research departments which focus on new product or service ideas, or on ways to sell existing products or services to new markets.

Valuable business ideas may also come from outside the business, for example from customers. Many businesses will have customer service hotlines to encourage feedback, and their websites may have comment and feedback pages. Not only does this help the business understand what customers want now, but it also gives them vital clues as to what customers may want in the future.

Businesses can be set up to produce goods (manufacturers), to supply services, to distribute goods (**wholesalers**) and to sell them (**retailers**). Coming up with an idea is only half the battle; now the problem is to see if it might work.

How do they know it will work?

The actual chances of success of what may appear to be a great business idea are comparatively low. Coming up with the idea is just the first stage. The ideas now need to be screened, developed, tested and re-tested before they can be launched onto the market.

People need to be able to spot gaps in the market and then to develop new ideas for products or services. Sometimes they have to think of different ways of satisfying a particular customer need.

Regardless of how clever new product or service ideas are, on average around 80% of them fail. This is because people often do not

---

KEY TERMS

Wholesalers ▶ businesses that take stocks of products from a number of suppliers and sell them on to other businesses, such as retailers.

Retailers ▶ shops (and now also websites) that sell products direct to customers or consumers.

Market research ▶ the process of gathering information about customers, competitors and market trends.

For example: Blue badge protector

In the UK, 2.5 million disabled people have blue parking badges. Thousands of blue badges are stolen from cars every year. Gowrings, a business that adapts cars for wheelchair users, learnt about the theft problem from their customers and immediately spotted a gap in the market. They came up with a simple solution: a steel case for the blue badge, with a lockable steel cable that is fed through the case and around the steering wheel of the car. A thief would have to use bolt cutters to steal the blue badge.

really understand the market they are entering. Also, in a lot of cases, people do not understand what their potential customers want, nor the strengths and weaknesses of their competitors. Careful **market research** is important, but this can often be difficult for a new business start-up that lacks resources.

Ground-breaking new products may require a significant level of long-term investment by a business. Once a gap in the market has been identified, probably through market research, the original idea will be developed. The new idea will then be turned into an initial design, and a brief will be prepared, outlining the product's major characteristics and functions. Then working samples – or prototypes – will be made and tested. These can be passed on to groups of typical consumer, to gauge their reactions and deal with any faults that may only become apparent when they are being used.

Assuming that all these stages have been passed successfully, the product will then move towards manufacture. The business will need to decide how many units to produce, and where to produce and organise the materials required to construct the product. The business can then go into full-scale production and launch the product onto the market.

A new product or service does not just have to be a great idea. It needs to look right, be easy to produce and to work. A great idea may not look, feel, smell or taste right. Many great ideas fail. Some products are too expensive to make, which will make them too expensive for customers to buy; others cannot be made quickly and efficiently, or may have to be handmade, such as pottery or jewellery. Functionality is important too – not only does the product have to work, but it also has to be reliable.

> Coming up with a great idea and proving that it will work is no guarantee that the business will be able to get started. It needs financial backing and the idea must be protected. If the idea is not protected, someone, somewhere, is going to copy it or come up with the same plan.

QUESTION TIME
6 minutes

In 1978, James Dyson saw that powder particles clogged vacuum cleaner bags. He came up with the idea of a system that would remove the powder particles. It took five years and 5,127 prototypes for him to come up with the first bagless vacuum cleaner. The first versions were sold in Japan for US$2,000 each. With the money he made, James Dyson set up a research centre in the UK and decided to manufacture his own model. It then took him 14 years to get his first product into a shop. Dyson is now believed to be worth at least £1 billion. The business has an income of over £500 million a year.

5

1 What is meant by a prototype? *(2 marks)*

2 How did James Dyson make sure that his business idea got all the support it needed? *(4 marks)*

Looking for a gap in the market

What is a niche?

A niche is a segment or a small part of a larger market. Smaller businesses often target these niches, trying to exploit a part of that market.

Usually a niche market involves creating a product or service that is not being offered by mainstream or larger businesses, so potential demand is not being met by any current supply. Larger businesses may not be particularly interested, because the sales in that niche market may be low in comparison to the markets they are already supplying.

Research by small businesses involves finding out precisely what the people represented by a market would buy if they knew that a particular product or service were available. The idea is that there is a demand for a particular product or service, and that the business or the entrepreneur (see 'Reasons for starting a business' on pages 10–11) recognises this.

How do you spot that gap?

There are many different ways of identifying a gap in the market:

- **Timing** – any business could consider changing its opening hours. By opening later, earlier, or for longer, new customers could be attracted to the products and services offered. For example, when some retailers such as Marks & Spencer have a sale, they will open their stores at 7am to attract customers before they go to work.
- **Size** – if the business made the product in a different size, would that appeal to a new market?

For example Lush

The handmade cosmetics company Lush produces a range of small tins of solid perfume that can be carried in a pocket or a purse. This is in addition to their traditional-size liquid perfumes.

- **Adapting** – an idea that may have proved successful in another part of the country or abroad could be brought to an area or a country where it is not currently available.
- **Location** – although an increasing number of products

TECHNIQUE	EXPLANATION
Updating an old idea	• Some products and services may have sold well in the past, but for some reason have stopped selling. Other products may have been selling well overseas for many years. With slight adjustment, it may be possible to give an old idea a new lease of life
Using the Internet	• Many of the supposedly great Internet start-up ideas were not particularly unique. Many of the early ideas failed. The Internet can, however, give extra value or a competitive edge that makes a particular product or service unique
Solving customer problems	• Many larger suppliers do not really satisfy the needs of customers. They are simply too large to pay attention to individual customers. For smaller businesses this is an ideal gap in the market, providing they are prepared to meet the needs of customers and match their expectations
Creating inventions and innovations	• Inventors and innovators come up with a product or service idea and then try to see if there is a sufficient market for it. Some may come across a particular customer problem and then aim to solve it. In many cases there may not be a need for what has been invented, no matter how clever it is
Marketing other people's ideas	• Reading business magazines and looking at websites may give an entrepreneur a basic idea for a new product or service that could be adapted
Being different	• Finding a USP – a unique selling point (or proposition) – is the goal of many businesses and entrepreneurs. A USP is something about the product or service that is unbeatable and gives the business a competitive advantage that cannot easily be copied

and services are sold over the Internet, many customers still prefer traditional forms of shopping. In a typical high street or market town, small retailers cluster around major shops or markets. On the outskirts of Norwich, for example, several smaller businesses can be found close to larger retailers like Sainsbury's, Boots and Pet World.

The table below shows some other ways that gaps in the market can be spotted, and gives examples of how that technique has worked for small businesses.

> A niche needs to be small enough for big businesses not to bother with, but big enough to make the effort worthwhile. The niche may just be too small, or the people in that niche may not have the money to spend, no matter how good the idea, product or service.

EXAMPLE

- The classic board game 'Monopoly' has been transformed. It is now possible to buy a 'Monopoly' game of Paris, of a Premiership football team or even of towns in Cornwall, rather than the traditional game of London streets

- Online employment agencies offer business clients information on wage rates and updates on employment law. They can also give applicants interview tips and other career advice

- Smaller businesses can create a close relationship with the customer, providing them with a personal service rather than the standard level of service offered by larger businesses

- The classic example is the 3M Post-it notes. When the Post-it was created, there was no obvious market for glue that would not permanently stick. But nowadays there are few office desks in the world without a pile of Post-it notes

- Many of the home-working ideas that are offered, suggesting that people can get rich quick, are in fact fake and illegal. Ideas are likely to have been protected by law before they ever appear in the media

- James Dyson's original USP was a bagless vacuum cleaner. Amazon's USP was one-click shopping

QUESTION TIME
7 minutes

Surfing could be big business for the south coast resort of Bournemouth. An artificial reef costing £1.1 million is being built to create a wave-maker. Surfers can pay £500 just to get the basic equipment they need. Now tiny 'surf pod' apartments are being built and sold at around £100,000 each, with pull-down beds, balconies and car parking. The first 45 were sold in 40 minutes! More surf pod developments are planned.

1 **What kind of customer would buy a surf pod?** *(4 marks)*

2 **Why might the demand for surf pods be affected if the artificial reef is delayed?** *(3 marks)*

Identifying a product niche or market niche

What is a product niche?

Identifying a product niche means finding a type of product or service that is not being made or offered by an existing business. At the very least, the products or services being offered already are not quite what is needed or do not do the job required.

A product niche needs to be:

- different from the mainstream product or services
- achievable, in that it can be made or provided (maybe it is not being made or provided at the moment precisely because it is unachievable)
- a product that can be sold for slightly more than the usual price for a similar product
- versatile enough to be sold to other markets in the future.

What is a market niche?

The total supply and demand for a product or service is called a 'market'. Part of the market is known as a 'segment', and a small segment is called a 'niche'. Some niches are tiny – e.g. the market for cars is huge; the market for jeeps is smaller (a segment); but the market for pink jeeps is tiny (a niche).

A market niche needs to be:

- big enough, with people in it who have enough money to spend
- potentially growing, not shrinking
- of little interest to bigger businesses
- something that smaller businesses can do or cater for with the skills and resources they have
- something that the small business can defend, because the moment it looks as if a bigger business might make money from it, they will muscle in.

For example Ergo-Shark left-handed mouse

A left-handed keyboard (basically a normal keyboard, but with the number pad on the left) sells for two or three times more than a standard keyboard.

The Ergo-Shark left-handed mouse looks fairly standard, but the two clickable parts are reversed. It is also more expensive than the usual mouse.

Many small businesses find successful product niches for which they can provide products or services that are either specially made or put together for specific customers. This works particularly well if the products are handmade, custom-built or 'bespoke' (individually made). Good examples would be creating house name signs, offering specialist gardening services (such as tree pruning), or customising cars by adding sports wheels or respraying with designs. It might not be possible for larger businesses to offer this kind of individual service.

For example Guardian Drink Holder

At a club in Cardiff, Luke Andrews' drink was spiked when he left it unattended. He collapsed and was ill for three days. As a result, Luke designed Guardian Drink Holders – a simple but stylish drinks holder that can be fitted in the toilets of pubs and clubs, so that people can take their drinks with them when they go to the toilet.

The holders are safe, hygienic, convenient and robust. They even have antibacterial technology built into them. They can be placed near hand driers and games machines and can hold bottles or glasses.

It took Luke three years to get from prototype, through trials to manufacturing. In 2008, after finding £150,000 to develop and manufacture the idea, he is ready to make 6,000 drinks holders a week. The holders have been taken up by several pub chains and individual clubs. They will also have advertisements on them.

8

How to exploit these niches

To exploit a niche, the small business has to specialise. It will need to produce just one particular product, or to provide a specialist service. In the beginning, the business must prove itself to its customers – assuming that there are customers out there who want the product. Reliability, attention to detail and customer care will all be vital. A poor reputation travels fast around a tiny market such as a niche market. Getting a bad name for quality and service will doom the business to failure.

At the same time, the niche has to be worth focusing on. It needs to be profitable and reliable as a source of work and income for the business. The small business is not going to be selling hundreds of products or providing services to thousands of customers, so each sale has to count. This means that each sale has to give the business a good profit. This is called a 'high profit margin' – which means a big difference between the costs and the sales price.

A business working in a niche needs to do three things to be successful:

- Create or identify the niche – find or make a demand for the product or service.
- Expand the niche – adapting what is offered or adapting the customer base should mean more customers.
- Protect the niche – the business needs to establish itself as the expert, the leader in that niche, and must be ready to fight off competitors.

Niche markets are always at risk. They might disappear or be attacked by bigger businesses. A business could go for multiple niches instead of sticking to a single one. For example, by developing two or more different niches, even a small business has a better chance of survival.

When a business enters any market for the first time, they often aim at a niche first, rather than the whole market. They do this to avoid taking on the big competitors, who will defend themselves by dropping prices or outspending the new business on advertising. If the new business takes just a little bit of the market, the big competitors may not notice until it is too late.

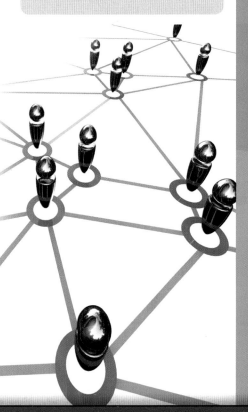

QUESTION TIME
12 minutes

The Guardian Drink Holders designed by Luke Andrews (see opposite) won a Gold Medal at the British Inventors Show in 2005 and the Silver Medal at the Export International Inventors Show in Switzerland in 2006. The antibacterial technology kills off 99.9% of bacteria, including E. coli and MRSA, both of which are dangerous infections. Each unit currently costs £14.99.

Using the information above, and the additional information on the opposite page, answer the following questions:

1 **What type of business might want to buy the product and why?** *(8 marks)*

2 **Give TWO reasons why customers of a pub, restaurant or club might want to see these products in toilets and restrooms.** *(4 marks)*

9

Reasons for starting a business

What is an entrepreneur?

Entrepreneurs are people who take risks and bring together all the resources necessary to make a business successful.

For our purposes, enterprise is about running a business and entrepreneurship. Enterprise is about being inventive and imaginative. It also means being able to create new ideas and solve problems.

Many people think that an entrepreneur is anyone who starts a business. However, there are several different types of entrepreneur, and each of them has a different role. There are people who:

- take an existing business into a competitive market where they reinvent the product or service to make it different, such as Stelios Haji-Ioannou, the founder of easyJet
- take calculated risks to start businesses because of their belief in the product or service, such as Duncan Bannatyne of the Bannatyne Group of companies (as seen on the television programme *Dragons' Den*)
- start one or more businesses, and then use similar techniques and brand names to launch new ones, such as Sir Richard Branson and his Virgin Group of companies.

The role of the entrepreneur can be complicated. It might involve:

- developing new markets, by either satisfying the needs of customers or creating a new demand for products and services
- discovering new sources of materials, such as developing a new way of producing something
- coordinating employees, resources and money to create products and services in an efficient and innovative way
- introducing new technologies, industries or products
- creating employment (this is one of the many reasons why governments are very keen on entrepreneurs).

Entrepreneurs need to have a broad range of skills or attitudes to life, in order to ensure their success. They need:

- drive and ambition
- self-confidence
- to take responsibility
- not to fear failure
- to take risks
- to take the longer view of things
- to use feedback
- to solve problems
- to set goals for themselves and the business.

What are the risks and rewards?

Managing risk is a key skill for an entrepreneur. Risk-taking is not always dangerous: there is often a reward in the form of profit. Risky business decisions have to be considered and measured against the possible returns, or rewards. The entrepreneur will ask:

- Are the potential profits sufficient to take the risk in the first place?
- Does the situation require us to take a risk?
- What is my attitude to the risk?
- Can we afford to take the risk?
- Are we capable of dealing with the risk?

For example **Samata Angel**

Samata Angel is a British-born Ghanaian fashion designer. She was given the Young Entrepreneur of the Year Award at the 2008 Precious Awards. Samata was praised for her determination, dedication and entrepreneurial skills and talent. Aside from running her fashion design business, with clients like Gwen Stefani and Jennifer Lopez, she has even found time to write a book called *The Emerging Clothing Designer's Guide to Making it Happen*, which helped to raise her profile.

RISKS	REWARDS
• The entrepreneur may only be able to reward themselves with a low salary, or perhaps no salary at all, in the first few months because the business may not be making enough money and what money is being made needs to be reinvested in the business	• If the correct decisions are made at the right time, then there is enormous potential for growth and wealth
• The entrepreneur may lack adequate resources to pursue ideas and opportunities	• The entrepreneur will gain a huge range of experience in different aspects of business
• It may not be possible to employ staff with skills to do everything that is needed, due to lack of funds	• The entrepreneur will develop a broad network of partners, suppliers and customers
• The entrepreneur will have to cope with a wide variety of different tasks and responsibilities, so this may put a lot of pressure on them	• The entrepreneur and employees will have pride in their success and a great sense of achievement
• Start-up businesses have the highest rate of failure of all types of business, as many lack the funds and experience to succeed	• The entrepreneur will have achieved independence and control over a business

Risk management involves looking at the risks associated with the greatest possible losses and the greatest possible likelihood of them occurring. An entrepreneur will look at these risks first, then consider less probable risks where losses would be lower. The process of managing any risk involves identifying the potential risks at the outset. The risks, if they happen, will inevitably cause problems.

There is a big difference between an entrepreneur and an established business in their attitudes to risk. On the one hand, an entrepreneur will tend to view risk as a means of maximising the possible rewards of a potential success. It is on this basis that the risk will be assessed. On the other hand, a more established business will look at risks in terms of

minimising possible failure.

Over 300 businesses close down each week. This means that around 17,000 businesses fail each year. Balancing risk means assessing the potential rewards against the ultimate fear of ruining the business and losing any hope of saving it. The key risks and rewards are outlined in the table above.

> Research carried out by the Cranfield School of Management shows that entrepreneurs who are risk-takers are far more likely to achieve higher sales growth. However, they caution that over-confidence among entrepreneurs is also a major cause of failure.

QUESTION TIME
8 minutes

Paul Benjamin opened the first branch of Benjys sandwich shops in 1989. The Benjamin family sold the business for around £40 million in 2000. It grew into a chain of sandwich shops and van-based franchises, delivering sandwiches to offices and other venues.

In 2006 the company had a turnover of £33 million and ambitions to open 250 stores. The company ran into trouble in 2007, with debts of £22.9 million. By February 2007 almost all the branches were closed. The main reasons for the setbacks were rent rises and tough trading conditions.

1 Why might the Benjamin family have sold out? *(4 marks)*

2 What might be meant by 'tough trading conditions'? *(4 marks)*

11

Franchises and social enterprises

What is a franchise and why are they popular?

Many new businesses fail in the first few years. One way in which this risk can be reduced is to effectively buy into the success of an existing business.

Franchising means using an existing company's business idea and its name. The franchisor is the business that owns the original company. It then sells the right to another person or group of people (the franchisee) to run a similar business (a franchise), usually in a different area.

The franchisor does not, of course, give this away for free. They charge the franchisee a fee to buy the franchise and then also take a percentage of the franchisee's profits.

There are many different franchises up and down the country, including The Body Shop, Benetton, Kentucky Fried Chicken, McDonald's and Burger King.

In effect, the franchisee is buying a **licence** to copy the style and the operations of the original business. Many franchises are very successful, earning money not only for the franchisee but also for the franchisor.

The franchisor usually offers a package of services and support, including:

- an existing well-known company name
- advertising that covers the area in which the franchisee operates
- training to help the franchisee start the business
- the necessary equipment, including shopfittings
- supplies of products and services that the franchisee will sell to their customers

For example Franchises

Dairy Crest milk delivery, Domino's Pizzas, Dyno-Rod drain clearing, McDonald's, Prontaprint, Spud-U-Like and Thornton's Chocolates are all franchise operations.

- the ability to buy products and materials at lower costs, taking advantage of bulk purchasing by all franchisees
- lists of existing or potential customers in the area in which the franchisee will operate
- support services, such as ongoing advice, loans and insurance.

When a franchisee buys a franchise, the franchisor is effectively expanding their business without any real financial risk to themselves. The franchisee pays the start-up costs and will be responsible for the running costs of the business. This enables the chain of companies to expand much faster than if the original business were trying to expand using its own funds.

Because the franchisee has made a financial commitment, they are very **motivated** and for that the business to be a success. The franchisor can concentrate on providing specialist support, rather than getting the new business off the ground.

A tiny proportion of franchises actually fail. The failure rate is around 6% to 7%, according to figures over the last 10 years. There are many reasons why the failure rate is so low:

- The franchisor carefully chooses who can buy a franchise.
- The franchisor states precisely how much money is needed by the franchisee, both to start up the business and to run it.
- The franchisee is following a tried and tested formula.
- The franchisor offers ongoing support if there are difficulties.

One of the other big advantages is the support from a national business and its ability to pay for national advertising and promotion. The money for this comes from the franchisees, because they are paying a percentage of all of their profits to the franchisor.

The key drawbacks for franchisees are that:

- franchises are not very flexible
- the franchisor keeps a tight control over the franchisee
- franchisees are not allowed to sell their franchises without the agreement of the franchisor
- a fixed percentage of the franchisee's turnover, rather than profit, is often paid to the franchisor.

12

KEY TERMS

Licence ▶ an agreement that allows one business to have certain rights to use something that actually belongs to another.

Motivated ▶ eager to work hard and do well in order to achieve success.

Many British franchises are members of the British Franchise Association. This organisation checks that its members use a strict code of business practice.

In the past, some franchises have failed because they are basically bad business ideas and the franchisors have misled their franchisees. The franchise is only as good as the franchisee. If it is run badly, then the business will fail.

If the franchise is run well and the franchisor monitors the franchisee, then there is less chance of the franchise failing. A poor reputation from a franchisee would adversely affect the reputation of the whole franchise business. The franchisor would seek to avoid this.

Franchises tend to be most common in the service sector. They include food outlets, clothing, business services, cosmetics and toiletry products.

What is a social enterprise?

Social enterprises are an increasingly popular type of business. They are distinct from commercial businesses, as their social or environmental purpose is central to their aims, rather than generating profits. The founders are usually passionate about wanting to change things, such as making social improvements or protecting the environment. Some social enterprises have specific or major goals, like saving a local post office, tackling global warming, dealing with homelessness or fighting to provide better healthcare or social care.

As they have social objectives, the founders and those involved with the enterprises are not interested in making a profit for its own sake and do not want shareholders telling them what to do. They reinvest all the profits they make back into the business or back into the community. Sometimes they aim to employ local or disadvantaged people.

Some social enterprises look for new ways of doing things, new products and new services. Some social enterprises are created because local government or the health service no longer provide that service but will pay for someone else to do it for them. The social enterprise steps in and provides a well-run service that meets the needs of the customers or clients.

What sets social enterprises apart from voluntary groups is that they believe that being competitive and profitable is the best way to provide the best levels of service, and they can achieve their social and environmental aims at the same time.

For example Social enterprises

The Big Issue newspaper, the Cafédirect hot drinks company, and Jamie Oliver's Fifteen restaurant chain are all social enterprises.

QUESTION TIME
12 minutes

Snappy Snaps, a chain of photo specialist stores, is a leading retail franchise that was founded in 1983. The founders identified three key points that helped make the franchise so successful:

- mutual support from other franchisees and a well-resourced franchisor for back-up
- eager and committed franchisees who use the established formula
- highly motivated, owner-operated franchises, providing excellent professional advice to customers.

1 Snappy Snaps franchisee success rates are around 90%. Why is the company so successful compared to other types of start-up business? *(8 marks)*

2 It requires at least £45,000 to start up a Snappy Snaps franchise, plus additional funds to rent or buy a shop. Why might a bank think that lending to a franchisee is generally less of a risk than lending to a start up business that is not a franchise? *(4 marks)*

13

What are business aims and objectives?

What are business aims and objectives?

Every business will establish short-term goals or aims. The short-term aims form the business's long-term objectives, setting out what the business wants to achieve in the future.

The objectives of different businesses are obviously going to vary. They can depend on things like how old the business is, how big it is, and the state of the market or markets in which it operates. Above all, they need to be realistic and achievable.

Objectives can also be affected by difficult economic conditions, when there might be high unemployment and the company's regular customers simply do not have enough money to spend.

A business can settle on many objectives, but really there are two main ones:

- to survive, which means making enough money to cover its costs – survival in itself is not enough in the long term
- to make a profit, so that the business owner can take out a wage, or employees can have a share in the profits, or shareholders can receive a reward for their investment (see also pages XX–XX).

Breaking even

The first thing a business has to do is to make at least as much money (income) as it spends (expenditure). Once it does this, the business has broken even. Any more income it receives will be profit. However, simply making a profit might not be enough. The business has to excel in one area or more in order to satisfy its **stakeholders**.

Making a profit

The first way to judge the success of a business is by the size of its profit. The more profit a business makes, the better it is seen to be performing. However, profit is only one measure of success.

An extremely large business, with expensive assets (such as large buildings or expensive machinery), is likely to make a large profit. But is this profit really so large compared to what it cost the business to produce it?

For example

A business may have assets, such as factories and equipment, worth £100 million and may make a net profit of £10 million.

By dividing the net profit by the capital employed, we can calculate the return on capital employed as a percentage. In this case, it would be 10%.

$$\frac{\text{Net profit}}{\text{capital employed}} \times 100$$

So in our example:

$$\frac{£10 \text{ million}}{£100 \text{ million}} \times 100 = 10\%$$

Another way of judging the success of a business is to look at its sales compared to the total sales in the market. This market share percentage can be calculated as follows:

$$\frac{\text{sales of the business}}{\text{total sales in the market}} \times 100$$

For example

If the total sales in the market were £150 million and the business achieved sales of £15 million, then it has a 10% market share.

If sales do increase, it is worth checking to see if the total sales in the market have also increased. If they have, then the business may not in fact have increased its market share.

Creating jobs and wealth

Another measure of business success, certainly one measured by government or potential employees, is job creation. It brings new wealth to an area and is also good for the government, as less money needs to be paid out in benefits.

A business can also create wealth in other ways. This can be measured in terms of what it owns, such as the land, factories or offices. Theoretically, the more a business owns, the more money it should be able to make. Wealth can also be measured by what the business is providing for its employees in terms of increasing their skills and making them more productive. Other businesses associated with the company are also affected by its wealth – suppliers receive more orders from a wealthier business. And the local area benefits from the wealth, because employees spend money on shopping, housing and taxes.

KEY TERMS

Stakeholder ▶ an individual or group with a direct interest in the business, such as an employee, owner or shareholder.

Dividend ▶ a share of the profits, paid out on each share held by the shareholder.

Shareholders of a business will be looking to see how much of the profit made by the business is passed on to them through **dividends**. Businesses do not always pass on all of their profits via dividends. They may keep – or retain – some of the profits to give them a cash reserve. This is known as 'retained profit'. They will retain this profit to invest in a specific project or buy a particular asset, or to help cash flow in the future.

Shareholders will also be looking at sales growth. This shows that the business is being very active and seeking out new customers, or encouraging existing customers to consume more.

Another type of stakeholder will be affected by increased sales – employees. They will be busier and there will be a need to employ more people.

Why are business aims and objectives important?

Aims and objectives are often written with clear benefits in mind, such as:

- To increase …
- To reduce …
- To improve …

They are often described as SMART targets:

S PECIFIC *they have a clear focus*

M EASURABLE *it is easy to determine when they have been achieved*

A TTAINABLE *they are realistic and not impossible.*

R ESULTS-ORIENTATED *they focus on the results rather than the methods*

T IME-SPECIFIC *they have a clear end date*

Defining the aims and objectives is important. They give the business greater direction and focus; they allow all employees and managers to have a greater understanding of the purpose of the business and they help external groups to understand the business. Clear aims and objectives can often help businesses solve problems.

Aims and objectives can be applied across the whole business, as can be seen in the diagram.

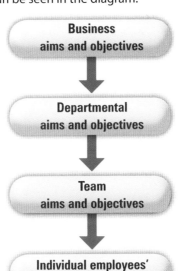

Business aims and objectives

↓

Departmental aims and objectives

↓

Team aims and objectives

↓

Individual employees' aims and objectives

The business aims and objectives might be very general, but the aims and objectives of individual parts of the business are clearer steps. If individuals achieve their aims and objectives, then the team reaches its aims, and so on.

QUESTION TIME
8 minutes

A business operates in a market with total sales of £120 million. It has sales of £6 million. The market increases in value to £150 million total sales and the business manages to increase its sales to £8 million.

1 Calculate the business's original market share. *(4 marks)*

2 Calculate the new market share of the business. *(4 marks)*

15

Types of business aims

YOU WILL FIND OUT:

- about survival, profit and growth
- about market share and customer satisfaction
- about ethical and sustainable businesses

Survival, profit and growth

Survival

For a small business, survival in the first few months, or even years, can be a challenging aim in itself. As we saw in Section 1.1.5, start-up businesses are far more likely to fail in the first year or two than a more established business.

New businesses often find it difficult to set aims and objectives. For a new business, before anything has been sold to a customer, everything is an expense, so they need to be extremely careful about their spending. They may therefore see survival as the only thing they can aim for in the beginning. Even this is hard to achieve, as it is very difficult for new businesses to break even.

Profit

In the longer term, the new business must, like any other business, try to make a profit. This is also difficult.

As all business activity costs money. Businesses need to pay for items such as **stock**, wages and salaries, and other running costs. To cover their costs, businesses must sell the goods and services they produce. However, if the income that a business receives from selling its products is less than its costs, the business will make a loss. If the income of a business is the same as its costs, the business will break even. Only if its income is greater than its costs, will the business make a profit.

A business cannot afford to continue to make a loss. It needs to make a profit to pay for what it

has bought and to put the money back into the business to develop it, pay off loans and pay tax.

Making a profit is a common aim, as it gives the owners of the business a reward for investing in the business. It also allows them to reinvest in the business, to make it even more successful in the future.

But not all businesses aim to make a profit. If businesses such as social enterprises or charities make more money than they spend, they put all of it back into the business or organisation.

Growth

Growth is another aim of most businesses. They might want to open more stores or move to larger premises. They might want to increase their range of products and services, to buy more efficient equipment, or to advertise to a wider group of customers.

Growth can be measured in many different ways, but the two key ways are:

- **Increased turnover** – this means that the value of the sales being made is greater than before. For example, instead of selling £15,000 of products a month, the business now sells £20,000 of products a month.
- **Greater profit** – the business is actually making more money on each sale it makes. Instead of making £5 every time it sells a £20 item, it is now making £6 per item. It will be able to do this if it can make or buy the item cheaper than before.

In order to increase its market share, a business may decide to reduce the price of its products in order to attract customers from other suppliers. However, in the short term, reducing the price may lead to lower profits. The business must decide whether to sacrifice short-term profit in the hope that achieving its aim of increased market share will lead to higher profits in the future. This can mean that objectives can sometimes conflict with each other.

Market share and customer satisfaction

The market for a product consists of all the buyers and sellers of that product. All businesses operate in the markets for their products. The more buyers – or customers – that a business has for its product, the higher the volume of sales it will achieve. Higher sales can mean more income and therefore more profit.

The market share of a business is the value of its sales as a percentage of the total sales by all businesses operating in that market (see also the equation on page 14). Another aim of most businesses is therefore to increase their market share in order to make more profit. However, in achieving that extra market share, the business may have to drop prices for a while to attract more customers. This might force a competitor out of the market, because they cannot

16

compete by selling at that price. Once that happens, the business that dropped the price can charge more again and make back the lost profits.

Most customers will be looking for a business that can offer them the best quality at the lowest price. To attract and keep customers, a business must always aim to provide a high-quality product. However, there is no point in providing the best product if no one can afford to buy it, so a business also needs to balance the costs involved in improving the quality with the price it will need to charge for it. Customers will expect value for money.

Customer satisfaction is another important aim. This means that the customer is pleased – or even delighted – with the products that the business sells them and, as importantly, is satisfied with the service provided by the business. So the business needs to consider staff training (giving the customer advice and support), its systems (making it easy for the customer to buy from and communicate with the business) and good service after the product has been sold (ongoing help and advice). If a customer is satisfied, they will come back to the business and buy again, and will tell their friends and colleagues about their positive experience. Poor customer service can mean that customers will not return and will tell their friends about their bad experience.

——— K E Y T E R M ———

Stock ▶ materials that will be used to make products, work in progress (part-made products) or finished products waiting to be sold.

Ethical and sustainable businesses

Growth and expansion are often seen in a negative light. By using profits to stimulate greater growth and to increase profits, businesses are often accused of being greedy and having little regard for social, ethical and environmental concerns.

Low wages, for example, are not ethically acceptable. Nor is the use of underpaid overseas employees. These both bring the business into conflict with the law and attract bad publicity on television or in the newspapers. Businesses need to balance growth and profit by showing that they care about these issues. Most businesses have to show a degree of social and ethical responsibility, regardless of whether these beliefs are genuine.

Being ethical means doing things and making decisions that are morally correct. This does not just mean not doing something illegal. It means thinking about buying things from other ethical businesses, not exploiting suppliers or employees, not damaging the environment, not treating animals badly, checking where materials and stock come from and making sure that it too has been ethically produced.

Sustainability is another aspect of a business taking on social and environmental responsibilities. It means running a business that does not affect the environment, cause pollution or use up scarce resources that cannot easily be replaced.

QUESTION TIME
14 minutes

Two friends decide to set up a DVD home delivery service. They borrow £8,000 to buy their stock and £6,000 to buy two mopeds to deliver the DVDs to their customers. They also rent a small unit on an industrial estate, which costs them a total of £4,000 each year.

As an introductory offer, customers can borrow as many DVDs a month as they wish for £120 per year.

1 How many customers would they need to cover all their costs so far? *(4 marks)*

2 If the two friends wanted to earn £12,000 per year each, how many more customers would they need? *(4 marks)*

3 Suggest what new services the business might offer to attract more customers. *(6 marks)*

The purpose of setting objectives

Why do businesses set objectives?

There are good reasons why a business should set objectives, rather than simply plodding along and hoping for the best:

- It helps with decision-making – the decisions have to be properly thought out.
- Targets can be set, which helps motivate employees and managers.
- The business can measure its own progress.
- The business can make sure that all of its different parts work together to achieve the objectives.

This is why some of the most successful organisations produce very clear general **mission statements**.

It is no good for a business to have aims and objectives if it does not really know how to achieve them. A business needs to set out its strategies and tactics in a **business plan.**

A strategy is a major plan used by a business to set out its long-term objectives. A good example would be: 'We want to be the best-known retailer in the high street in five years' time, by offering first-class customer service'.

Tactics are the individual parts of a strategy. They are short-term and flexible. An example would be: 'In order to become the best-known retailer in the high street, we need to open at least ten new stores each year'.

In order to meet objectives, the strategy states what the business needs to do and the tactics describe how to achieve the strategies. Setting aims and objectives will help the business to understand its purpose and give it a clearer view of its future.

The two most common objectives of business organisations are survival and making a profit. These objectives do not apply to organisations that do not need to generate money in order to keep running, such as a government department, which is funded by the taxpayer. No business can survive for very long if it does not cover its costs. It must at least do this, otherwise its money will run out and no one will lend it any more. Making a profit simply means selling products and services for more than they cost the business to buy, make or provide to customers.

How do businesses choose their objectives?

In order for a business to achieve its long-term objectives, it needs to make short-term plans. The table opposite shows examples of how short-term plans can help a business in achieving its long-term objectives.

Some businesses will design a mission statement that tries to express the purpose of the business and what broad products and services it offers. The mission statement is designed to give the management, employees, customers and potential investors a quick guide to the aims and objectives of the business. It also allows the business to be described in no more than three or four sentences.

When we look at business plans later in this unit (see pages 24–9), we will see that mission statements are also a good starting point in helping to explain the direction in which the business wants to be moving and the way in which its future is mapped out.

For example Tesco's mission statement

Tesco PLC's mission statement is: 'To create value for customers to earn their lifetime loyalty'. Tesco recognises, as do many successful businesses, that customers are of vital importance. If they are treated in the right way, they will come back and shop with the business again.

LONG-TERM OBJECTIVE	SHORT-TERM PLAN
Expand into Europe	• Investigate different countries and their markets • Find suitable premises • Recruit staff for overseas work
Develop new products	• Investigate the market • Research possible competition • Plan to buy new machinery • Recruit new staff
Become the best	• Improve products and services • Investigate the competition • Retrain the sales team • Plan a major advertising campaign
Reduce waste	• Find out how much waste is produced now • Find out where the waste is produced • Find out how similar businesses deal with waste • Bring in a waste management consultant

A mission statement should say what the business is, what it does, what it stands for and why. Out of this mission statement, the business can then identify its objectives and aims, as well as the strategies and tactics that will help it to achieve these.

A mission statement can therefore state:

- the purpose of the business
- who the business serves
- the type of customers
- the needs that the business fulfils
- how those needs are fulfilled
- the values of the business.

By using a mission statement as the building block of the aims and objectives, the business can produce measurable results.

> Strategies are the broad ways in which the business can accomplish its mission. Goals and actions flow out of each strategy.

A mission statement is broadly a shortened version of more complex objectives. It needs to mean something – otherwise it has no value to the business. It needs to state a purpose and how that purpose will be achieved. If it clearly states the aims and objectives of the business, then the strategies and tactics to achieve them can be created. If the mission statement is vague, it may be impossible to come up with a way of achieving those aims and objectives.

KEY TERMS

Mission statement ▶ a paragraph, a set of points or even just a sentence that summarises what the organisation stands for, as well as its principles.

Business plan ▶ a detailed report of a business's future proposals. It also examines the present market and provides financial details. The business will use its business plan to help in meeting its aims and objectives.

QUESTION TIME
10 minutes

The Dartmoor Pony Heritage Trust's aim is to save the Dartmoor pony. The charity's mission statement is: 'To save the indigenous Dartmoor Pony from extinction and to maintain its presence on Dartmoor, thus protecting our heritage for future generations'.

There are only around 400 of these rare ponies left in the wild. The charity has set up a visitor centre, where it runs educational programmes for schools. It also has a 1,000-acre grazing site on Dartmoor for the ponies.

1 How clear is the mission statement? Why might it be difficult for some people to understand? *(4 marks)*

2 Suggest THREE aims and objectives of the charity, as indicated in the mission statement. *(6 marks)*

19

Using business objectives to measure success

YOU WILL FIND OUT:
- why it is important to be successful
- who cares about success

Why is it important to be successful?

It is easy for business start-ups to fail. The first few months or even years, when the business is small, are the most difficult. The company may lack finances, resources, and the skills and talents needed to survive.

There are many reasons why things can go wrong:

- **Lack of systems** – no systems or procedures are in place to sort out problems. Problems are dealt with as they arise, because the business could not predict them.
- **Lack of direction** – the company owners do not know where the business is heading; they have no clear goals. Survival is their main goal.
- **No financial planning** – no one looks at how much money is being made and spent until it is too late.
- **Relying on one or two people** – small businesses are often built around the skills of one or two people. If they leave or are ill, the company falls apart.

- **Not knowing who the customer is** – the business has not identified its key customers and does not know how to tell them about its products and services.
- **Not knowing about the market or the competition** – the business may not realise that tastes are changing or that a major competitor is taking all the customers.
- **Lack of communication** – the business owners do not explain what is needed to their employees or suppliers, or they are useless at communicating with customers.
- **Lack of quality standards** – the company has no way of ensuring that quality levels are maintained.
- **Lack of money** – the business is simply spending too much and earning too little.
- **Concentrating on the job, not the business** – the owners are so busy doing the job that they forget all their other business activities and responsibilities.

Success is vital for businesses and social enterprises for many different reasons. For example:

- The organisation may have borrowed money to set itself up. This needs to be repaid. If the business fails, it may still end up having to pay the money back.
- Investors are relying on the business to be careful with their money.
- Businesses and social enterprises provide employment.
- They contribute to the local economy by paying Council Tax and spending money with other local businesses.

The bigger a business becomes, the more important it is for it not to fail, because so many people and other organisations are relying on its continued success. These different groups, some closely related to the company and others less so, are known as 'stakeholders' (see also Section 1.2.5). They have an interest in the business and are concerned that it does well and survives.

20

Who cares about success?

Everyone in the business and everyone related in some way to the business should care whether or not it is successful. Some may rely on the business to pay wages; some may be owed money by it; others may have paid the business money and are expecting it to provide them with products or services. All of these groups are examples of stakeholders: for one reason or another they need the company to be a success and would suffer if it failed.

In difficult economic times, business failures are all too common. Nearly 2,000 businesses failed in 2008. In 2009, this figure is expected to rise to over 32,000. In recent times the worst year for business failures was back in 1992, when 34,000 businesses failed.

Every time a business fails, people lose their jobs. The business owners find themselves in debt. Investors lose the money they put into the company. Suppliers who have provided the business with products and services do not get paid. Customers who have paid for products and services to be supplied, lose out. Property owners who rented the building to the business lose money, and many other groups and individuals are affected.

No matter how big or small the company, failure affects far more people than just those directly involved in it.

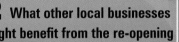
All businesses rely on other businesses. They are all part of a network that supplies products and services to one another, as well as to their customers. One business failing and owing other businesses money can have a knock-on effect. If a really large company fails, owing lots of money to several smaller businesses, then the effect can be disastrous.

QUESTION TIME
10 minutes

In 2003, the village shop in the small village of Woodton in East Anglia closed down. Villagers had to go to other villages and towns to do their shopping. In 2005 the shop was reopened, and now sells everything from newspapers to local farm produce. The village, with 650 homes, now has its own place to buy groceries.

1 In what ways might a shop such as this be important to the local community? *(6 marks)*

2 What other local businesses might benefit from the re-opening of the shop? *(4 marks)*

21

Stakeholders and their objectives

What are stakeholders?

A stakeholder is an individual or group affected in some way by a business, or with an interest in its activities. Many groups will have a stake in the success of a business and will benefit if the business does well or suffer if it fails.

Each type of stakeholder will have a slightly different view of the business. Some may actually work within the business (internal stakeholders), while others are external to it (external stakeholders).

Internal stakeholders

- **Employees** have a stake in the business because their livelihoods rely on its success. If the business does well, they may receive more money and benefits. If it fails, they may have to take a pay cut or even lose their jobs. Increasingly, organisations encourage employees to become shareholders, to reinforce the link.
- **Managers** at different levels of an organisation are ultimately responsible for the decisions that affect its success or failure. Managers are often rewarded with high salaries and **bonuses**, or with additional benefits, such as private healthcare or company cars.
- **Directors, owners and share-holders** are often interchangeable, with some kind of financial stake in the business. They might own shares or be outright owners of the business. The directors and owners will make day-to-day decisions that affect the future of the business.

    Shareholders look to these people to make the right decisions, so that they receive a share of the profits. Shareholders literally own a

Employees · **Managers** · **Directors/owners** · **Shareholders** · **Trade unions** · **Customers** · **INTERNAL** · **BUSINESS** · **EXTERNAL** · **Local community** · **Suppliers** · **Banks and lenders of finance** · **HM Revenue & Customs** · **Government** · **Pressure groups**

share of the business. Shares might go up or down in value, depending on the success or failure of the business. Shareholders receive a dividend as their part of the profits.
- **Trade unions** are employee organisations that support employees at work. They ensure that employees are treated fairly and receive reasonable pay and benefits. They are stakeholders because they represent employees, who are key internal stakeholders.

External stakeholders

Most businesses have a complex network of external stakeholders. Some have a relatively close relationship with the business; others influence the business without becoming involved on a daily basis.

- **Customers** want low prices and the best quality available. They weigh up what they can gain from a choice of businesses. Customers are always looking for new products and services and want businesses to offer what they need.
- Businesses buy goods and services from **suppliers**. A builders' merchant will buy from businesses supplying timber, bricks, concrete, and a host of other products. The business and the suppliers rely on

one another. The business needs the supplier to have in stock the products it needs; the supplier needs to be paid by the business.
- **The Government** will often directly influence a business because it passes laws that the business must take note of and apply, such as health and safety regulations or laws about payment. The government is involved in collecting taxes from businesses via Her Majesty's Revenue & Customs. Businesses are also influenced by regulations from the **European Union**.
- Wherever a business is located, it will have an impact on **the local community**. Some impacts will be positive (such as buying products and services from local suppliers); others negative (such as increased traffic, or a threat to other local businesses due to competition).
- **Banks and finance providers** lend to businesses so that they can fund special projects or expand. Banks and other finance providers will not want a company to make decisions that could affect its ability to pay back the loans. Before agreeing to lend it any money, they will look closely at its profitability.

22

Bonuses ▶ additional pay made to directors, managers and other employees, as a reward for their efforts towards the success of the business.

European Union ▶ an agreement between many European countries to make trade between them easier, to allow people to move around freely and to gradually have more similar laws.

All the stakeholders in a company have their own expectations, so the business itself must balance the wishes of the various stakeholders. Higher wages would please employees, management and trade unions, but would not please owners and shareholders. The increase would cause business costs to rise and the profitability of the business would probably fall.

If the business focused solely on providing profits for its owners, then it would find itself in difficulties with its employees and the trade unions. These groups would consider themselves to be exploited and undervalued. This could in turn affect their performance and the overall profitability of the business.

Pleasing all groups at all times may be impossible. However, an organisation must try to take into account the needs of each stakeholder group. This becomes even more complicated when the external stakeholders are brought into the equation.

Why are stakeholders important?

A business or a social enterprise needs to take account of the needs of all its stakeholders. Some stakeholders will be employed by the business and will rely on the owners making the right decisions so that they get paid and keep their jobs. Others, like the local community, may be affected by the activities of the business, having to put up with extra traffic, more noise and pollution but also benefiting from more jobs and money for local people and other local businesses.

More pay for employees (which would please them) means higher costs. This probably means less profit, so less money for investors and shareholders. It is possible to balance things; the business might offer extra pay for employees if sales targets are met. This means that the business has made better profits than before, so everyone can share in the success – employees and shareholders alike.

It may not always be possible for a business to satisfy all of its stakeholders.

What do stakeholders want?

Each stakeholder group is looking for something slightly different from a business:

- The government wants the business to stick to the laws and regulations.
- Investors want the business not to take too many risks. They want a return on their investment.
- Customers want quality products and services at a fair price.
- Local communities want to limit any negative impact on the local area.
- Suppliers want the business to be fair in its dealings with them.

A business normally tries to rank the importance of its stakeholders, working out how powerful they are and what influence they have on the business. But each business, regardless of its size, has an obligation to all its stakeholders.

QUESTION TIME
12 minutes

The Millennium Dome (now the O₂ Arena) was built after a massive campaign to find out the opinions of local stakeholders. Letters were sent out to 7,000 local residents and 120,000 leaflets were distributed, asking for views. The concern was that the massive venue would disrupt the lives of the local community, but the developers claimed that it would also bring benefits.

23

1 Suggest THREE ways in which the building of the venue might disrupt the local community. *(6 marks)*

2 Suggest THREE ways in which the venue has brought benefits to the local community. *(6 marks)*

What is a business plan?

What is a business plan?

A business plan is essentially a document that describes a business, along with its objectives, strategies, the market in which it operates and the business's financial forecasts.

A business plan usually has two key functions:

- to act as a basis for securing external finance or funding
- to be used within the business as a way of measuring actual performance against forecasted figures.

The business plan should give details of how the business is going to be developed, when it will happen, and who is going to be responsible. It should also show how money will be managed. In many cases, potential lenders or investors will not read much of the business plan beyond the executive summary, which covers the key points of the entire business plan and outlines the business opportunity through to financial forecasting. Ideally, the executive summary should be no more than two pages long.

A business plan is important, as there may be a wide range of different individuals or institutions wishing to find out about the company's intentions. These could include:

- banks
- external investors, including **venture capitalists** or **business angels**
- providers of grants
- someone who may wish to purchase the business
- potential business partners
- employees.

It is important that the business plan is constantly updated and changed as the business grows. The plan should include:

- an executive summary
- a short description of the business opportunity
- the business's marketing and sales strategy
- profiles of the management team and key personnel
- an overview of the business's operations, including premises, production and use of IT
- financial forecasts.

What does it do?

Sets out the vision

The business plan needs to get across clearly what the business actually does, as well as its vision for the future. It should begin with an overview of:

- when the business started, or when it intends to start, and any progress made
- the sector in which the business operates and the type of business
- any relevant business history
- the legal structure of the business.

Provides clarification

As far as the products and services offered by the business are concerned, investors will seek clarification on:

- what makes the business's products and services different and what benefits they offer
- the type of customers
- how the business intends to develop the products and services
- whether the business holds any **patents**, **trademarks** or design rights

- any key features about the sector in which the business operates.

Explains the market

Investors will also want to see that the business plan shows full awareness of the market place. The business plan should describe:

- **the features of the market** – its size, development and current issues
- **the target consumer base** – identifying who the customers are and how the business knows they will be interested in its products and services
- **the competition** – who they are, how they operate, and what market share they have
- **future developments** – any anticipated changes in the market and how the business and its competitors are likely to react.

Marketing and sales involve promotion and sales of a business's products and services. It is important that the marketing and sales strategy in the business plan is realistic and achievable. Investors will ask:

- How will the business position its products and services in the market place?
- Who are the customers? What are their characteristics and how will the business attract new customers?
- What is the business's pricing policy? Will different customers be charged different prices, and will offers be available for bulk purchasing?
- How will the business promote its products and services? What type

of marketing and sales methods will be used?
- How will the products and services be distributed to customers?
- What sales methods will be used, for example a website, face-to-face, through retailers or by telephone?

Shows the financial forecasting

Investors will want to know how much capital is needed, what guarantees lenders may have, how the business intends to repay funding, and what the business's sources of revenue and income will be. The financial forecasting should include:

- a cash-flow statement – showing the projected flows of cash into and out of the business for at least the first 12–18 months
- a profit-and-loss forecast – showing projected sales and the costs of providing products and services, as well as **overheads**
- a sales forecast – the income that the business expects to receive from sales.

KEY TERMS

Venture capitalists ▶ investors who provide cash for start-up businesses and small businesses that wish to expand, in exchange for a share of the business.

Business angels ▶ individuals who invest at an early stage of a new business, usually in a high-risk, high-potential growth area.

Patent ▶ a legal document designed to protect new inventions, covering how the invention works, what it does, and how it is made.

Trademark ▶ a name or a symbol that identifies a product or a company.

Overheads ▶ unavoidable costs, such as rent or rates, which have to be paid by a business, regardless of the level of sales being achieved.

QUESTION TIME
10 minutes

1 Why is a business plan as important to an existing business as it is to a start-up business?
(10 marks)

25

Some organisations feel that business plans unnecessarily restrict the activities of the business. They may be written at a time when the business is unaware of the realities of the market or the industry in which it will be operating. Then it may only be when the business is involved in delivering products and services to customers that it becomes aware of the complexities of the market. At this point, it may have to adapt more quickly and radically than the business plan had anticipated.

The purpose of a business plan

The purpose of a business plan

A business plan is a written statement about a business. It is written by the owners or the managers, and states what they intend to achieve and how they intend to do it.

The main purposes of a business plan are:

- to seek sources of finance
- to gain finance
- to monitor progress.

A basic business plan needs to cover:

- the structure of the business
- the products and services offered
- the types of customers and how they will be approached
- the growth potential of the business
- how the business intends to finance the operations.

As well as stating the business's objectives and identifying its financial requirements, the business plan will also include a section on its marketing plan.

The marketing plan

The marketing plan will assist the owners of the new business by:

- focusing on the main factors that need to be addressed in order to remain competitive
- identifying and examining the business's expansion opportunities
- preparing a series of measures to address any future problems
- setting identifiable goals and listing potential results
- identifying criteria to be met in achieving the business's goals and objectives
- setting out a series of measures to allow the monitoring of progress
- supplying the information required by providers of finance.

It is vital for a business to research a market that it believes contains profitable opportunities. It will want to find out:

- What is the size of the market?
- Is the market growing?
- Is the market supplied by out-of-date or inefficient companies?

- Is the market a niche that has not been considered by the competitors?
- Is the market dependent on certain pricing levels that determine whether or not customers buy?
- Is the market already supplied by a competitor's branded products or by products that do not command much customer loyalty?
- Is the market dominated by lots of competitors or by just a few large ones?

It is unlikely that everyone in a particular market will want to buy a new business's products or services. Sometimes it is more appropriate to focus on a segment of the market. There are several links in the selling chain between the business and the customer, such as distributors, agents or dealers, and retailers. The business could focus on one of these links.

Knowing how this market structure works will enable the business to establish, or estimate, the potential value of the sales to this market. Direct routes can enable the business to fix a selling price and estimate the sales. When there is a network

For example Freeview

A prime example of a product or range of products filling a market gap is Freeview. Prior to the launch of Freeview, customers could view only terrestrial television – the five main channels – for free. They could also pay a monthly subscription to a satellite or cable provider, to receive a much larger range of TV stations.

With the development of new digital TV stations, the stations wished to increase their audiences. Freeview came on the scene to provide the solution. For the cost of a set-top box and no subscription, customers can now access over 30 digital TV channels.

Profit is made by the manufacturers of the Freeview boxes, but it also increases the audience of the digital TV channels. This allows the TV channels to charge higher advertising rates.

26

of distributors in the market, the business has to make the selling price low enough to allow each layer of the distribution network to earn its income, but still offer the product to the customer at the right price.

Establishing customer needs, competition and gaps in the market

A business will want to know what products customers are buying, why they buy them, what they are prepared to pay for them and who they are currently buying them from. A new business will do its utmost to identify its particular target group of customers and meet their needs, wants and preferences. It will also want to make its products or services more appealing to the customers than those of the competition.

Many businesses, before they spend time and resources on developing products and services, look for what is known as a 'market gap'. A market gap is an opportunity for a business to provide a product or service that no other business or competitor is currently providing. The business will outline in its business plan how it intends to exploit the gap.

Showing that the business should be a success

All parties involved in the start-up of a business will want to be optimistic about the future and will have high expectations of a successful trading business. The business plan offers the business owners an opportunity to identify a series of objectives, with the aim of improving the overall state of the business in the future.

For new businesses, this essential objective-setting may not only be a basic requirement of any providers of finance, but may also be fundamentally important to the eventual success or failure of the enterprise because it gives the business direction.

For an organisation entering the market as a new business, their first objective may be to supply their products or services. An analysis of present market conditions and the comparative success of existing businesses operating in related areas will be of prime importance in meeting this objective. It will be included in the business plan. The business will also have to look at distribution, to see whether it can identify cost-effective methods of getting products and services to potential customers.

QUESTION TIME
10 minutes

1 Why might it be difficult for a start-up business to provide all the information needed in a business plan? *(6 marks)*

2 Give two examples of products or services that have filled a market gap. *(4 marks)*

27

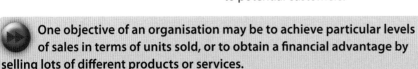

One objective of an organisation may be to achieve particular levels of sales in terms of units sold, or to obtain a financial advantage by selling lots of different products or services.

The need to achieve high sales levels is particularly important to a business that produces inexpensive products. This objective could be met by a business supplying its own-label products to wholesalers and retailers. This would allow higher levels of production, which in turn would drive down the cost of each product (unit) produced.

The main sections of a business plan

What are the main sections?

Ideally, a business plan should include:

*   **an executive summary** – an overview of the business. It is vital to include this, because many lenders and investors will only read this section of the plan
*   **a description of the business opportunity** – what does the business intend to sell or offer, and why? Who are its customers?
*   **the business's marketing and sales strategy** – why will customers buy from the business, and how does the business intend to sell products and services to them?
*   **profiles of key personnel** – showing the qualifications and experience of the business's managers (and owners, if they are involved with the business)
*   **a description of the business's operations** – including the proposed premises, work facilities, management information systems and IT
*   **financial forecasts** – essentially translate all the previous sections into numbers in terms of income, expenditure and profit.

Above all, the plan should be relatively short, so it is more likely to be read. A well-presented plan will give the reader a positive impression.

The key points in good presentation are:

*   number the pages
*   include a contents list
*   start with the executive summary
*   use a sensible and large enough font
*   write the plan so it addresses an external audience
*   edit and re-edit the plan to make sure it makes sense
*   show the plan to expert advisors, such as accountants, and ask for feedback
*   avoid using jargon
*   put all data, such as balance sheets and other tables, at the back of the report as appendices.

Importantly, the business plan must be realistic. It may need updating later and it is a useful tool for judging the relative successes of the business.

It is important for the owner of a new business to assess their own skills from the outset, and to be aware of the resources available to them. They may have idealistic visions of what they want to do in the future, but without adequate skills and resources they will not succeed in such a competitive world.

Essentially, the skills they need to possess are an ability to:

*   **evaluate their own strengths and weaknesses**
*   **work independently or with other people**
*   **plan**
*   **manage their time effectively**
*   **set targets**
*   **review progress**
*   **make decisions**
*   **solve problems.**

28

Why are these sections needed in a business plan?

Potential investors will usually want to see a business plan before they even consider funding a business. As a result, many business plans are written solely for this purpose, but a good business plan needs to look at how the business will develop over a longer period.

A business can use a business plan to help allocate resources. This can also assist in attracting new funds as time goes by. The business plan will show how funds will be used.

By getting into the habit of having an ongoing business plan, which is regularly updated, the business can also monitor how it is measuring up to its business objectives. In this way, the business plan can be used to identify where the business is at any precise moment, and in which direction it needs to move in order to grow. It can also ensure that the business meets its key targets and manages its priorities.

Businesses should therefore adopt a continuous and regular business planning cycle that ensures that the business plan is kept up-to-date. This can monitor the extent to which the company is meeting its objectives and where it may be making mistakes. Businesses usually try to assess their progress every three to six months.

Good business plans should incorporate sets of targets and objectives. Most business plans will have overall strategic goals (broad, long-term objectives), but these need to be broken down into specific, measurable targets. This assists the business in understanding what needs to be achieved and by when. The business can also use the targets to monitor the performance of employees, products and services. Targets are useful, as they help individual employees to understand how they can assist a business in meeting its objectives and how they fit into the organisation. Individuals' progress can also be appraised using targets and objectives.

Many businesses use an annual business plan that is broken down into four quarterly plans. Targets can be set for each quarter. Businesses that are very sales-orientated may even break down their plans into monthly or weekly targets and reviews.

Aspects of a business plan need to be regularly assessed and updated. The whole plan does not need to be radically reappraised on a regular basis.

QUESTION TIME
10 minutes

1 **Why is it important for a business to include sets of targets and objectives in a business plan?** *(9 marks)*

29

Uncertainty and risk

Why are start-up businesses at risk?

It is generally accepted that the first three years, and in particular the first year, present the greatest risk to a new business. So many things could go wrong.

The business may lack sufficient resources, finances, or skills and expertise to be successful. Many small businesses are over-optimistic about how they will perform once they are up and running, and will have made serious financial commitments that they simply cannot cover from the revenues received.

In addition to having to cope with expected costs, a business may often encounter unexpected costs that it could not reasonably have predicted. For example:

- It may need to seek new suppliers.
- The premises may need to be refurbished.
- Key members of staff may leave unexpectedly and will need to be replaced.
- The financial providers may lose confidence in the business's ability to pay back any loans they have taken out.

While the business needs to monitor its income and expenditure, there are other, stronger forces that could influence its success – established and probably larger competitors, which will move quickly to try to destroy new businesses as they emerge. Existing businesses know that small businesses are vulnerable in the first year or so of their existence. The small business is still learning and it may make costly mistakes that the competition can exploit. Larger competitors can afford, at least in the short term, to reduce their prices. A new business may then be tempted to reduce its prices, but this will be at a much greater cost to it than to the larger competitor.

How can the business plan help?

Many of the problems facing a start-up business begin with not getting things right in the business plan. Sometimes lack of skill or information causes problems; sometimes the issue that proves to be incredibly important has simply not been thought through.

The table on the right sets out the most common problems, what they mean and how the start-up business can avoid them.

PROBLEM WITH BUSINESS PLAN

Vagueness

Broad statements

Over-optimism

Ignoring risks

Inconsistencies

Unrealistic assumptions

Sloppiness

Lack of market knowledge

Lack of knowledge of competitors

Dismissal of competitors

Poor focus

30

EXPLANATION	SOLUTION
• The business plan does not have sufficient detail to explain what the business is about	• Be clear about the business's purpose and its aims and objectives
• Broad, general statements that are not backed up by market research, facts or figures	• Always be able to prove what is written in the business plan
• Although business plans should be positive, investors need to know that their funds will be safe if problems occur	• Show that the business has a back-up plan
• It is important that the business has thought about what could go wrong and what could be done if that happens	• Show that the business has a back-up plan
• Statements in one part of the business plan do not match up with facts and figures in other parts of the plan	• Check everything – at least twice
• Figures need to reflect the real world – often they do not	• Do not be over-optimistic
• Business plans should be spell-checked, and well presented. Calculations need to be double-checked, as figures that do not add up will create a very bad impression	• Get someone else to check the business plan
• Evidence of market research is often absent. Good market research may cost money, but is an investment	• If you cannot afford to pay for someone else to do the market research, do it yourself
• The business needs to be aware of competitors, as well as their strengths and weaknesses	• Identify all potential competitors. Find out what they are good at and what they are bad at
• The business needs to be aware of what competitors do well and how this will be countered. It is not sufficient to claim that the business's products or services are superior	• Even small competitors are a threat. Always research them
• There is no clear direction to the business	• Be clear about the direction of the business – use a mission statement and a series of aims and objectives

Investors will want to know that the business can make a profit, if that is the objective of the business. Suppliers will want assurance that their time and effort will be well spent. Major customers will want to be sure that the business can deliver what they need, when they need it and at a price they can afford in the long term, as they will often wish to establish a long-term relationship with the business as a supplier.

QUESTION TIME
10 minutes

An essential part of a business plan is to identify the cost and sources of necessary resources, including premises, equipment and materials.

The new business needs to examine a number of different premises to find the most suitable. Some businesses may need to be located where there is a constant stream of passing trade, which means being close to where customers shop. Other businesses may need to be close to their business customers, in order to make it simple to deliver products and services as required.

1 **Why might it be difficult for a start-up company to choose the ideal location for its business?**
(9 marks)

31

What are the options and what is a legal structure?

What are the options?

This unit focuses on three different types of business structure:

- sole traders
- partnerships
- private limited companies.

Each type of structure has a number of advantages and disadvantages. Each one also has implications for the business owners. Some are easier to set up, but more financially risky than others; some require the owners to complete more paperwork. Others are not really appropriate for particular situations. On the following pages, we will look at each type of legal structure, the **liabilities** facing the owners, the legal issues, and the pros and cons.

Having decided on one type of legal structure, the business can switch to a different one in the future. For example, a sole trader may decide to take on a partner to help with the workload, or a sole trader's business may grow sufficiently to become a private limited company, with other investors and shareholders involved in the business. Switching the other way round – from private limited company to sole trader for example – is unusual.

The type of legal structure does not tell us anything about the actual size of the business.

For example Electricians

An electrician could easily be a sole trader or a private limited company. The choice is the owner's. Several electricians working together are unlikely to be sole traders, unless most of the electricians work for one electrician as his or her employees. They are more likely to be a partnership or a private limited company.

Nor does the legal structure tell us about the income of the business (its turnover); or how much money the business is making after it has paid its bills (its profit); or the size of the business (how many employees or outlets it has). It usually follows, but not always, that smaller businesses are sole traders and larger businesses are private limited companies.

Why is the choice of legal structure important?

Different types of legal structure place different responsibilities on the business owners. They may also give the owners greater access to potential investors or funds.

For example Finance

Banks are more likely to lend to a private limited company than to a sole trader, as they see this type of legal structure as more established (legally). They will also have a better idea of the finances of the business, as it has to produce very clear summaries of its financial position.

Choice of legal structure can also determine just how fast a business can grow. Many businesses begin as a sole trader or a partnership, but quickly realise that they should be a private limited company.

Above all, it is a question of separating the business, legally, from the owner. Sole proprietorships and their owners are not legally different. If the business fails, the owner stands to lose everything. If a private limited company fails, the owners stand to lose only the money that they have put into the business.

What is a legal structure?

The legal structure of the business sets the level of potential risks and liabilities of the business. It determines how tax is worked out. There are also costs in establishing and maintaining the legal structure.

KEY TERM

Liability ▶ a debt or financial obligation for which someone is responsible. A liability can be either limited or unlimited. If the owner has unlimited liability, then any money owed has to be paid back, even if it means that the owner has to sell their house and belongings to pay for it. Limited liability means that the owner will stand to lose only the amount of money they have invested in the business.

The legal structure of a business will often help to determine what options are realistic for a business:

- Being a sole trader is the simplest way to run a business. Keeping accounts is relatively straightforward because income and expenditure have to be recorded. The profits belong to the owner, but the owner is personally liable for any debts.
- A partnership is two or more people sharing the risks and responsibilities. They share the profits and the debts. A limited liability partnership is similar to a partnership, but liability is restricted to what each of the partners has invested in the business.
- A private limited company exists in its own right. It can use the letters 'Ltd' after its company name to show its legal structure. It is separate from the owners and can raise money in its own right.

As with any business decision, it is important to investigate the options and consider the advantages and disadvantages, then make a decision that is right for the business. Many business owners also seek advice from accountants, lawyers or business advisors.

QUESTION TIME
10 minutes

John decided that he wanted to run his own computer repair business. He originally wanted to take on a friend as an employee, but his friend wanted to have a share in the management of the business. John knew he and his friend would be responsible for any business debts, but they were not planning on borrowing very much from the bank, so this was not an issue for them. A few months after the business had started, John's friend suddenly decided to leave.

1 What type of legal structure do you think John's business was in the beginning? *(2 marks)*

2 If John and his friend were personally responsible for any business debts, what kind of liability would they have? *(2 marks)*

3 Once his friend leaves, what options for a new legal structure might be open to John and why? *(6 marks)*

Sole traders

YOU WILL FIND OUT:

- what a sole trader is
- what the liabilities are
- what the legal issues are
- what the advantages and disadvantages are

What is a sole trader?

Sole traders are also called 'sole proprietors' or 'self-employed'.

A sole trader is a person who owns a business and does not share ownership with anyone else. They have unlimited liability. In other words, they are completely responsible for all the debts of the business. A self-employed person means an individual who works for himself or herself and is not employed by a business. There are enormous numbers of sole traders in Britain today, perhaps more than three million.

Being a sole trader does not necessarily mean that the business does not have a large **turnover**, nor does it mean that it does not make a high profit. Sole traders do all sorts of different things, such as running shops, being hairdressers, plumbers, electricians or writers, or running bed and breakfast accommodation.

Sole traders are usually specialists who provide a particular service that does not have a market big enough for a large business to become involved in. They often have very specialised skills, or use specialist tools.

If a business is a sole proprietorship, it does not necessarily mean that only one person is employed or directly involved in the business. In fact, many sole traders employ a large number of people.

Many people set up their own businesses so that they can be their own boss. They often see a business opportunity and usually start quite small. They must be prepared to work long hours, take risks and take all of the responsibility. Since 2000 the number of businesses in Great Britain has increased by 600,000, but the number of employers has increased by only 50,000. The remaining 550,000 businesses are sole traders. It is important to realise that sole traders do also employ people.

When a sole trader starts their business, they will need some **start-up capital**. This is money for sorting out the business premises, or for buying stock or materials, tools and transport. These expenses may be quite low at first. Many sole traders use their own savings or an **overdraft** from the bank.

As a business gets going, it also needs to cover its day-to-day running costs, such as:

- replacing stock that has been sold
- paying the owner some money to live on
- covering the costs of rent, business rates, wages, lighting and other essential bills.

This money is known as 'operating capital' – it is cash required to cover the running costs. Eventually, the business should get itself into a position where it is earning enough money to pay its running costs.

What are the liabilities?

As far as the law is concerned, there is no difference between a sole trader's business funds and that sole trader's private money. If the business does not earn enough money to repay a loan, then the sole proprietor of the business will have to find the money. They are still liable for the repayments. This is called 'unlimited liability'. This means that there is no limit to the amount that the sole proprietor might owe if the business is in debt.

What are the legal issues?

The main legal requirements of a sole trader are to keep appropriate business accounts and records. These will be necessary in order to supply a tax return to Her Majesty's Revenue & Customs, who will collect tax on the sole trader's profits.

Also, as with all businesses, sole traders are required to comply with legal requirements concerning consumer protection. As the sole trader has unlimited liability, there is no distinction between the sole trader's business and private financial affairs. The sole trader will be ultimately liable for any debts that the business incurs and legally they will be obliged to sell off any of their own personal assets to pay creditors, should the business fail. This is a major reason why some people are reluctant to become sole traders and why they consider other forms of legal business structures instead.

--- **KEY TERMS** ---

Turnover ▶ the amount of money received by the business as sales revenue in a year.

Start-up capital ▶ money that is needed to begin the business.

Overdraft ▶ the amount of money the bank allows the business to borrow even if it has no funds in its bank account.

What are the advantages and disadvantages of being a sole trader?

The advantages and disadvantages of being a sole trader are outlined in the following table.

ADVANTAGES	DISADVANTAGES
There are no particular legal formalities to complete before commencing to trade	Finance is limited to the owner's savings or profits or any other money he or she can borrow
There are no particular legal requirements governing the layout of their accounts, so the sole trader could do the accounts themselves	The owner has sole responsibility for debts. If the owner falls into financial difficulties, it may be necessary to sell his or her own personal possessions to meet the business's debts
The annual accounts do not have to be audited (that is checked by an independent accountant), so the business does not have to meet this expense	Responsibility for a range of activities falls upon the one person who runs the business. In other words, the owner is entirely responsible for running the business – dealing with paperwork and customers, filling in tax returns and having day-to-day contact with any employees or subcontractors
The owner has the freedom to run the business in his or her own way	The success of the business is always dependent on how hard the sole trader wishes to work
	Any unforeseen accident or illness could seriously affect the business, since all responsibilities rest on the shoulders of that one person

> ▶▶ Becoming a sole trader is very straightforward. For many people, it gives them a level of independence where no one else is involved and they can make decisions alone.
> Unlimited liability is the major drawback, as can be the relatively long hours. Raising cash is also a difficulty, and sole traders may need to develop a range of skills in a variety of different areas, including accounts and the management of employees.

QUESTION TIME
10 minutes

Carol runs a small clothes shop as a sole trader. She sells around £120,000 worth of goods in a year. She pays tax on her earnings. Carol has unlimited liability. If she were to become a private limited company, then she would have to find another investor. She could bring in someone who knows about retailing and fashion. She wants to grow her business, but is worried about losing control of it.

1 What is unlimited liability?
(3 marks)

2 Why might Carol fear losing control of her business if she changes the legal structure to a private limited company?
(7 marks)

Partnerships

YOU WILL FIND OUT:

● what a partnership is

● what the liabilities are

● what the legal issues are

● what the advantages and disadvantages are

What is a partnership?

One option for sole traders wanting to grow their business is to take on a partner. Partners are joint owners of the business. Legally there have to be between two and 20 partners in what is known as an 'ordinary partnership'.

Each partner takes a role in running the business. In most ordinary partnerships, the partners have unlimited liability, just like a sole trader. Sole traders sometimes enter into partnerships because their own resources are limited and it is a way of bringing new funds to the business.

Many businesses actually start as partnerships. It is easier to borrow money from banks because several people are involved. This means that the bank can draw on the **assets** of several people, if the loan is not repaid.

As well as bringing in new finance, partners can contribute new skills and expertise. They will take responsibility for different aspects of the business, and can also share the responsibilities of running the business – so if one partner is unavailable, due to illness or holidays, then the others can take on their work and responsibilities.

The law assumes that all partners are equal, regardless of how much work a partner does, or the amount of money they have put into the business. Most partnerships are ordinary partnerships. As far as the law is concerned, there is an assumption that responsibility, profit and capital are equally shared by all the partners – and they have equal responsibility for the debts (unless the deed of partnership says otherwise).

A deed of partnership

If the situation is different, then partners can draw up a legal contract called a 'deed of partnership'. The deed of partnership deals with the fact that partners work different hours and put in unequal amounts of money. It covers:

- the names of the partners and the purpose of the partnership
- how much money or capital each partner has put into the partnership
- how profits and losses should be divided (this is usually in the same proportion as the amount of capital put in by each partner)
- how many votes each partner has at partnership meetings
- how disputes between partners are handled
- arrangements for any of the partners wanting to leave the partnership, or for a new partner wanting to join
- how the partnership can be **wound up** if necessary
- what happens if a partner dies
- how the partners can withdraw their share of the profits.

What are the liabilities?

Aside from ordinary partnerships (which can only have a maximum of 20 partners) there are two other types of partnership, which can each have more than 20 partners:

- **Limited partnerships** – can have some partners who do not take a role in running the business, but who own part of it. They are called 'sleeping partners'. The sleeping partners in limited partnerships have limited liability, but one member of the partnership has to have unlimited liability.
- **Limited liability partnerships** – all of the partners have limited liability, and this restricts their potential losses to the amount of money that they have invested in the business.

What are the legal issues?

Ordinary partnerships, just like sole proprietorships, are easy to set up. Some legal documents are needed, such as a deed of partnership, and only two people are needed. Ordinary partnerships do not need to involve solicitors or accountants.

Limited partnerships or limited liability partnerships can be as complicated as a limited company (see pages 38–9). They have to have their accounts checked and the accounts need to be sent to the Registrar of Companies (Companies House).

In most partnerships, each partner has an equal say in how the business should be run. In some partnerships, however, some partners are given more power and responsibility than others. The exact amount of power and responsibility is spelled out in the deed of partnership. Together the partners should be able to make the right decisions, as they will have a good mix of skills and expertise. This gives them an advantage over a sole trader.

It is also easier to raise money, because banks and other lenders of finance are more inclined to lend money to partnerships than to sole traders. If the structure is a limited liability partnership, then it can attract other investors to put money into the business.

KEY TERMS

Assets ▶ items of value, such as property and vehicles, which can be seized or sold in order to pay off an outstanding debt.

Wound up ▶ to wind up a business is to close it down, dispose of its assets and pay off any debts.

When a partner leaves the partnership, the partnership automatically ends. A new partnership needs to be formed and often the remaining partners will disagree about what should be done. If a partner with vital skills leaves, then the business could suffer; but if the weakest partner leaves, then the partnership could find a better partner, with a wider range of skills.

Family partnerships often break up because the children do not want to take over the business. This means the partnership often closes when the partners retire or die.

It is relatively difficult and complicated to leave a partnership. For one thing there is the question of getting back the money that was originally invested in the business by the partner. This could seriously undermine the partnership at what might be an important time.

A partner cannot pass on their share of the partnership or sell their share of the partnership to another person without the agreement of the other partners.

QUESTION TIME
10 minutes

1 What are the key differences between an ordinary partnership and the other two types of partnership? *(8 marks)*

2 What is a deed of partnership? *(2 marks)*

What are the advantages and disadvantages of partnerships?

ADVANTAGES	DISADVANTAGES
• It is easier for partners than sole traders to raise capital, because all of the partners can pool their resources, giving access to more capital than one person could raise	• In an ordinary partnership, a partner is personally liable for all of the firm's debts and the actions of other partners
• Partners can share their expertise and their workload	• Disagreements can arise between partners about the amount of effort that each of them puts in
• Partners can arrange to cover one another at times of illness or holidays, or even during lunch breaks	• Partnerships can only raise limited amounts of capital by comparison with businesses like limited companies
• A partnership (like a sole trader) does not have to publish its accounts or have them audited	• Decision-making can be slow, since all partners have to be consulted
• Additional capital can be raised by introducing more partners into the partnership	• The death or retirement of a partner can bring a partnership to an end
	• All profits must be shared

Partners share profits, so there is always a link between the amount of hard work and effort put in, and the rewards. It is important to remember that the share of the profits may not be equal, particularly if there is a deed of partnership. For most partnerships, liability is also a concern; risks taken by one partner can have a direct impact on the other partners, so partnerships need to be built on trust. Raising cash is slightly more difficult compared to limited companies, but each new partner can bring in additional funds.

Private limited companies

What is a limited company?

There are two different types of limited company:

- **Private limited companies** – their shares are not traded on the **Stock Exchange**. It is easy to identify a limited company, as they have the letters 'Ltd' after their company name
- **Public limited companies** – their shares are available for sale or purchase on the Stock Exchange. They have the letters 'PLC' after their company name.

Both types are limited liability businesses. The letters 'Ltd' or 'PLC' tell you about the type of ownership of a business, but you cannot make assumptions about their sales revenue, their profit or the number of people they employ. It is not even true to say that public limited companies are always bigger than private limited ones. (We will look at PLCs in more detail in Unit 2.)

What are the liabilities?

Sole traders and partnerships can find it difficult to raise money and to expand, because potential investors are worried about unlimited liability.

All owners of limited companies have limited liability, so people are happier to invest in the business. There is no separation between a sole trader's business and the sole trader himself or herself, while a company is separate from its owners. This is where companies differ from sole traders and partnerships.

Companies have shareholders, who are the owners. The limited liability means that they cannot be forced to pay the debts of the company. They stand to lose only the value of the shares they have in the company. If a company ceases trading, then its assets are used to pay off its debts. If there is anything else left over, then the shareholders receive a share of it.

What are the legal issues?

The annual general meeting

Shareholders legally control a limited company but rarely take day-to-day control (there might be thousands of shareholders in a PLC). Each year the shareholders elect directors at the **Annual General Meeting (AGM)**. The directors represent the wishes of the shareholders.

The directors

The directors cannot do everything in a business, so they use managers to run the company for them. The board of directors begins by appointing a managing director. Directors with day-to-day responsibilities are called executive directors, because they carry out – or execute – the wishes of the board of directors.

For smaller businesses, often the same people are the shareholders, the managers and the directors of the company. As far as the law is concerned, they are shareholders and directors, but because they are involved in the day-to-day running of the business, they are also its managers.

Incorporation

Because limited companies have a separate legal existence from the owners of the company, all limited companies have to be 'incorporated' – referring to the legal process of setting the business up as a limited company. Incorporation means that the company can enter into agreements using its own name, rather than the names of its owners. If the company breaks the law in any way, the company can be fined, rather than the owners.

All British limited companies also have to register with the Registrar General, also known as the Registrar of Companies. This means that before it can even start trading, the company has to complete a number of important documents and submit them to the Registrar. Only then will the limited company officially exist and be able to engage in business as a separate, legal identity.

There is a choice at this stage as to whether the business will be a private limited company or a public limited company. Both have limited liability, but both types of company have advantages and disadvantages (see opposite).

The memorandum of association

Key documents need to be created before incorporation can take place. The first is the memorandum of association. This includes:

- the company name and whether it is a private limited company or a public limited company
- the registered office of the company
- a statement that says the share-holders will have limited liability
- the amount of each type of share the company can issue, which is known as **authorised capital**. In most cases, the company will

state that its authorised capital is greater than its actual needs. This will allow the company at a later date to raise more money, by selling shares without having to change its memorandum of association

- an 'objects' clause, which is the description of the main activities of the company – legally the business should not do things that are not covered by this clause.

The articles of association

The articles of association show how the company will be run, including:

- the voting rights of shareholders
- how often annual general meetings will be held, and their procedures
- how profits will be shared
- the number, rights and duties of the company directors.

What are the advantages and disadvantages of private limited companies?

ADVANTAGES	DISADVANTAGES
• Shareholders have limited liability • It is easier to raise capital through shares • It is often easier to raise finance through banks • When additional capital is required, additional shares are offered to the public • Suppliers tend to feel more comfortable in trading with legally established organisations because they are considered to be more reliable • Directors are not liable for the debts of the company, provided they follow the rules • The company name is protected by law • The ill-health or death of a shareholder does not necessarily affect the running of the business, because the shareholder may not have any day-to-day responsibilities in the business	• The formation and running costs of a limited company can be expensive • Decisions tend to be slow, since there are a number of people involved • Employees and shareholders are distanced from one another • All the affairs of the company are public • Legal restrictions

--- **KEY TERMS** ---

Stock Exchange ▶ an electronic market that allows investors to buy and sell the shares of public limited companies.

Annual General Meeting (AGM) ▶ a meeting of ordinary shareholders that is held once a year, at the end of the financial year.

Authorised capital ▶ the total amount of money that a company can raise by issuing shares.

QUESTION TIME
10 minutes

1 Who owns a limited company? *(2 marks)*

2 Why might investors be less likely to put money into a business that has unlimited liability? *(6 marks)*

3 Many private limited companies are described as being 'family-owned'. What do you think this term means? *(2 marks)*

39

Many private limited companies are family-run, and limited liability does take away some of the financial risks. These types of companies can effectively choose their own shareholders, as the sale of shares has to be approved by existing shareholders and offered to them first. Private limited companies are often seen as a halfway house between a partnership and a public limited company.

Public limited companies' shares are openly traded through a stock exchange. This means that they can raise capital by issuing shares. The key disadvantage is often the vast number of shares that have been issued, meaning that smaller shareholders cannot exert a great deal of influence. Many shareholders of public limited companies are criticised for appearing to be interested only in short-term profits, with no interest in the long-term success of the business.

Choosing a location

Key reasons for location

The location of a business can have long-term implications for its success. Before a business decides where to locate itself, a number of factors need to be considered.

The main reasons for choosing a location could be:

- to be near to the market for the products or services being offered
- to be close to the raw materials
- to have a pool of potential employees in the area
- the cost of land or buildings
- government support in the area
- transportation links.

The larger the organisation, the greater the risk of making the wrong choice. A small business may only need small premises and its exact location might be less crucial.

Another factor is whether the business is involved in the primary, secondary or tertiary sector:

- a **primary sector** business needs to be where the raw materials are, or can be grown
- a **secondary sector** business needs to be close to those resources
- a **tertiary sector** business needs to be close to where its customers are located.

Industrial inertia

Certain areas are always associated with particular types of business. A business in a particular industry will tend to attract similar businesses to the area. There will be a ready pool of skilled employees and perhaps the location is just right. Once a business has settled, it is rare for it to move. It is very expensive to close down and start up again somewhere else. If a business does move, it is often only within 10 miles of the old site. This is known as 'industrial inertia'. Once an area has become well known for a particular sort of industry, education and training in the area are likely to be geared up to provide suitably skilled or qualified employees for that industry.

Other businesses will move into the area to supply the industry, or to provide it with services. This means that over time all the conditions are there to make businesses reluctant to move premises.

Demography

Demography is the study of the size of a population and changes in that population. There are two key ways in which demography can affect the location of a business:

- **closeness to the market** – businesses in the tertiary sector will want to be located close to the highest possible percentage of people in the population who will buy their products and services
- **the availability of suitable employees** – a business will need to ensure that there is a sufficient pool of potential employees in the area closest to the factory or other business premises they wish to open.

For example

You might find a large number of retirement homes in coastal towns along the south coast of England, such as Hastings or Bournemouth.

The cost of employing people

Linked to demography is the cost of employing people. Many British businesses choose to locate in the Far East for this reason – there is a pool of skilled employees available and the cost of hiring them is much lower than hiring similarly qualified people in Great Britain.

Sometimes skilled employees already exist in an area because similar businesses are already in operation. In other circumstances, skilled labour has to be attracted or trained.

Infrastructure

The infrastructure of an area includes anything man-made, such as:

- railways
- roads
- airports
- ferry ports
- housing
- schools
- other businesses
- premises for businesses.

A business will look for features in the infrastructure that match its needs.

The company may set up on what is called a 'brownfield site', which is a site that has had buildings on it before. Alternatively, it may build on a 'greenfield site', which is undeveloped land. In both cases, building from scratch means having to sort out a water supply, electricity, gas, sewerage and telephones. Sometimes a business may find ideal premises that are now vacant because another company has moved on or closed down.

A business that does not have to be close to suppliers or close to its customers is often referred to as a 'footloose' business. This means that it can locate literally anywhere, either to suit the wishes of the business owners or in a location that is cheap and affordable.

KEY TERMS

The primary sector ▶ creates or recovers raw materials, including agriculture, fishing, forestry, mining and quarrying.

The secondary sector ▶ also known as the manufacturing sector, transforms raw materials into products.

The tertiary sector ▶ also known as the service sector, is involved in distribution, retail, transport, healthcare and financial services.

For example

A business that transports containers of products brought in from other countries would need to be located near a port. Locating that business inland would simply not be appropriate.

QUESTION TIME
10 minutes

'**B**usiness incubation' is an environment that provides full support for businesses on one site, with all the necessary resources and facilities that businesses need. It is a concept that is found around the world. In Britain alone, there are around 300 business incubators, supporting over 20,000 creative and innovative businesses.

One business incubator called Kirkcaldy, built and managed by Fife Council Development Services, provides offices. Eleven businesses moved to the centre after it opened in spring 2008, attracted by the high-quality business space, on-site business support services and the 'easy in, easy out' lease terms.

Another business incubator in Fife, called the Business Impact Suite, provides hot-desking (shared workstations used by several employees) and a range of support services in a state-of-the-art business facility. There is space for up to 12 hot-deskers, with high specification computers and printers, filing cabinets, and telephone and Internet access.

1 Why might a small business start-up be attracted to using a business incubator? *(6 marks)*

2 What is a lease? *(2 marks)*

3 What does the term 'hot-desking' mean? *(2 marks)*

Start-up location decisions

Why is location so important?

For any business, including a start-up enterprise, location can be crucial, as this may have a direct bearing on the future of the business. Ideally, a business will look for a location that offers the opportunity to maximise revenues (income) and minimise expenditure (costs).

A useful way of looking at location decision is to consider 'push and pull factors':

- **push factors** – include a high level of competition from other businesses in the area (or a rising level of competition); rising costs (such as rents and rates); poor communication systems (both poor road networks and issues such as the non-availability of Broadband); and low or falling demand locally for the products and services offered by the business
- **pull factors** – include government incentives to locate in the area (grants, low-cost loans, subsidised rent, etc.); low labour costs; good or improving communication systems; and a healthy, growing or developing market for the products and services offered by the business.

What needs to be considered?

A number of different push and pull factors can apply to new or existing businesses, as seen in the table below.

FACTOR	EXPLANATION	EXAMPLE
Closeness to the market	• This is particularly relevant if the business deals with products that have a short shelf life, are perishable or have high transport costs	• A sugar factory reliant on sugar beet deliveries is close to areas where these are cultivated
Communications	• Transportation links can be important, but the quality of the information technology infrastructure also needs to be good for most modern businesses	• Many warehousing facilities belonging to large manufacturers, and supermarkets are located close to major motorways
Raw materials	• Locating close to the source of raw materials means that transportation costs and the time for deliveries to arrive is reduced	• This is an important factor for businesses involved in steel-making or reliant on large quantities of fuel such as coal
Workforce	• Businesses need to have access to a reliable and trained pool of employees. Some businesses are more reliant on this than others and some look for areas with traditionally low wages	• Manufacturing and processing
Waste	• With increased concerns and legislation regarding waste disposal and the treatment of toxic by-products from production, location can be tied to the location of plants capable of handling hazardous waste or dealing with recycling materials	
Power	• Great Britain has a comprehensive and reliable power supply, making this factor less relevant to British business	• Some businesses will locate in areas where they can negotiate discounted or favourable energy rates with power suppliers
Land	• Land is a scarce commodity on a small island such as Britain. Property prices are also high, particularly in built-up areas and areas that have a good infrastructure, useful workforce pool and proximity to markets	• For smaller businesses, the option of locating in central London may not be available due to the high rents and rates
Incentives	• Both central government and the European Union offer incentives to businesses if they choose to locate in particular parts of the country. These areas are usually those with higher than average unemployment rates or a tradition of under-investment in the infrastructure	

42

Businesses are not always driven to make location choices on the basis of push and pull factors. There are exceptions to the rule:

- footloose businesses – are businesses that are not tied down by traditional location factors, so can locate in any area they choose, such as a website development company
- industrial inertia – this is when a business located in a particular area, as a result of significant benefits from that area, chooses to remain there even when the original benefits are gone, despite better options elsewhere.

QUESTION TIME
10 minutes

Choosing the right location can be something of a balancing act. Ideally, the location should be convenient for your customers, employees and suppliers – without being too expensive.

For shops and other retail businesses, location is of critical importance. Your location must attract customers.

If you rely on passing trade, you want to be in an area where enough people who want your product or service can see you. For example, newsagents are often located in or around train stations. You could also benefit from customers who are attracted by other shops in a shopping centre.

For employees, the best location will be easy to travel to. Good public transport links make it easier for employees who don't live within walking distance. Employees also tend to prefer working somewhere with good local facilities.

You may want to be near suppliers for a quick, flexible service. Deliveries may be easier if there are good road and transport links.

You may not want to be too near your competitors, though clusters of similar businesses sometimes attract more customers. Your neighbours and your location also affect your image.

Location has a major impact on cost. If you need premises in a prime location, the extra costs may be justified.

Source: www.businesslink.gov.uk

43

1 Explain what is meant by the term 'passing trade. Give TWO examples of businesses that would benefit from passing trade. *(4 marks)*

2 Why might a number of similar businesses in the same location be an attraction to customers? *(2 marks)*

3 Explain what you understand by the term 'prime location' and give TWO examples. *(4 marks)*

What have you learnt?

This section should have given you a good general introduction to the issues involved in starting a business. We have looked at:

- why people start businesses and how they come up with business ideas
- the value of setting business aims and objectives, and how different stakeholders can influence them
- business plans and the kinds of risks facing start-up businesses
- legal structure, including sole traders, partnerships and private limited companies
- location.

Understanding the importance of these basic issues, centred on setting up a business for the first time, will be extremely useful as we look later in Unit 1 at different aspects that help determine whether a business is a success or a failure.

Completing the 'Question time' exercises at the end of each topic will help you get some valuable practice for the examination. The way the questions are structured and written, along with the marks, is exactly the same as the way it is done on the examination paper.

We cannot predict what will be on the examination paper, so it is best to revise thoroughly. Your teacher or tutor will be able to give you a

photocopy of the 'Unit Revision Pack' from the Teacher Support Pack when you have finished the unit – it is full of other revision ideas and exercises, as well as mock examination papers for you to try.

Don't worry about the examination: by the time you've finished the unit, you'll be ready for anything!

Integrated questions from Section 1

Try these exam-style questions. They bring together all the different topics studied in the sections, just like the examination papers do. The only difference is that here we are using examples of real businesses.

44

FRANK ROBERTS AND SONS LIMITED

QUESTIONS
10 minutes

For more than 100 years the Roberts family has been producing some of the finest bakery products in the heart of rural Cheshire. Each week over 2 million of the finest breads are baked for retail and catering customers throughout Britain, Europe and beyond.

Initially the business started in the Cheshire town of Northwich in 1886, and moved to the nearby village of Lostock Gralam in 1900. The company developed steadily through the difficult First World War years (1914–18), and the delivery service was expanded at the end of the 1920s. By 1941 there were 26 employees, with six vans, supplying over 60 shops in mid-Cheshire.

It was then discovered that land was available beside the new bypass in Rudheath. This was ideally situated for the major roads and for the planned M6 motorway, which was built 11 years later.

In 1952, all staff were transferred to the new bakery. About 600 loaves per hour could be produced and 12 people were employed. Between 1952 and 1962 bread production trebled. In 1962, over 100 people were employed and there were 20 vans.

By the early 1970s, demand was again outstripping supply and another extension for the bakery was completed. This was to house a new oven and cooler, with a capacity of 3,500 loaves per hour.

In the 1990s, the bakery expanded further, culminating in a major extension in 2000, giving the bakery the potential to bake almost 8,000 loaves per hour.

Source: adapted from www.frank-roberts.co.uk

1 Why might Roberts and Sons be described as a privately run family business? *(2 marks)*

2 Each time the business moved, it was able to expand its production. Why was it important for the business to be able to expand its production? *(4 marks)*

3 Locating near to the M6 before it was built was a risk. Why was this risky and what were the long-term benefits? *(9 marks)*

4 The business motto is 'Fresh approach – traditional values' and one of their main objectives is maintaining a culture of 'pride in our product'. What is meant by these ideas and what do they tell customers about the business? Does it help generate customers? *(5 marks)*

45

Market research on a limited budget

YOU WILL FIND OUT:
- what marketing is
- what needs to be considered

What is marketing?

Marketing is much more than just coming up with some clever advertising to sell a product or a service. Marketing does have very strong links with sales, but it also involves:

- researching markets to find out what customers want to buy
- designing and then developing products that match customers' needs and wants
- ensuring that the quality and price are suitable
- making sure that the customer knows that the product or service exists and where they can buy it.

Thousands of new products are launched every year. To make sure that the product or service is a success, everything begins with **market research** and a close look at the types of customers – or markets – who might be interested in it.

What needs to be considered?

Market segments

The term 'market' is a broad one, but it means a group of people or organisations that either already buys or might buy a product or service.

Each market is made up of many individuals or organisations. Each of them has their own different characteristics. For this reason, the first thing to do when carrying out market research is to identify parts – or 'segments' – of each market that have very similar characteristics.

Types of market

Markets can be classified geographically:

- **local market** – customers who live within the immediate area of the business
- **national market** – customers who buy from different branches of a business that are scattered around the country
- **international market** – customers who are located in other countries. They may have different needs from those at local or national level.

Characteristics of buyers

Businesses need to find out as much as they possibly can about who buys their products and services. This helps them develop the most suitable way of encouraging that type of customer to buy products from them or to buy more products from them. There are many ways in which finding out about the characteristics of buyers can help.

- **Age** – Different age groups have different needs and different spending habits. Some products and services, such as MP3 players, are aimed at particular age groups and might not be of interest to other age groups.

- **Gender** – Men and women also have different tastes, needs and spending habits. For example, men are the target market for aftershave, while women are the target market for fragrances. As these are basically the same type of product, the advertising has to be different for each gender.

- **Income** – How much money a customer has to spend is a major consideration. Those on high incomes have different spending patterns to those on low incomes. Some retailers, such as Harrods,

For example **Computer users**

A computer manufacturer might have two markets: personal home users and businesses. They might identify that one segment of the home user market is teenagers who like to play online games. The market research would aim to build up a profile of the typical characteristics of this segment.

46

cater for high-income customers, whereas Poundstretcher, Aldi or Lidl cater for those with lower incomes.

- **Ethnic, cultural and religious groups** – A business might segment its market so that it can provide for any special requirements of a particular group of people from an ethnic or cultural background. For example, an Asian radio station might be a segment of a national radio network. Foods can also fall into this category, such as kosher foods aimed at Orthodox Jewish customers.

- **Buying habits** – Another way of segmenting markets is to look at the buying behaviour of customers. Some always buy the same product and are loyal to a **brand**; some switch from brand to brand, depending on the offers available; some choose purely on the basis of price at the time; some focus on quality; and others buy purely because the product or service is the most fashionable.

- **Socio-economic groups** – Businesses will target particular socio-economic groups. This is a way of segmenting the market according to the occupation or job of the head of the household. Using this segmentation method, households are split into five categories, graded A to E, with C split into C1 and C2. The A group has the highest income and the E group is the poorest in society. Many of the products and services are aimed at those in the middle.

KEY TERMS

Market research ▶ the process of gathering information about customers, competitors and market trends.

Brand ▶ a named product, with a recognisable name, packaging and type of advertising.

Understanding customer behaviour is vital to a business, as it defines the way in which the business needs to operate and develop. By matching their business strategy to their customers, businesses can increase revenue and identify new opportunities.

Many organisations collect a vast amount of data about their customers, but few of them actually analyse the patterns of behaviour. Customer behaviour data can be identified from purchasing behaviour, returns and cancellations, complaints, frequency of verbal communication, web-browsing behaviours and a host of other sources.

One of the most basic types of market research is the Awareness, Attitude and Usage (AAU) Study. This is used to assess the general state of the market for a particular brand, product or service. Normally, the survey draws on the opinions of customers (both consumers and business customers).

QUESTION TIME
10 minutes

Patrick and Aleisha design greeting cards. They make cards they like without thinking about customer tastes. They have discovered that certain styles of card sell really well, but these are the ones they find boring to make. They often run out of these and are left with their favourite styles that do not sell.

1 How could Patrick and Aleisha work out what type of cards customers want? *(4 marks)*

2 To what extent do you think that the products Patrick and Aleisha offer match the needs of their customers? Explain your answer. *(6 marks)*

47

Reasons for conducting market research

Why is market research necessary?

It is vital for a business to understand its markets and its customers. If it understands who it is selling to and why, then it can begin to work out what future demand might be.

Market opportunities represent chances for businesses to identify and then supply demand for products and services. Identifying particular demands can be complicated. If the business finds a worthwhile market opportunity, it needs to be geared up to be able to supply it.

A business will begin by looking at its own strengths and weaknesses. It will then examine the opportunities and threats presented by the market and the competitors. The business needs to understand as much as it can about the market, in particular its trends. It will achieve this by carrying out research. Some research can be purchased or is available free of charge on the Internet through government agencies. Other, more focused research may need to be done by the business itself.

A company also needs to be clear about the current business climate. It must predict what other businesses might be doing and how ready customers are to buy its products and services. Above all, it needs to examine the amount of competition already in the market and judge whether it is the right time to enter that market.

Markets change constantly, as do customer tastes and demand. A business needs to keep track of these movements, to ensure that they can match the predicted market trends as and when they occur. This is difficult, as it requires the business to invest time, money and effort in market research.

> ⏩ In carrying out market research, a business will try to make some kind of judgement about its potential share of the market. It will need to seek information about its competitors' businesses and their products. This will enable it to position its product and set pricing levels. Many small businesses operate in a market where there are lots of suppliers and no one individual organisation has more than about a 5% share.

How can it be done cheaply?

The question facing a start-up business is just how to collect enough information to actually help it – without spending a fortune. There are four main options:

- doing the research themselves
- getting someone else to do it for them
- paying for research that already exists
- using free information.

Doing it themselves

Doing the research themselves is perhaps the cheapest option. It will involve time and effort and a considerable amount of planning. The business also needs to be clear about what it is trying to find out, so research objectives are vital. These could include:

- How many people might buy our products or services?
- Where do people buy them at the moment?
- How do our prices compare?
- Have people ever heard of us?
- What could we do to convince people to buy from us?

Obviously, the business could ask several questions and they need to ask the right type of potential customers. The business will probably have an idea about the segments it is aiming to attract.

48

Paying for new research

Another option is to get someone else to do market research for them, but this could be expensive. There are hundreds, if not thousands, of market research specialist agencies that can design research, organise it, collate it, draw conclusions and make recommendations. The bigger the research programme, the more expensive it will be. They can also organise for research to be carried out in multiple locations. For most start-up businesses, this is simply too expensive to consider.

Buying existing research

An alternative for a business is to buy research that has already been collected. There are organisations that routinely carry out market research and produce reports on trends in particular areas of business. The business could buy copies of these reports and use them to base decisions on. Problems with this type of research are: it may not answer specific questions and will probably cover too broad an area; it will certainly not focus only on the local market and customers. It can also be expensive, but not as expensive as paying for fresh research.

Using free information

There is one other option: to look through published information from the Office for National Statistics, local government and other sources. Here the business could find out employment figures, numbers of local businesses and a host of other sets of data. Even *Yellow Pages* is useful. By looking up different types of business, it is possible to see how many competitors and potential business customers are out there, and whether there are other types of business that might be interested in the products and services. What *Yellow Pages* does not tell you is how big the other businesses are, or whether they are major players in the market.

Broadly, then, the market research options are to use:

- **primary research** – new research collected either by the business itself or on behalf of the business. This is fresh data that has never been collected before
- **secondary research** – research already collected by another business or organisation that can be used for a fee or for free.

Another distinction can be made in market research between **field research** – research that is collected by going out and questioning customers and suppliers; and **desk research** – research that is carried out by searching through existing sets of data, like statistics or reports.

QUESTION TIME
10 minutes

Patrick and Aleisha (introduced on pages 46–7) have decided to carry out some market research to find out exactly what customers want. They will then start making their designer cards to match the needs of their customers. They hope this market research will help them to increase their sales.

49

1 What might be the main purposes of their market research? *(4 marks)*

2 Suggest how Patrick and Aleisha might carry out their research in the cheapest way to achieve their two objectives. *(6 marks)*

Market research methods

YOU WILL FIND OUT:
- about telephone and postal surveys and questionnaires
- about customer and supplier feedback and focus groups
- about Internet research

Telephone surveys

Telephone market research is largely viewed with suspicion by the people who are telephoned. Direct sales organisations often begin their conversation by saying that they are carrying out market research, when in fact they are making a sales call.

Dedicated telephone research can give important, rapid and cost-effective data to a business or a specialised company doing research on its behalf. Its success depends on the accuracy of the telephone list and the researchers' ability to match the people on the list with the characteristics of the target group.

A trained market researcher works from a script, to ensure that the respondents answer the required questions. There is no face-to-face contact. The researcher types the answers directly into a database, saving both time and effort.

Telephone surveys have become an important aspect of market research, mainly because of their speed. However, there is a high failure rate, owing to unanswered calls, the wrong person answering the phone, or calls being made at inappropriate times.

Postal surveys

Postal surveys – also known as 'mail-out surveys' – involve sending out a number of questionnaires to a target group of potential respondents. The questionnaires are designed to be completed by the respondents in return for a gift, a voucher or entry into a competition. Usually, a business will choose some of its customers, or it can purchase a mailing list from a specialised market research company that provides names and addresses of people that match the profile of the target group. This form of market research is now being overtaken by email surveys.

The questionnaires must be well designed, with clear and unambiguous questions. They can have visual prompts or even include samples of new products in the package to the respondents. The key advantage of postal surveys is that questionnaires can be sent out at a relatively low cost. They can also be useful in asking questions that could be difficult to ask on the telephone.

Questionnaires

Questionnaires can be a simple, inexpensive way of collecting data.

In designing and administering a questionnaire, it is important to:

- **define the objective of the survey** – organising the questions to get the answers needed
- **decide on the sampling group** – how many people and whether they are representative
- **provide a mix of different questions** – multiple-choice, yes and no answers, etc.
- **get the questionnaire out** – how respondents will be asked, for example face-to-face or by post
- **sort out the information** – how the completed questionnaires will be analysed.

How a questionnaire looks will have a direct impact on the number that are completed. The better the quality, the higher the response rate will be and the more data will be collected. Poorly designed questionnaires are often too complicated, too long or boring.

It is better to opt for as short a questionnaire as is practicable, ruling out questions that do not provide useful information. Short questionnaires will cut out the boredom factor for respondents, cut down interviewing time and reduce overall costs. Ideally, the questionnaire should not take more than 20–30 minutes to complete.

> It is always a good idea to test out your questionnaire before you launch into the research project itself. Choose a small sample from your main sample and test the questionnaire on at least 10 to 12 individuals. Ideally, get them to complete the questionnaire without prompting. Any problems at this stage can be rectified and will not leave you with the problem of dealing with deficient questionnaires once you have dozens to analyse.

Customer and supplier feedback

A major goal in marketing is to keep the current customer base satisfied and enthusiastic about the products and services being offered. Research can be used to test the relative levels of satisfaction in an organisation's products and services against those of its major competitors.

In addition, gaps in satisfaction can be identified between what is currently available and what might be the ideal or desired product or service. This may open up opportunities for new product development and a way for the organisation to offer recognisably different products and services to those of its competitors.

After a basic customer satisfaction study or survey is completed, it can be repeated regularly. This focuses a business on customer satisfaction, as well as providing immediate feedback on potential problems – hopefully resulting in the greatest net gain in satisfaction.

Focus groups

Focus groups involve selecting and interviewing a group of individuals who are representative of a larger target group. Typically, these individuals represent a business's customers, distributors or potential customers, or simply match a typical customer's age, gender or income level. Focus groups encourage discussions on the group's views and experiences of a product, service or topic.

In effect, this is a form of group interviewing. A moderator (taking the role of the group leader) guides the group through a series of questions, prompting conversation and discussion. The moderator ensures that all individuals have an opportunity to contribute. Focus group research can provide useful insights into people's shared understandings, but also indicates how some group members can dominate and influence others. It is important that the moderator is not only a good leader, but also has excellent interpersonal skills.

Focus groups are all about attitudes, beliefs, experiences, feelings and reactions. It is difficult to obtain data about these factors in any other way, although some could be gleaned through observation or one-to-one interviews.

Internet research

Email surveying – by bulk sending (or 'spamming') – can reach an enormous number of people quickly. The response rate can be very low, but the sheer volume may result in a large number of responses.

The geographical location of the respondent is not a barrier, although this can mean having to produce questionnaires in other languages, if the target groups are located in many different countries.

The response rates for this type of survey used to be relatively high. But potential respondents are now less likely to complete the questionnaires, as they receive thousands of spam emails and might delete them without reading them.

Compared to many methods, the Internet is a far cheaper method of collecting data, but the questionnaire has to be created and programmed, which could push costs up. The main advantage of the online questionnaire is that the data can be instantly exported to a database and incorporated into the research findings for analysis.

The success or failure of online questionnaires depends largely on the time taken to carry out the research, the questionnaire's complexity, sample profile (whether the sample is more or less likely to respond and/or have access to a computer) and budget.

A business can use Internet research to evaluate its:

- website (design, navigation, useability)
- online products or services
- competitors.

QUESTION TIME
10 minutes

1 **With so many different market-research options available to a start-up business, which method might be the best to begin with, and why?** *(6 marks)*

2 **Why might the Internet not provide accurate data for a start-up business wanting to base its assumptions on customers and the market?** *(4 marks)*

51

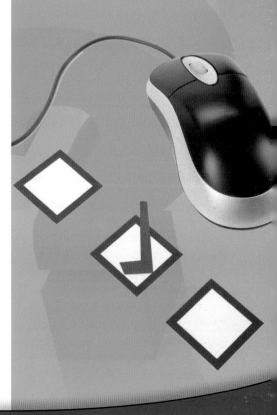

Using the marketing mix

What is the marketing mix?

In order for marketing to be effective, businesses need to look carefully at a combination of four factors: product, price, place and promotion.

They need to find a balance between ensuring that information about the products or services reaches the target market and that the market can easily make a purchase.

The business also needs to balance costs and effectiveness. If the marketing mix is wrong, then a good product could fail because of a poor pricing strategy. If the distribution is wrong, then any money spent on advertising the product will be wasted. Ideally, a successful mix will achieve the marketing objectives of the business while giving customer satisfaction.

The aim of the marketing mix is to position the product or service in the market in a way that makes it attractive to target customers. The business needs to be able to assure customers that the product can satisfy their demands far better than any competing products. However, many factors can limit or influence the marketing mix used.

Market research

Market research involves examining the needs, demands and expectations of the potential market and then trying to create or offer products and services to match these requirements. A business will usually carry out routine market research to discover trends and changes. Market research will also identify the key characteristics of the target market and indicate ways in which the market can be reached.

Finance

A business may need to make a considerable investment in a product or service before it even launches it onto the market. The development phase of new products and services is expensive and is not initially offset by income from sales, although this may happen later if the product or service is successful.

Finance also determines the type of marketing that the business can afford. Mass marketing through advertising is the most expensive form of marketing. Cheaper alternatives are possible, particularly with the advent of the Internet, where targeted email campaigns can be run at relatively low cost.

Technology

Technology directly affects the options open to a business in terms of how it markets and distributes its products and services. There is a wide range of different promotional opportunities – from conventional television and newspaper advertising, to digital advertising in the form of banner advertising on websites and direct-mail emails.

Why is the balance important?

Businesses will use different combinations of the marketing mix, depending on the type of customer they are aiming their products and services at and the size of those markets.

The marketing mix for industrial markets needs to focus not only on awareness but also on cost, quality, reliability and availability.

KEY TERM

Non-durable ▶ a product that is designed to be used up fairly quickly, for example food products or office photocopier paper.

The marketing mix for consumer markets offers a different series of opportunities. Most purchases fall into two main categories:

- convenience goods, which are bought fairly frequently and tend to be **non-durable**
- shopping goods, which tend to be durable; customers take longer to decide about them before making a purchase.

The marketing mix can be influenced by the type of customer, or how they are categorised or segmented:

- Some businesses will categorise their customers by their spending power. Higher-income customers will look to shop in exclusive stores, while lower-income households will visit most high street stores.
- Age is another determinant: toys are promoted on commercial television during children's programmes, while sportswear or cars may be promoted on sports channels.
- Gender also affects the marketing mix. The product, packaging or promotion may be aimed specifically at either men or women.

Each part of the marketing mix is of equal relevance and each segment of the market will respond to its own blend of the marketing mix. The fashion industry, for example, tends to focus either on quality and exclusivity or on cheap products that are available in a wide variety of outlets.

> Products can be modified according to the marketing mix. For example, the grooming product Lynx is targeted at men, while Impulse body fragrances and anti-perspirants are targeted at women. Essentially these are the same product.

An integrated marketing mix

Marketing orientation

Marketing orientation is about focusing on satisfying customer demands and expectations. Market-orientated businesses are often referred to as being 'consumer-centred' or 'consumer-driven'.

Most businesses have a marketing department that focuses on research, the analysis of competitors, strategy and promotion. But a marketing-orientated business takes this one stage further, by examining how it can continue to provide products and services that respond to any changing needs, wants or demands of their customers. It invests heavily in product development and in communicating with its customers.

For example Levi's

Levi's, the jeans manufacturer, brought out hipster jeans when market research showed that female customers tended to wear their jeans lower than their male customers. A new line of products was created specifically to cater for women wanting to wear their jeans on their hips rather than their waist.

Product orientation

Businesses with a product orientation tend to stress the product's features and technical strengths and expertise, rather than the demands of the market. The major problem is that a product-orientated business may find that there is no demand, regardless of how good their product or service may be, as they have not identified consumer demands before launching the product.

Production orientation

Production orientation refers to businesses that use efficiencies to produce low-cost products in high volumes. The problem arises when either supply exceeds demand, in which case prices have to be dropped even further to encourage sales, or demand exceeds supply, in which case there may be no additional capacity to produce extra products and take advantage of increased sales.

Sales orientation

Businesses may also have a sales orientation. This focuses on the needs of the seller rather than the needs of the buyer. The business tries to convince a potential buyer that they really need to buy a product or service that they would not normally think of purchasing.

For example CDs

In the music industry, consumers want to consume or purchase music and are not particularly concerned about the way in which this music is delivered to them. The market has moved from vinyl records through cassette tapes to CDs. Now, many music consumers purchase downloadable music, which places CD manufacturers under threat, as they are product-orientated.

QUESTION TIME
10 minutes

1 What are the four elements of the marketing mix? *(4 marks)*

2 A small business is looking to open a retail outlet selling repaired, second-hand washing machines, dishwashers and fridges. Suggest how it might profile its potential customers and how this might influence its marketing mix? *(6 marks)*

53

Elements of the marketing mix

YOU WILL FIND OUT:

● about product

● about price

● about place

● about promotion

Product

The term 'product' describes a range of different factors about a product or a service, including how it is branded and designed, its quality, its appearance and any special features. It also refers to the different types of that product available and the service given to customers after a sale has been made. All of these elements are an integral part of the term 'product'.

There are very few businesses that sell only one product or service. In fact, most sell a range of products, often with the same product name. This is known as a 'product family'.

For example

You can buy several different versions of Nestlé's KitKat and different flavours of Pringles potato crisps.

Other businesses sell a wider product range that might include ice cream, soap powder and medicines. Each product range, taken together, creates the product mix of the business – in other words, everything that it sells under different brand names and ranges to different types of market and customer.

The most important thing for a business to do is to make sure that their products stand out from the competition.

For example

We know and recognise Coca-Cola's brands by the packaging and colours.

A vital part of product differentiation is the product's name and the way it looks and often the way it is advertised. Businesses want customers to recognise their products immediately and choose them first, without even considering the competition.

> Packaging not only protects a product, but also helps give the product a recognisable appearance. A business will use lettering, designs, shapes, sizes and colours to attract the customers' attention. The product's brand name is often written as a logo, which will appear on all advertising to help customers recognise it.

Price

Choosing the right price for a product or service is always one of the most difficult things for a business to do. Generally speaking, the higher the price, the lower the demand for the product.

In many markets, businesses need to try to set their prices so that they at least match the prices set by the competition. If rivals are charging a particular price for a very similar product, then the business knows that it will lose out on sales if it charges more. It will have to decide whether

to match the rival's prices or charge less to try to increase its market share.

Although businesses would love to sell all their products at full price, this is often impossible. They will offer discounts and special offers and have sales, where prices are slashed.

Sometimes, to attract customers, businesses will sell 'loss leaders' – products with a very low price that make virtually no profit. This is common for new products or services. The business may start with no market share and needs to build this up rapidly. Using low prices to achieve this is called 'penetration pricing'.

'Price skimming' is another strategy. Launching a new and perhaps fashionable product, the business can charge a high price, knowing that people will pay it, and drop the price later to attract more customers.

Alternatively, the price might start at a reasonable level and gradually increase as the product or service becomes more popular. Marketing specialists call these types of products 'cash cows', because they make the business so much money.

Place

This means choosing the right location or distribution method to allow the maximum number of potential customers to have the opportunity to buy the product or service. This used to mean getting products or services into as many shops as possible. Now, with the Internet, providing advertising works and customers visit the website, the place might be a virtual place, where the customer can order online.

For traditional outlets, being in the right location is still vital. A large

54

supermarket, for example, needs to be close to a large population centre, have a large car park and a good road network. A takeaway restaurant needs a convenient situation either where customers can park or from where cheap delivery trips can be made. Most shops need to be convenient and accessible, so parking is essential, as is 'passing traffic' – cars or pedestrians walking past the retail outlet.

The key to choosing the right place also means having the product available at the right time. There is little point releasing a new toy or a mobile phone in January, because the vital Christmas market will have been missed. Nor is there any point in advertising a product and then failing to let the customer find it by messing up the distribution. Businesses will always try to choose the best type of distribution for their products and services. They will create networks of distributors and retailers.

Promotion

Promotion is any method that the business uses to try to communicate with its customers. It will usually try to tell them that a product or service is for sale, and will explain the key benefits and how it would serve their needs. Marketing communications also try to persuade customers to buy the products for the first time, or to buy them again.

Although many businesses have their own marketing departments, many larger ones will use advertising agencies, which specialise in getting marketing messages across to customers. They will be able to design advertising,

place the advertising in the media and carry out market research for the business.

Promotion consists of two major areas:

- **above-the-line promotion** – advertising in the media, such as television or newspapers
- **Below-the-line promotion** – which includes special offers and the product's packaging.

We have already seen that packaging is important in attracting customers to a product or service. Many colours and designs of brands are instantly recognisable, such as Heinz baked beans. The first task of promotion is therefore to get the packaging right, then to make sure that customers remember what it looks like.

Direct mail is a thriving business, both for printers and for newspapers and the Post Office. Leaflets, brochures and envelopes are pushed through our letterboxes daily, offering us products and services. Some businesses buy lists of potential customers from other businesses. They will buy lists of people who most closely match their own target market segments, so they can focus on sending them promotional information.

⏩ Sometimes it is very difficult to tell the difference between very targeted messages and junk mail. Junk mail is sent randomly to anyone, regardless of whether or not they would be interested in the product or service.

QUESTION TIME
8 minutes

Over 20% of people spend one to two hours online every day, 60% spend between two and four hours online a day, and 18% spend five or more hours online a day. All of them are looking for interesting websites and many of them are buying products and services.

1 A business website tells the customer nothing about the actual size of the business or how long it has been trading. Why might this be a problem for a potential customer? *(4 marks)*

2 How can a start-up business get people to visit its website? *(4 marks)*

55

The marketing mix and small business

YOU WILL FIND OUT:
- about products and customer needs
- about price, demand and competition
- about limited budget promotions
- about e-marketing

Products and customer needs

A start-up business needs to offer products and services that match customer demand. If it has carried out market research, it should know what customers are expecting or what they cannot easily obtain elsewhere, in order to find a gap in the market.

The business will soon discover whether its market research was correct – either it will make sales or find it has few interested customers. In either case, it needs to react quickly to the realities of the situation. Wise start-up businesses selling products will not have bought in huge amounts of stock of one particular type, as they may be left with stock they cannot sell. Most suppliers will accept **returns**, if they are sent back in good condition. In a relatively short period the business will begin to realise how many different types of products it needs to stock and how often it needs to reorder. Having a good relationship with a supplier helps a great deal, particularly if they can make fast deliveries if stock is running out.

For product-based businesses, if a customer asks for a product that is out of stock, it could be ordered from a supplier. A service-based start-up does not have this option; it needs to adapt what it offers, or offer a broader range of services.

KEY TERM

Returns ▶ ordered products that are returned to the supplier, who will then reduce the value of the returns from the total amount owed by the business.

⏩ Broadening the range of products or services – either in response to customer demands or because there are not enough customers for the range currently being offered – is known as 'diversification'. This means that the business is offering a broader range than before, catering for a different group of customers and their needs.

Businesses will tend to diversify into areas that are close to what they currently offer, such as a photocopy and printing service offering to print photographs or selling stationery. In time, the business may discover another area to diversify into that may have nothing to do with their main business. It may decide to move into that gap in the market, as there is a demand for it.

Price, demand and competition

There is a major link between price, demand and competition, and these can radically affect the chances of a start-up business.

A start-up business will have decided on its pricing policy, based either on what customers are prepared to pay or the prices charged by the competition. If the competitors drop their prices, the business needs to respond. If it does not drop prices, then it could lose sales, unless it has another advantage, such as convenience or better services. A new competitor, or an existing one trying to grab more of the market, is always a threat, particularly to a new business only just establishing itself.

Demand is never predictable, especially if the economic situation is not good or there are changes in fashion, tastes and technology. Demand can drop off gradually or suddenly. A start-up business cannot persist in trying to sell products and services when there is no demand. For example, a small electrical retailer cannot continue selling televisions that are not flat screen; most customers do not want them any more.

The more choice a customer has in buying a product or service, the more likely they are to shop around for a good deal. Overall, the demand may stay the same, but the supply is bigger than the demand.

The level of competition can directly affect the fortunes of a start-up business. It would be foolish to enter a market dominated by bigger, richer, more established businesses. It needs first to find a niche, do some market research, get established and then, perhaps, take on the bigger businesses.

Limited-budget promotions

Start-up businesses can rarely afford to pay for the kind of promotion they would really like, unless they have huge financial backing. So a new business needs to start small with its promotions and make sure that every penny counts.

Promotions could include:

- **Advertising in the local press** – free newspapers or local newspapers are distributed in most areas. Compared to national newspapers, the prices for advertising are reasonable and the papers will have a wide local audience.

For example Price, demand and competition

A small business opens and sells only organic farm produce. Bigger retailers notice the demand in the market and start offering their own organic products. Unless the demand increases, more businesses are competing for the same level of demand. There is oversupply in the market and someone, somewhere, is going to lose out. If the start-up business cannot offer something special, they will be the losers.

- **The Internet** – a good website is essential, but useless if no one ever visits it. The site needs to be publicised and the business can swap banner ads or links with other local businesses. Website design can be done by the owners, and website hosting can be cheap. A website host is a business that provides space on its own server for another business's website, so that it is accessible via the Internet.
- **Personal recommendation** – this is the cheapest type of promotion, providing that the business has delighted and satisfied its customers. A good experience with the business is bound to get around the area, as customers tell their neighbours, friends and family.
- **Business cards and leaflets** – handing these out on busy shopping days or near other businesses that sell similar products is always a good idea. The business needs to make sure that discarded cards and leaflets are picked up, or they may find themselves in trouble for creating litter. Also, competitors may not be very pleased if someone is outside their shop telling customers to shop elsewhere!

E-marketing

As we will see on pages 58–9, the Internet offers even the smallest start-up business opportunities that start-ups could never have dreamt of ten years ago. Most homes in Great Britain have access to the Internet – and a start-up business could reach literally billions of potential customers across the world. The most common forms of e-marketing to consumers are: emails, short message service (SMS) and banner advertising. The key benefits of e-marketing are:

- The business could achieve global reach.
- A properly planned e-marketing campaign can cost much less than traditional methods.
- If the business is using email or banner advertising, then the effectiveness of each of these can be measured.
- As the website is open all the time, any marketing effort could attract customers at any point of the day.
- Personalisation is possible – offers can be targeted at particular types of customer.
- One-to-one marketing is possible by sending information directly to mobile phones or personal digital assistants (PDAs).
- Marketing campaigns can be more interesting, incorporating music, videos and interactive features.
- There should be a better conversion rate (the number of enquiries from customers that are converted into sales). If a customer responds to an email, they can click on the link and be taken straight to the online shop.

QUESTION TIME
10 minutes

1 How might a start-up business find out whether it is wasting its money by advertising in a local newspaper? *(4 marks)*

2 How could a start-up business benefit from e-marketing? *(6 marks)*

Business-to-consumer (b2c) marketing has two elements: building traffic to the website; and then maintaining customer loyalty. Online shoppers are notoriously price-sensitive. They demand high levels of customer service and can also easily be lured away from the website, making it difficult for even the largest brands to remain competitive.

57

Using ICT in international marketing

International marketing and trade

Marketing no longer ends at the borders of a territory or a country. The Internet allows global marketing initiatives to take place. Even the smallest start-up business can now reach a global market place. It can also reach parts of markets that were closed to it through traditional bricks-and-mortar retail outlets or the use of sales personnel (such as door-to-door sales personnel or telesales). Global marketing is so important that there are now university degrees in it. Many job advertisements stress global marketing responsibilities.

At a most basic level, a business's website can be translated into several different languages and adapted to meet country-specific demands.

Businesses will sometimes enter into join ventures with smaller businesses in different parts of the world. They will collaborate in their email campaigns and in placing banner advertisements. Businesses begin the process by learning about the likes and dislikes of business and consumer populations in each of their target countries. They will also need to understand local languages, legislation and regulations.

The Internet is growing even in less-developed countries. This allows marketing communications to take place with an ever-growing world population. The number of computer owners is broadly doubling every three to five years. India and China in particular are major growth areas.

By using the Internet to deal directly with customers, rather than using **intermediaries**, a start-up business is able to appreciate many of the key aspects of its customers. By understanding their needs and their usage rates, as well as their preferred methods of purchasing and delivery, it is possible to target these customers in a much more effective manner. The more information that is captured regarding their purchasing habits, the better the business begins to understand the customer – their interests, the frequency of their visits to the website, and how many of those visits result in a sale. Encouragement, such as money-off vouchers, can then be given to customers whose purchasing frequency is dropping.

E-commerce

In the UK, a fully functional website can be designed by website specialists for between £5,000 and £8,000. However, it is perfectly possible, with a minimum of experience, for a business to create a basic website itself, albeit with limited functions. The more expensive part of developing websites is the addition of secure shopping areas and online transactions.

Businesses can purchase off-the-peg website designs with fully functional shopping carts. These can then be customised to incorporate the business's own logo, designs, text and product photographs.

Website design software can cost from as little as £50, although businesses recognise that lower-cost software is often not as flexible as the more expensive and better designed software options.

An essential part of e-commerce is completing a transaction by allowing customers to pay immediately and then to receive confirmation of the transaction by email. Many businesses use a standard order form in a secure part of their website, which the customer completes, detailing their card payment details.

KEY TERM

Intermediaries ▶ other businesses, such as distributors or retailers, that operate between the business and its customers.

For example easyJet

Instant online sales and ordering facilities are a huge benefit to customers. They can secure a product or a service, having established its availability. Customers of businesses like easyJet have to purchase their tickets online. This not only attracts immediate discounts on conventional telephone sales, but also allows the customer to view flight times and availability around their

preferred times of travel. They can choose according to their own requirements and preferred pricing. The secure ordering system takes the customer through the process and then sends an automated confirmation email, which the customer prints out for reference and to present at the check-in desk at the airport.

While a start-up business may be able to use its website to attract new customers in different markets around the world, it also faces more competition from other businesses that would not have been competitors in the past. It will acquire new competitors in each new country it deals with, all hoping to take advantage of the Internet.

▶▶ **Provided customers have confidence in the security of the system, they are able to make transactions without having to visit a traditional retail outlet. Even businesses that have always relied on their retail outlets, such as Argos, have turned to online sales as both an alternative and an addition to their overall sales offerings.**

www.argos.co.uk

QUESTION TIME
12 minutes

The major disadvantage of buying products online is that a delivery cost has to be incorporated into the price. Many businesses will either have a small, standardised delivery cost, regardless of the size of the order, or they will have built the delivery cost into the price of the product sold via the website. However, many businesses now recognise that adding unreasonably high delivery costs at the online point of sale deters customers from completing the transaction.

59

1 **Suggest THREE services that could be provided online by a start-up business. Explain the reasons for your choices.** *(6 marks)*

2 **Is it wise for a start-up business to rely on online sales alone? Give your reasons.** *(6 marks)*

What have you learnt?

This section has introduced you to marketing, and the use of information technology in marketing.

We have looked at:

- ways in which start-up businesses can do market research with limited budgets and the different options open to them
- the marketing mix – product, price, place and promotion. We discovered that they are all interlinked and together they determine just how a start-up business sets its prices, decides what products and services to sell, where they will be sold and how they will tell their customers that they are available
- the limited ways, largely due to lack of finances, that the start-up business can make the best use of promotional budgets and get their messages out to the broadest possible audience
- the opportunities that the Internwet and e-commerce can offer to even the smallest start-up business.

Hopefully you will have tried out all the 'Question time' exercises in this section. They should give you a pretty good idea of the types of questions to expect in the examination. You can nearly always count on something to do with marketing in the examination; it is an important subject and spreads into many areas of the start-up business.

Your teacher or tutor will be able to give you other useful resources from the 'Unit Revision Pack' in the *Teacher Support Pack*, including lots of extra ideas for revision and a mock examination paper. Expect to find questions on Section 1 (setting up a business) as well as on marketing (Section 2). The examiners like to mix up the questions on the paper, asking you different things about different parts of the course.

Stay focused and try to remember what you did in Section 1.

Integrated questions from Sections 1 and 2

Try the exam-style questions opposite. They bring together topics from Sections 1 and 2.

60

SPECIALIST CLEANING SERVICES

QUESTIONS
20 minutes

Specialist cleaning services are a prime example of a business with a fast-repeating customer base. In other words, customers require the services of the business on a regular basis. Just about everyone is a potential customer.

As well as this vast market, there is no requirement for expensive investment in premises or office staff. You can run your business from home, using your own mobile phone. This makes specialist cleaning an ideal start-up for anyone who wants to run their own business.

Creating their own business (either full-time or part-time) allows people to unlock their potential. They can control their own lives and increase their income in direct relation to the effort they put in. Some people want to increase an existing income or to add to a business that offers similar services. Others want to maximise their earning potential by developing a strong specialist business.

1 What is meant by a 'fast-repeating customer base'? *(2 marks)*

2 Why is there no need to have an office or premises? What other vital equipment will be necessary? *(2 marks)*

3 Why might this type of opportunity appeal to a potential small business start-up? *(6 marks)*

4 What kind of market research might be necessary before deciding to launch a specialist cleaning service? *(4 marks)*

5 How might a business start-up like this promote its services, and who might be its main customers? *(6 marks)*

61

Finance and support for a small business

YOU WILL FIND OUT:

- why finance is crucial
- about sources of finance
- why finance can be a problem

Why finance is crucial

Setting up any business needs money. Most small businesses are initially funded by money provided by the owners. A sole trader may use their savings, or several individuals may put money into a business and create a partnership or a private limited company. This is usually the only money that is available, unless they choose to turn to banks to help them find the funds to buy the necessary equipment and stock, and obtain premises from which to operate.

New businesses tend to find it more difficult to raise capital. Once the business has developed, it is far easier to attract investors and to obtain loans because the business will have its own **assets**.

The state of the economy is also important. When the economy is doing well, it is easy to raise finance from borrowing, and investors are keener to become involved. If the economy is not doing well, and potential investors are unsure of a business's long-term prospects, they are likely to choose to put their money in more secure investments.

Once the business has a track record of success, it will attract investors and lenders, who will be confident that the business will be able to pay back a loan or provide them with a share of future profits.

Businesses need money in order to invest in equipment, stock and premises. They also need money to pay regular bills. This is known as **working capital**.

It is only once a business becomes established that income filters into the company from purchases made by customers.

Sources of finance

The sources of finance depend on the stage of development of a business, the type of business, the current state of the economy and, in the case of an existing business, how successful it has been to date. For most start-up businesses, the key sources of financial support are:

- personal savings
- family and friends
- private investors
- bank loans
- grants
- business angels
- venture capital funds.

In the early stages, start-up businesses tend to either fund themselves or rely on friends and family while they develop the business idea. The major issue is that they will have to do a great deal of work before they can even put a business plan together. Typically they will have to:

- get an understanding of the market they will be working in
- collect information on their target market, customers and competitors
- make decisions about the products and services they will offer.

All of this work needs time and money – something a potential business start-up may not have available.

Why finance can be a problem

With so many potential expenses, finance can be a real issue. Even when the business plan has been written, the business has no track record, it has never made a sale, and there is no guarantee that the business idea will work.

The owner may have to find someone who is willing to guarantee any bank loans that might be made. This means finding an individual with an asset (like a house) who is willing to risk their property as a guarantee that the loan will be paid back by the start-up business.

KEY TERMS

Assets ▶ items of value, such as property and vehicles, which can be seized or sold in order to pay off an outstanding debt.

Working capital ▶ money used to finance wages and bills and other day-to-day costs.

Interest ▶ a charge added to the amount borrowed, which is also paid to the lender.

62

Finance, no matter where it comes from, is a scarce resource. To obtain it, the start-up business needs to compete for it with a host of other businesses and individuals. Some of these competitors will be seen as less risky than a start-up business, so they will get the loans first.

There is a major difference between a loan and an investment:

- A loan is given to a start-up business for a set period of time. They will have to pay back the loan, plus **interest** on the loan.
- An investment is made in exchange for a share of the start-up business. The investor will want to know that their money is safe and that they will see their original investment grow as the business grows.

As we look at the different types of finance available to start-up businesses, we will see that compared to more established businesses the options are far more limited. However, it is at the very beginning of the life of a business that finance is needed. An office or shop needs to be bought, leased or rented; stock and equipment have to be purchased; training needs to be undertaken; staff must be taken on; and a host of other expenses covered. Most of these expenses will have had to be paid for before the business makes a penny. This will leave a huge hole in the finances of a new company.

Once a business is trading, it should be making money. This can then be used to pay off loans and bills. But at the same time the money is also needed to expand, to replace sold stock, to buy new equipment and other things. At this stage, however, the business has a track record; it can show finance providers that it can make money and is not as big a risk as a start-up business. Getting to this stage is often impossible for new businesses. They simply fail before they can attract any additional funding.

As we will see on pages 72–3, the problem revolves around cash flow: just how much money is going in and out of the business. If the start-up business gets this wrong, it will run out of cash. With nowhere to go for extra money, it will be forced to close down before it has really started.

> Any initial investment is a risk. If the owners of the start-up business invest their own money in the business, then they are taking the ultimate risk. They could lose everything if the business fails. However, other finance providers will see the owner's own investment as a sign that they have sufficient faith in the business to risk their own funds. This may make them more willing to make funds available to the company.

QUESTION TIME
8 minutes

A business seeking to borrow funds from banks, business angels or government agencies has to show that the money is safe in their hands. Poor management skills are the reason why 80% of owner-managed businesses fail. So this is the first thing lenders look at when considering a loan. Before they lend money, lenders will also want to see that the owners have:
- a good track record
- expertise and skills to adapt to changing circumstances
- good product or service quality
- good financial controls
- good growth prospects
- ability to repay the loan.

1 Why might it be difficult for a start-up business to prove any of these six points to a potential lender? *(6 marks)*

2 In what document might lenders find evidence of these points? *(2 marks)*

63

Sources of finance

YOU WILL FIND OUT:

● about bank loans and overdrafts

● about mortgages

● about loans from friends and family

● about grants

Bank loans and overdrafts

Banks can usually provide two different types of finance: loans and overdrafts.

Loans

The business will borrow an amount of money and pay it back on a regular basis, in instalments. The bank will charge interest on the money that has been borrowed.

Often banks will demand security on the loan. Security is often in the form of assets owned by the sole trader, partners or shareholders of a business. The bank can seize these if the business fails to pay back the loan. Sole traders often have to offer their own homes as security, or **collateral**.

Loans tend to be for a fixed term, with interest payments due on a monthly basis. The longer the period of the loan, the more interest will have to be paid over the term of the loan. The business needs to make sure that it can afford to pay the monthly instalments and that these repayments do not eat into its working capital, affecting its ability to pay other **current liabilities**.

Overdrafts

Banks also offer overdrafts. This means that a business can write cheques or make payments in excess of the amount of money that it actually has in its account. The bank will set an overdraft limit, which is the maximum amount that the business can go overdrawn – or 'into the red'. If a business has a £1,000 overdraft facility, this means that it can write cheques to the value of £1,000 – even if its bank account is empty.

Overdrafts, in particular, can

be an extremely expensive way of borrowing money. Overdrafts not only have to be agreed with the bank or building society (in terms of the amount that the business can be overdrawn), but they attract a relatively high level of interest.

Mortgages

A mortgage is used by a business to buy buildings or premises. It is a legal agreement between a bank or financial service provider and the business, which gives the lender certain legal rights over the property being purchased with the mortgage. The bank or financial service provider has the legal right to repossess the buildings or premises, if the business is unable to make the required mortgage repayments.

A business mortgage is like a special type of business loan. The lender will gain legal rights over the property until the business is able to fully repay the loan. Small business mortgages usually last for up to 20 years. The business will need to show that it will be able to repay the mortgage, so it will have to prepare business plans and financial plans and work out the market value of the property. The business will have to put up between 20% and 30% of the purchase price as a deposit. Some smaller businesses may only be required to put up 10%, but their interest rates will be higher.

The advantage of purchasing a property, as opposed to renting it, means that the business can rent out part of the

building to another business and can generate extra income. Also, mortgage repayments are often cheaper than rent, particularly if the repayment schedule has fixed monthly payments.

There are also disadvantages, such as extra responsibilities for the property. A mortgage can be quite draining on the finances of a small business. Another problem is that having a mortgage on a property means that it is more difficult to relocate, as the property would have to be sold before the business could move.

Loans from friends and family

Loans from friends and family are also a potential source of funds for a start-up business. Friends and family are more likely to be able to offer a low-interest loan, or one with no interest attached at all. They will probably consider lending over a longer period than other sources, and may be willing to adjust the terms

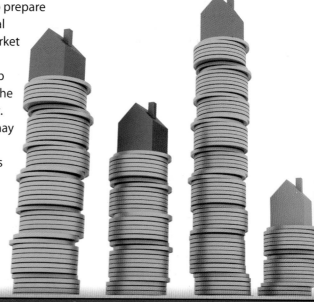

64

of the loan. They will also be a good judge of character and are less likely to need a detailed business plan.

If the business has been turned down by other sources of finance, it is wise for the start-up owner to be open about it. Family and friends should only lend what they can afford to lose. There can be difficulties, as relationships are at stake if problems do arise.

Some start-up owners will sign a formal agreement with friends and family. These set out the terms of the loan in writing. This helps to avoid misunderstandings that can arise if the loan has been agreed verbally.

Grants

Great Britain's financial markets are among the most dynamic and flexible in the world, meeting the needs of most small businesses. However, some small businesses, particularly start-ups, can struggle to access finance. Small businesses with high growth potential may also have difficulty in raising the relatively modest amounts of capital needed to fund their ambitions for growth. Grants are available from a number of sources. A grant is different from a loan, as it is not expected to be repaid.

Some of the key types of grant available in Britain are listed below. Later in this section we will look at other sources.

The Government Grant for Research and Development

This initiative provides grants to help individuals and small to medium-sized businesses to research and develop technologically innovative products and processes.

Early Growth Funds

This grant aims to increase the availability of small amounts of money for innovative businesses and smaller manufacturers.

Regional Venture Capital Funds

This is an England-wide programme that provides up to £500,000 to small to medium-sized businesses that show growth potential.

Small Firms Loan Guarantee

This service is provided by the government. The government guarantees bank loans taken out by start-up and small to medium-sized businesses.

As a short-term source of borrowing, the business can also buy 'on credit' – it can buy goods from a supplier and sell them before the payment is due to the supplier 30–90 days later.

> Once a business starts trading, it will begin to make money. It can keep back some of the profits, rather than paying it to the owners or shareholders. This means that the business will have cash available. This type of cash, known as 'retained profit', is far cheaper than borrowing from a bank.

─── K E Y   T E R M S ───

Collateral ▶ assets used to guarantee the repayment of a loan.

Current liabilities ▶ debts that a company currently owes to its suppliers; they are due for payment by the end of the financial year.

QUESTION TIME
8 minutes

According to the World Bank, Britain is the best location for start-up businesses in Europe, having over four million small businesses. Britain has better support and back-up than any other European country. There is less paperwork to complete, workers are more flexible, and there is more support from the government and advisors.

The London 2012 Olympics alone will bring £10 billion into the economy, and start-up businesses are aiming to take a share of that money.

1 The London 2012 Olympics will have around 7,000 contracts with direct suppliers and will offer around 75,000 business opportunities. Suggest FOUR ways in which a small business could get involved with the Olympics. *(4 marks)*

2 An estimated half a million extra tourists will be visiting London to watch the Olympic Games. Suggest FOUR opportunities for types of service that a small business could provide directly for these tourists. *(4 marks)*

65

Sources and types of advice available for small businesses

YOU WILL FIND OUT:

● about support and advisory services
● about private support services
● about financial and insurance services

Support and advisory services

There is plenty of help and advice available to businesses – ranging from trade associations related to a particular industry, through to government organisations, such as Business Link.

Trade associations

Trade associations are organisations that represent the interests of their members in a particular industry, for example the travel association ABTA, which represents travel agents. Members pay a fee and in return receive support and services from the organisation. The trade association will provide assistance in the application of law and in dealing with problems, as well as trying to convince the government to consider the industry when it makes policies and laws.

Chambers of Commerce

In most towns in Great Britain there is a Chamber of Commerce. It is rather like a trade association, except that it has members involved in almost every different type of business. Chambers of Commerce represent the wishes and the needs of local businesses, routinely interacting with local government and central government. They can also act as a means by which businesses can receive grants and training from central government or the European Union.

Business Link

This is a national organisation with offices in each area of Great Britain. The offices are designed to help local businesses and to provide them with services, training, support and advice, for example in writing business plans, in exporting and importing, and in dealing with European regulations.

Confederation of British Industry

The Confederation of British Industry (CBI) is a British organisation that works as a **pressure group** to influence the government, so that it produces favourable policies and laws for business. The organisation also carries out research into how trends in the future might affect businesses.

Institute of Directors

The Institute of Directors supports business leaders, providing information, advice, training and publications. It also represents the concerns of businesses to the government.

Government agencies

The primary government support for businesses comes from the Department for Business Enterprise & Regulatory Reform (BERR). It has an enormous range of information, advice and support for businesses in every different industry. Specific information is available to different business sectors, such as computer games, manufacturing and telecommunications. BERR analyses the market and provides information about new opportunities and threats that could affect the industry. It works closely with different trade associations and Business Link.

BERR is also concerned with regional economic development. This is of great interest to many businesses that may wish to locate or relocate in an area suffering from high unemployment and lack of investment. To encourage businesses to settle there, the government may give them financial incentives. The Selective Finance for Investment

KEY TERMS

Pressure group ▶ an organisation that tries to influence the government, the European Union, other businesses and individuals to be favourable towards their members or their cause.

Direct debit ▶ an instruction to a bank to pay money to a person or organisation each month, usually to pay bills; direct debits can be set up for varying amounts.

Standing order ▶ an instruction to a bank to pay money to a person or organisation each month, usually to pay bills; unlike direct debits, standing orders are for fixed amounts that cannot be varied.

Premium ▶ the cost of taking out the insurance; it has to be paid to the insurer.

project, for example, offers a minimum of £10,000 for businesses to establish, expand, modernise or relocate in a particular area identified as needing assistance.

European Union

There is also assistance for businesses from the European Union, which concentrates on aiding areas where people's incomes are well below the European average. Normally European funds can be accessed via organisations such as Business Link.

Private support services

A wide range of other businesses are also concerned with supporting or providing services to business. These include:

- **accountants** – who can help prepare financial data
- **solicitors** – who can help with legal matters, chasing of debts and business contracts
- **computer services** – which can provide computer maintenance and repair, as well as helping to organise a business's website
- **communication services** – which could include telephone companies, the Post Office, courier services, Internet service providers, advertising agencies and mobile phone providers.

Financial and insurance services

Businesses will also need assistance in handling money. Banks can help them to:

- deal with cash
- process cheques
- process **direct debits** and **standing orders**
- process debit card and credit card transactions
- exchange currency
- transfer money to and from abroad.

Businesses will also need insurance to cover them against potential risks, such as fire or theft, or to cover them if there are accidents at work. A business will pay an insurance company a **premium**, depending on the risk involved.

> Business consultants aim to assist businesses in improving their performance. This is usually achieved by analysing any problems that the business is experiencing and developing strategies to deal with them. Consultants can help businesses by identifying good practice, offering training on using new technology, and developing new strategies and marketing techniques, for example.

QUESTION TIME
10 minutes

Sally has just left school after her GCSEs. She wants to go straight into work, running her own small cleaning business. She is very confident that she can find more than enough customers to keep her busy.

Sally has managed to save £2,000 from holiday and weekend work. She has worked out that she will need an additional £6,000 for a van, equipment, materials and insurance.

1 In the role of a small-business advisor, suggest to Sally which organisations she might approach for support, advice and sources of finance. *(10 marks)*

67

Basic financial terms

What are gross profit and net profit?

You will need to know about price, sales, revenue, costs, profit, and how they relate to one another. None of these terms are as difficult as they may seem. The following example will help you understand why.

For example Gross profit and net profit

A business sets its price for a product at £10. Over one month it sells 1,000 of these products. That means its revenue from the products is:

£10 × 1,000 = £10,000

But the business had costs. It had to buy the product from a supplier (£4). All of its other costs (wages, rent, electricity, etc.) cost £5,000 for the month. So its costs for the whole month, including the 1,000 products from its supplier, is:

1,000 × £4.00 + £5,000 = £9,000

So if we deduct the costs from the revenue, we will have the profit:

£10,000 − £9,000 = £1,000

Now, before the owner can take that £1,000 and spend it on champagne and fast cars, there is tax to pay for. That's why this figure is called the gross profit – that is the amount the business made before it paid tax.

If the business is due to pay 20% tax, for example, we now take 20% off its £1,000. This gives us £800. Now the business owner can decide what to do with the £800, which is called the net profit – that is the profit after tax.

Basic financial terms

Let's go a stage further and look at price, revenue and profit in a bit more detail.

Price

Setting an initial price for its products or services is one of the most difficult tasks facing a business. It needs to take account of the costs incurred. It also needs to consider the prices charged by key competitors. The best price that a business wishes to charge may not be possible if competitors are charging considerably lower prices.

It is difficult for a new business to set prices, because its products and services may not be well known. Its costs may be comparatively high, because it will not have the advantages of producing products or providing services on a large scale. Equally, it cannot charge high prices because neither the company nor its products and services are established in the market.

Revenue

Calculating revenue is relatively simple. Sales revenue – or income – is equal to the total number of products or services sold, multiplied by the average selling price. In other words, all a business needs to know is how many of its products or services have been sold, or might sell, and the price they will charge.

KEY TERMS

Gross profit ▶ the difference between a business's costs and its sales revenue before tax is paid.

Net profit ▶ the gross profit minus other costs; it forms the basis for tax calculations.

Overheads ▶ expenses, such as rent or rates, which have to be paid by a business regardless of the level of production.

68

Profit

We have already seen that a business incurs costs that must be paid. Clearly these have a direct impact on the profitability of a business. There are, however, different types of profit.

- **Gross profit** – Gross profit is only one calculation of profit. It simply shows how much it costs a business to generate a certain amount of revenue.
- **Operating profit** – The operating profit is the business's gross profit minus its **overheads**. Overheads are all the other fixed costs that may not be directly associated with the business's output or the cost of achieving sales. This is often a far more accurate measure of the profitability of the business.
- **Pre-tax profit** – A business may also calculate its pre-tax profits, as it may have one-off costs, such as the refurbishment of a building. These costs are deducted from the operating profit to give the pre-tax profit.
- **Net profit** – The most important type of profit is the profit achieved by the business after it has paid Corporation Tax – its net profit. This is the amount of profit that it can choose either to pay out to shareholders or to reinvest in the business.

Profits are a key measure of the success of a business. Profit means that the business can attract additional funds to invest in assets. It may also attract new shareholders. Although many businesses do borrow money, profit is the source of more than 60% of all of the finance used to help businesses grow.

We can see that there is a direct relationship between costs and profit. Costs cut into the revenue generated by the business and reduce its overall profitability. Adjustments can be made to the revenue generated by a business, either by increasing the price of products or services sold, or by increasing production while keeping costs the same. In both cases a business would make more profit. However, if additional costs were incurred by increasing production, and these were equal to the revenue generated, then no extra profit would be made.

Businesses look for ways to gradually increase profit and to sustain that level of profitability. Often the danger for small businesses is that they create an increase in profitability and then incur additional costs in order to maintain that level of profitability.

QUESTION TIME
10 minutes

A business works out that it has overall costs of £4,000 per month. On average it sells 500 products that cost an average of £4.50 each. The business's average selling price for each product is £9.99.

1 Is the business making a profit or a loss? Calculate the profit or loss figure. *(4 marks)*

2 Suggest how the business could increase its profits. *(6 marks)*

69

> Pricing policy differs from business to business and from sector to sector. Effectively, the more competitive the market in which the business operates, the tighter the pricing policies have to be in order to continue to compete and attract customers.
>
> If, for example, a key competitor were regularly offering a similar product for £10, then a business could not confidently expect to sell exactly the same product for £15. Customers would simply not buy from the higher-priced supplier unless there was a particularly good reason to do so.

Calculating profit and loss

YOU WILL FIND OUT:

● about profit quality

● about net profit calculations

● why these calculations are useful

● about profit and ethics

Profit quality

We have already seen that gross profit is the difference between sales revenue and the cost of those sales. It is useful, however, to see precisely how these two figures work together, as it will reveal precisely what the ratio is of gross profit to sales.

The formula to work out a **gross profit margin** as a percentage is:

$$\frac{\text{gross profit margin}}{\text{sales turnover}} \times 100$$

This is a particularly useful formula if we are comparing two different years, because it may show us whether sales costs are increasing or decreasing in relation to the value of sales revenue.

Net profit calculations

A similar set of calculations can be made to see the ratio of net profit to sales turnover. The ratio is shown as a percentage and calculated by dividing net profit by sales turnover and then multiplying by 100.

——— **KEY TERMS** ———

Gross profit margin ▶ gross profit divided by sales turnover and then shown as a percentage.

Net profit margin ▶ net profit divided by sales turnover and then shown as a percentage.

Externalities ▶ costs or benefits of an activity that are not actually paid for or received by the business engaged in that activity. For example, a negative externality might be a factory polluting a nearby river as a result of its operations; there will be clean-up and health costs that the business might not have to pay.

For example Profit quality

In 2008, a business has sales of £88,000 and sales costs of £12,000. In 2009, sales revenue has increased to £98,000 and the cost of sales has increased to £18,000.

The first thing to do is to work out the gross profit.

2008 The gross profit is £88,000 – £12,000 = £76,000

The gross profit margin is therefore: $\frac{£76,000}{£88,000} \times 100 = 86.36\%$

2009 The gross profit is £98,000 – £18,000 = £80,000

The gross profit margin is therefore: $\frac{£80,000}{£98,000} \times 100 = 81.63\%$

From these figures we can see that the sales costs are increasing in relation to the value of sales. This indicates that the business is beginning to lose control of its costs, although it is still making a substantial gross profit.

For example Net profit calculations

In 2008, the net profit was £24,000 on a sales turnover of £88,000. To work out the ratio of net profit to sales, also known as the **net profit margin**, the following calculation is made:

$$\frac{£24,000}{£88,000} \times 100 = 27.27\%$$

In 2009, the net profit has risen to £28,000 and sales turnover to £98,000. Therefore:

$$\frac{£28,000}{£98,000} \times 100 = 28.57\%$$

Despite the fact that the business incurred higher costs of sales, the actual net profit margin increased by 1.3%. If succeeding years show higher percentage figures, then the business is moving in the right direction. If the percentage figure drops, then there are problems for the business. The higher the ratio, the more profitable the business.

Why are these calculations useful?

The amount of profit that a business makes, and the trends in the profit, show the business whether it is making the right decisions. They can also show where and when it might need to make an investment in order to make more profit.

The key point about any business is the balance of risk against rewards. There is little point in a business investing a large amount of money, if it is only going to end up with the same amount of profit. It needs to be assured of receiving a better return for the money it spends by reinvestment than it would get simply by leaving its cash in the bank – the lowest-risk option. These calculations can help it assess the risks.

A business may see a change in its gross or net profit, as well as its gross and net profit margins. Some of the reasons may be directly related to the fact that it has better or worse control over its own costs. Other factors that could affect the overall profit levels come from outside the business, such as a change in the tax rate.

Profit and ethics

Most businesses operate to make a profit for their owners and shareholders. To make a profit, the business has to charge its customers more than the costs it incurred in providing its products or services.

However, there are a number of businesses in Britain that do not aim to make a profit. These are social enterprises. Others try to offer their products at the lowest possible price and generate only enough money for reinvestment. In an ideal world, even those in favour of all businesses making a profit, recognise that customers should not be exploited and that the environment should not be harmed.

At the same time, businesses cause what is known as **externalities** – pollution and damage to the environment, for example. Although they pay tax and are regulated to stop excesses, it is often society that pays to put these damages right, not the business itself.

QUESTION TIME
10 minutes

1 Suggest THREE external factors that could affect the profit margins of a business. *(3 marks)*

2 In the first year a business shows a net profit of £50,000. In the second year this is doubled. Its sales turnover in the same two years has increased from £250,000 to £1 million. What does this tell us about the business? *(3 marks)*

3 Profit adds to costs for the customer, but it also leads to two other outcomes for the business. What are they? *(4 marks)*

71

> Costs can be categorised as fixed, variable, direct or indirect costs. Fixed costs are those that have to be paid by the business, regardless of how much money it may be making (such as rent and employees' wages).
>
> Variable costs relate directly to the amount of business the organisation is doing. If it is making and selling more, then the costs tend to go up (more stock, more electricity, overtime for staff, etc.).
>
> Direct costs are those that can be linked to the making or selling of the products, such as the cost of products or materials, the wages of people that manufacture them and the electricity used to run the production line.
>
> Indirect costs are those that cannot be linked with the making and selling process. Sometimes they are called 'overheads' and include rent, rates, administration and sales and marketing costs.

The meaning of simple cash-flow statements

YOU WILL FIND OUT:

- what a cash-flow forecast is
- about the importance of cash-flow management
- what a cash-flow forecast shows

What is a cash-flow forecast?

Cash is a business's most **tangible asset**. Cash-flow forecasts and cash-flow statements show the flows of cash both into and out of a business. The forecasts actually attempt to predict the flows, so that the business can identify when there might be a shortfall in cash (which may mean borrowing), or excess cash (which can then be invested).

Monitoring cash flow is a way of noting how money comes into and goes out of a business. It is split into two categories:

- **Receipts** – usually money that has come into the business by customers paying for products or services. It is important to remember that these are not **invoices**, but actual payments. Receipts can also be money put into the business by its owners.
- **Payments** – a total of all money paid out by a business. It would include payments to suppliers, wages to employees and other necessary expenses, such as rent and business rates.

The difference between the receipts and the payments is called the 'net cash flow'. If this figure is positive, then the business has had more receipts than payments. If it is negative, then the business has paid out more than it has earned.

A cash-flow statement is used as a monitoring tool and contains the actual figures as they become available, so that they can be compared to the cash-flow forecast.

--- **KEY TERMS** ---

Tangible asset ▶ an asset owned by the business that can easily be turned into cash in order to cover expenditure.

Invoices ▶ written requests for money, as payment for products or services supplied by a business. They are sent to the business's customers.

The importance of cash-flow management

Businesses need a good source of cash to pay bills as they become due. Delaying payment can be a major problem, particularly if suppliers are not paid, or employees do not receive their wages.

Cash-flow problems are one of the most common reasons why businesses fail. In fact, around 70% of businesses that fail in their first year do so because of major cash-flow problems. It is important to note that cash flow is not the same as profit. Profit is the difference between revenue and costs, but cash flow is the movement of money into and out of the business.

New business start-ups often suffer from cash-flow problems. They may buy new stock but may not have sold it until the bill for that new stock becomes due. They know that they can make a profit once the goods are sold, but have a cash-flow problem because the goods have not yet been sold and the supplier wants their money.

Businesses can survive in the short term without making a profit, providing they generate enough money to cover their expenditure. However, in the long term, profit is absolutely essential.

Cash-flow forecasts can help the business to:

- identify when there is a cash-flow shortage and how big it is
- arrange covering finance in advance
- balance their income and their expenditure to cover probable shortfalls.

72

What a cash-flow forecast shows

A cash-flow forecast, therefore, outlines the money that is coming into the business and the money that is flowing out of the business. It shows the anticipated inflows and outflows of cash over the coming months.

If a business's income in a given month is greater than its expenditure, then a positive cash flow will be shown. If the expenditure is greater than the income, a negative cash flow will be indicated. Usually a business will use an overdraft facility to deal with this. If it appears to be a longer-term problem, they may take out a loan.

The monthly cash-flow forecast lists:

- the cash inflows (the actual money coming in from sales and other sources)
- the cash outflows (money being used to pay for bills and other expenses)
- the effect on the overall cash balance that the business holds.

The closing balance on a cash flow becomes the opening balance for the next month. On a cash-flow forecast you will see figures in brackets, which represent minus figures.

QUESTION TIME
10 minutes

A business has cash sales of £25,000 in a month and has spent £15,000 on stock. It had an opening balance of £5,000. Other cash costs in the month totalled £4,000.

1 Which of the figures are cash inflows? *(4 marks)*

2 What is the closing balance at the end of the month? Show your calculations. *(6 marks)*

73

▶▶ A business will be able to judge how accurate its cash-flow forecasts are by comparing them with its actual cash-flow statements. This will reveal how good a prediction the business has made as to the probable inflows and outflows of cash over the given period of time. Usually a business will create a cash-flow forecast covering six to twelve months ahead. They will continue this process by making a projection, extending the cash-flow forecast. But as they receive more information from cash-flow statements, their predictions should become gradually more accurate.

The importance of cash-flow statements

YOU WILL FIND OUT:
- about cash inflows and outflows
- about opening and closing balances
- about statements and forecasts

Cash inflows and outflows

The ideal situation is obviously for a business to have more money flowing in than flowing out. If this is happening, the business can build up a cash balance, which it can use to deal with any future shortfalls in cash. It could also use this to expand and to set aside for paying off loans or making payments to investors.

For most businesses, the problem is that cash inflows often lag behind cash outflows. Therefore the trick is to be able to speed up the inflows and slow down the outflows. If the business becomes short of cash, it may become **illiquid** and it may have difficulties in remaining **solvent**. A cash-flow forecast, therefore, tries to estimate the expected inflows and outflows so that when a business is short of cash it can find cash from elsewhere, and if it has too much cash it can try to invest this money.

CASH INFLOWS	CASH OUTFLOWS
• Payments received for products and services from customers	• Purchases of stock, machinery, raw materials or fixed assets
• Receipt of a bank loan	• Payment of rent, wages and other operating expenses
• Interest received on investments or savings	• Payment of tax and **VAT**
• Investments made by shareholders	• Dividend payments to shareholders
• Increased loans or bank overdrafts	• Repayments of loans or reduced overdraft facilities

The table above outlines typical cash inflows and outflows.

Some payments have to be made on fixed dates, such as wages, loan repayments and tax. The difficulty is that the business may not be able to accurately predict exactly when it will receive payments from customers. It is important to remember that on the cash-flow statement, the actual payment date is relevant, as is the date when the customer is invoiced or even when the customer is expected to have to pay.

—— KEY TERMS ——

Illiquid ▶ this means that the business has assets that cannot be very quickly converted into cash.

Solvent ▶ solvency is a measure of a business's ability to pay its debts with available cash.

VAT (value added tax) ▶ a sales tax on many products and services; it is collected by the business and paid to the government.

Administrative overheads ▶ unavoidable office costs; administration supports the business by providing office and secretarial services.

Opening and closing balances

An opening balance is the amount of money that a business had in its bank at the start of a month.

The closing balance is the opening balance plus or minus the net cash flow. This shows the business precisely its precise financial position at the end of the month. The closing balance becomes the opening balance for the next month.

Statements and forecasts

Businesses will actually create two different cash-flow forms:

- a cash-flow statement – a record of the receipts and payments, as they take place
- a cash-flow forecast – an estimate or prediction of what the cash flow might look like in the future.

Cash-flow statements and forecasts tend to be done for a three-month, six-month or twelve-month period. As far as the forecasts are concerned, the further into the future they are planned, the less likely the figures are to be correct.

74

The purpose of making forecasts is to help with budgeting. They can be used to compare the actual results, as they occur, with the forecasted figures. This gives the business an opportunity to see how it is doing compared to the predictions that it made.

The table below shows a cash-flow forecast for a six-month period, January to June.

There are additional lines on this cash-flow statement. The capital from owners refers to money invested by the business owners. The payments are broken down into production, which is roughly half of sales, **administrative overheads** and payments made to purchase machinery.

> ⏩ A cash-flow forecast shows the business cycle. Income and expenditure are rarely timed to match one another. Inflows of cash will often lag behind outflows. Ideally, at some point, there should be an occasion when there is more money coming in than going out. By creating a cash-flow forecast, the business can begin to address these imbalances.

QUESTION TIME
12 minutes

1 Give TWO examples of typical cash inflows. *(4 marks)*

2 Give THREE examples of typical cash outflows. *(6 marks)*

3 Give an example of an external organisation that might want to see a start-up business's cash-flow forecast. *(2 marks)*

CASH FLOW FORECAST (£S)						
	January	February	March	April	May	June
RECEIPTS						
Sales	12,000	18,000	20,000	19,000	22,000	28,000
Capital from owners	10,000	0	0	0	0	0
Total receipts	22,000	18,000	20,000	19,000	22,000	28,000
PAYMENTS						
Production	6,000	9,000	10,000	9,500	11,000	14,000
Administration	4,000	4,000	5,000	5,000	5,000	6,000
Machinery	0	0	4,000	0	0	2,000
Total payments	10,000	13,000	19,000	14,500	16,000	22,000
Net cash flow	12,000	5,000	1,000	4,500	6,000	6,000
Opening balance	5,000	17,000	23,000	24,000	28,500	34,500
Closing balance	17,000	23,000	24,000	28,500	34,500	40,500

Identifying solutions to cash-flow problems

Reasons for cash-flow problems

Cash is a large part of what is known as 'working capital'. Working capital is the amount of money that is available to a business to pay for day-to-day running expenses. It is calculated by comparing what the business actually owns with what it owes. The problem is that much of what a business may own is tied up as a fixed asset, such as land, buildings and machinery.

A business may suffer from 'a liquidity crisis' for many reasons – cash-flow problems or difficulties with working capital. The major reasons are outlined in the table.

Resolving cash-flow problems

There are various ways in which the careful management of cash flow can either avoid cash-flow problems or deal with them promptly. Essentially, the options are to:

- encourage debtors to pay sooner
- cut down unnecessary expenses
- sell off debts to a debt collection agency
- try to delay payments to suppliers
- increase cash flow by selling off stock at a discount
- ask the bank to extend the overdraft
- obtain a long-term bank loan
- sell assets and then **lease** them back (known as 'leaseback')
- sell off any unused assets.

It is important to recognise that a problem with cash flow can be more dangerous than a drop in profits. A business needs to be

PROBLEM	EXPLANATION
Too much spent on fixed assets	Expensive vehicles and machinery can tie up a business's available cash in assets that are difficult to sell. A business may be advised to lease assets to ensure that more cash is made available
Too much stock	If it is holding too much stock in reserve, the business may find it difficult to sell stock fast enough to generate sufficient cash
Overtrading	This is when a business expands too quickly for the funds it has available. It may overcommit itself to additional wages or the purchase of assets. If sales do not match forecasts, it will face a liquidity problem
Seasonal fluctuations	Outgoings tend to remain relatively constant for most businesses. If the business only generates sales during the season, such as a theme park open only in the summer, then regular outgoings will drain their working capital out of season
Making too much credit available	Many businesses offer credit on products and services between 30 and 90 days after delivery. The longer the credit period, the longer the wait the business has for cash. It offers credit in order to attract sales, but it must make sure that customers are not given a longer credit period than the one offered by its suppliers
Using too much credit	A business may find itself overexposed to massive debt by taking advantage of long credit periods from suppliers. It hopes that the longer it has to pay, the more likely it will be to have the cash available. But taking too much credit could lead to a major cash crisis in the future
The unexpected	Non-payment by customers can affect cash flow, as can changes in the interest rate, levels of employment, the closure of a major supplier or customer and a host of other unexpected and unwanted events

aware of the impact that resolving a liquidity problem can have in the long term. For example, by selling and leasing back assets, this represents a long-term financial commitment for the business. The sale of unused assets may in fact inhibit the business's ability to grow in the longer term.

Speeding up inflows

One of the primary techniques in helping to solve cash-flow problems is to increase the speed at which cash flows into the business. In effect there are three different ways in which this can be achieved:

- **Negotiating shorter credit terms for customers** – this is a potentially difficult and

dangerous option, particularly in very competitive markets. The business may lose customers if it insists on reducing the length of credit available to its customers. In any case, larger customers demand longer credit periods. One way around this is to offer early settlement discounts to customers if they pay their invoices ahead of the due date.

- **Improved credit management** – by keeping a close eye on the payment of invoices by customers, the business can prompt customers to make payments on invoices when they are due. This will require the business to send out reminder letters and, perhaps, make telephone calls to persuade customers to pay their invoices.

Lease ▶ sometimes known as a 'rental plan' or a 'hire purchase agreement', the asset is made available to the business over an agreed period for a fixed, regular payment.

Commercial mortgage ▶ rather like a personal mortgage, this is usually taken out for 15 years or more. Many banks and building societies offer commercial mortgages.

- **Debt factoring** – a business has the option of selling the value of an invoice to a debt factoring company. The business will receive 80% of the invoice value as soon as it is sold to the company. The factoring company then collects the full value of the invoice at the end of the credit period. It will then pay the business the remaining 20%, minus factoring fees. Usually this means that the business loses 5% of the total invoice value.

Delaying outflows

Just as a business can seek to improve the inflow of cash, it can also attempt to reduce the amount of money that it spends. Again there are three ways in which this can be achieved:

- **Negotiating better credit terms** – suppliers can be approached to extend the period of credit for a range of products, services, components and raw materials used by the business. Although this only postpones payment, it can help the business over a difficult period when cash is in short supply. Suppliers will usually consider this as an option, but if they believe that the business is in difficulty, they may be reluctant. Equally, new businesses with little or no credit history will find it difficult to convince suppliers to extend credit terms.
- **Leasing instead of buying** – for most businesses, fixed assets are one of their biggest expenses. This is particularly true for new businesses that may need to

acquire specific fixed assets in order to begin trading. Expenditure on these fixed assets represents a significant drain, but as an option the business could choose to lease the asset, rather than buying it outright. Staged payments over the lease period can help with cash flow, and the business still has the option of owning the asset at the end of the lease period by making additional payments. Many businesses lease their company cars rather than purchasing their own fleet of vehicles.

- **Renting instead of buying** – another significant expenditure is the purchasing of buildings, which may either be on the basis of an immediate full payment or a **commercial mortgage**. Renting the buildings rather than purchasing them means that the business does not have to find the capital to finance the purchase.

> We have already seen that it is possible to delay cash outflows, but there are more permanent ways in which a business can cut or delay expenditure. These are by decreasing levels of stock, cutting costs and postponing expenditure.
>
> There are four ways in which a business can seek to find additional funding to cover any shortage of cash:
>
> - overdrafts
> - short-term loans
> - long-term loans
> - sale and leaseback.

QUESTION TIME
12 minutes

Brownhill Kennels has got cash-flow problems.

It normally invoices its customers within a day or two of providing services to them. The invoice states that the customer has 45 days to pay.

Looking over the invoices that it receives from its own suppliers, Brownhill sees that the average payment time requested is 30 days.

Brownhill also owns two vans, and has been looking into buying another kennel business in the area.

1 **Suggest to Brownhill Kennels how it might speed up its cash inflows and delay its cash outflows in order to improve its cash flow.** *(6 marks)*

2 **What other options might the business have in respect of its vehicles and buying the other kennels?** *(6 marks)*

77

What have you learnt?

This section has aimed to explain the importance of finance to a business, particularly a start-up enterprise. We have looked at:

- finance and support for small businesses and how it is particularly difficult for start-ups to attract the finance they need. There are many ways in which a start-up business can find help and advice
- financial terms and some simple calculations to work out the relationship between price, sales, revenue, costs and profits. You will also know how to work out whether a business is making a profit or a loss
- cash flow – how cash-flow statements and cash-flow forecasts are put together, where the information comes from, how it fits into the calculations, and what it means

- what a start-up business can try to do to sort out problems highlighted in the cash-flow statements and forecasts, although the solutions to these problems might be limited for new businesses.

If you have tried all of the 'Question time' exercises in this section, you will be getting a good idea of the kind of thing the examiner is likely to ask on the examination paper. You won't be asked to complete a cash-flow statement. You might have to do some basic calculations though, but the examiner will always, give you the formula you need to do them.

Your teacher or tutor will also be able to give you a copy of the 'Unit Revision Pack' from the *Teacher Support Pack*. It will help you identify all of the key areas to revise and will include a mock examination paper. The

support pack material will include information on this section, but it will also include questions from the first and second sections of this unit. This is to remind you that you won't get finance-only questions on the exam paper. The odd question will crop up among questions on the other four sections in this unit.

Finance is really nothing to worry about. It is an important part of business (some would say the most important), but as long as you understand the basics, and why finance plays such a key role, you are halfway there.

Integrated questions from Sections 1, 2 and 3
Try these exam-style questions. They bring together topics from Section 1 (Starting a business), Section 2 (Marketing) and Section 3 (Finance). This is a real business situation.

78

BOO.COM

There are literally hundreds of thousands of e-commerce websites on the Internet. For every successful site, there is a long list of failed businesses.

One of the early pioneers of e-commerce, Boo.com, collapsed in 2000. It sold famous brand-name clothes and fashion.

Boo.com's main target market was fashion-conscious 18–24-year-olds, but fashion and shoes have the highest rate of returns of any type of product, plus they do not have such a large mail-order market.

Boo.com raised a great deal of money from venture capitalists and from investors like Benetton. The owners had managed to spend £80 million on the start-up, but it soon became clear that their cash-flow forecasts were way too optimistic. Many of the products they sold were returned as faulty.

The business owed £12 million to advertising agencies alone; 400 staff lost their jobs and, in all, the business spent £125 million in just six months.

Boo.com had hoped to generate £70 million in sales in the first year and £700 million per year within two years, according to its forecasts.

QUESTIONS
17 minutes

1 What do you understand by the term 'e-commerce'? *(2 marks)*

2 What were the major financial problems of the business? *(6 marks)*

3 Boo.com raised a great deal of money from venture capitalists and from investors like Benetton. What is a venture capitalist? *(2 marks)*

4 Did Boo.com target the wrong type of customer with the wrong products? Give reasons for your answer. *(7 marks)*

The need for recruitment

YOU WILL FIND OUT:

● what recruitment is

● about full-time workers

● about part-time workers

● about temporary and permanent workers

What is recruitment?

All organisations wish to employ the most appropriate individuals as employees. To achieve this, they need to have a series of processes and procedures in place, to ensure that candidates will meet the requirements and needs of the organisation. This is known as recruitment.

The organisation's human resources department usually manages the recruitment process. It works together with the line manager (the manager to whom the new employee will directly report), deciding on the type of candidates it is looking for and identifying the key responsibilities and duties of a vacant position. For smaller businesses, this is usually the job of one of the owners or managers, who may not have the specialised skills to deal with the recruitment process.

Applicants will be sent documents that have been prepared by the organisation, laying out the requirements and challenges of the post. These are integral to the recruitment process.

Once a candidate has been shortlisted, they usually have a face-to-face interview. The impression they make at the interview will have a direct impact on the interviewers' choice.

The entire recruitment process must take into account various legal obligations, as well as any regulations laid down by the business itself.

Full-time workers

Full-time employment means that the employee works a full week – usually up to 40 hours a week, but often as much as 60 hours or more. The employee does this every week, apart from the time they have off for holidays. Typical full-time jobs include most teachers, local government officers and office workers.

Full-time employees are usually paid on a monthly basis, but sometimes full-time employees such as factory workers might be paid on a weekly basis. Factory workers have traditionally been paid in this way.

The contract of employment for full-time workers will state the number of hours that they are expected to work, the availability of **overtime** (and how much pay, or time off instead of pay, they will get for working overtime), and their holiday entitlements.

Around 60% of people in work in Britain have full-time jobs. Not all of them work standard hours from 9am to 5pm. Many work **shifts**, at home, at night, or even for three or four 12-hour days each week.

An increasing trend is for employees to work **flexi-time**. This means that employees can work around their other commitments, perhaps dropping children off at school or looking after elderly family members. For example, instead of starting work at 9am, they can start at 9.30am or 10am and perhaps finish work later. Employers are encouraged by government to allow employees – as long as they do their full weekly hours – to organise their time to suit their outside commitments.

Part-time workers

Part-time employment is common in the UK. It ties in with many employees' needs for flexible working arrangements. Traditionally, part-time work has allowed employees with outside commitments, such as childcare, to balance their working life and home life. The majority of part-time workers are women.

Normally, part-time work is no longer than 25 hours per week. Part-time workers have the same rights as full-time employees. They tend to work either part-days, such as mornings, afternoons or the middle part of the working day, or they may work evenings or weekends. Some may only work two or three whole days per week.

KEY TERM

Overtime ▶ additional hours worked by employees, usually at a higher hourly rate of pay than their normal pay.

Shifts ▶ when an employee works non-standard hours, such as starting at lunchtime and working through into the evening, or beginning earlier in the day and finishing after lunch, they work in shifts.

Flexi-time ▶ employees can choose what hours they work, as long as they meet daily, weekly or monthly required totals of hours.

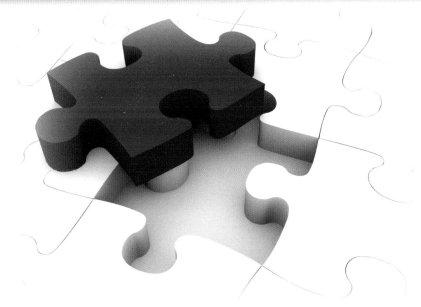

Temporary and permanent workers

When an employee begins working for an employer, their contract of employment will state whether the job is temporary or permanent.

If the job is temporary, the contract will state that the employee has been taken on to work for a specified period of time, such as six months or a year. At the end of the period, the contract has been completed and the employee leaves the job. In many cases, temporary contracts are given to employees to cover long-term sickness, maternity leave or the short-term needs of the employer to take on more staff. Both the employer and the employee enter into a temporary contract knowing that the relationship is for a limited period of time, although in many cases temporary contracts can lead to a permanent post. Typical temporary jobs include secretarial work, catering, and seasonal work when employers take on extra staff (for example in a shop during the busy run-up to Christmas).

The majority of jobs are classed as permanent, as there is no definite period of time that the employee is expected to work for the employer. The contract only ends when the employee chooses to leave the job or, for disciplinary reasons, the employer terminates the contract. However, permanent work is not necessarily secure. An employer may wish to terminate the contract because the skills or job of the employee are no longer needed, or perhaps because the business is about to close down.

Deciding on the exact mix of full-time, part-time, temporary and permanent workers is a major issue for start-up businesses. While many can benefit from permanent, full-time employees, they cannot be sure whether there will be sufficient work for them once they have taken on this commitment to pay wages and other benefits in the longer term.

Start-up businesses often decide to opt for part-time, temporary workers. This gives them more flexibility, but it is not seen as an ideal situation for the employees, who can be discarded easily and may look for more secure work elsewhere. Part-time, temporary workers may have little loyalty towards the business, which could be a major problem for the owners.

QUESTION TIME
22 minutes

Based in Swansea, Wheelies Direct is a cycle replacement service. They have 75 employees and two retail outlets, a workshop, a warehouse, a call centre and an online shop.

They favour a diverse workforce. They select older people for their call centres and younger people for the more physical roles in the warehouse, workshop and retail outlets. They are firmly in favour of equal opportunities and anti-discrimination, and believe that they have a competitive advantage by recruiting skilled employees.

1 Wheelies Direct has a mix of part-time and full-time employees. Explain the difference between these two types of employee. *(4 marks)*

2 Suggest TWO reasons why Wheelies Direct might hire temporary staff. *(4 marks)*

3 What benefits do older employees bring to businesses like Wheelies Direct? *(6 marks)*

4 Wheelies Direct has identified that skilled staff provide a competitive advantage. Discuss whether skilled staff are a benefit to a business like Wheelies Direct. *(8 marks)*

81

Recruitment methods

YOU WILL FIND OUT:

● about internal and external recruitment

● about personal recommendation

● about advertising

● about interviewing

Internal recruitment

Internal recruitment means filling vacancies from within the business. In other words, existing employees are either encouraged to apply or are selected for a vacancy. The business may choose this course of action because it believes it already has employees with the right skills for the job.

Details of the vacancy may be:

- advertised on a staff notice board
- placed on the organisation's intranet
- included in the organisation's in-house magazine or newsletter
- announced at a staff meeting.

There are advantages and disadvantages to using internal recruitment.

External recruitment

External recruitment is probably the most common method of recruitment. It means filling job vacancies with individuals from outside the organisation.

A business may choose to do external recruitment itself, by advertising a vacancy and then carrying out the selection process. By advertising the post, it will hope to attract the widest possible audience, including suitable candidates.

Most businesses tend to use external recruitment agencies on a regular basis. Sometimes this is a necessary feature of recruitment and selection, as many companies have a high turnover of employees – a large proportion of employees are constantly leaving the organisation for

opportunities elsewhere. Therefore, to take the strain off the organisation's human resources department, external agencies are used as a constant source of new employees.

> ▶▶ **Using internal recruitment means that fewer new ideas, attitudes and perspectives are brought into the organisation by new employees.**
> **With external recruitment, the choice of the media, the type of advertisement, the acceptable costs and the use of external agencies depend very much upon the nature of the post in question.**

Personal recommendation

As a start-up business gets busier, it may decide to approach its part-time employees to see whether they would be prepared to work full-time. If this does not deal with the immediate need to fill a vacancy, then employees, business colleagues, friends and family can all be asked whether they could recommend someone to approach.

For some businesses, personal recommendation is a slightly less risky way of taking on a new employee, as they are known to someone who is trusted by the business owner. They may have the talents that the business is looking for, particularly if such skills are hard to find.

ADVANTAGES
• Existing employees have greater opportunities to advance their careers and gain promotion and additional skills and experience
• The employer will know much more about the aptitudes and abilities of the internal candidates, reducing the chance of selecting an inappropriate candidate for the post
• Internal recruitment tends to be a far more rapid process than external recruitment, and is far cheaper
• Restricting the vacancy to internal candidates can also help retain employees who may otherwise have left

DISADVANTAGES
• The number of potential candidates for the post is limited to only those in the business
• There may be far better external candidates, who have more experience and better qualifications
• Employees, whether they are competent or not, will feel that they have an automatic right to be given a more senior post
• If an internal candidate is selected to fill a vacancy, a new vacancy instantly arises

82

Advertising

External advertising for vacant posts normally takes place when the business has exhausted its search for a suitable internal candidate. While many businesses write and place advertisements in the media themselves, others use agencies to do this for them.

Recruitment advertisements in local or regional newspapers can be relatively straightforward, featuring simply the job title, a brief description of the role, the closing date and necessary contact details. While these small advertisements – known as 'display' advertisements – may be suitable for recruiting relatively unskilled workers, something more is required to attract experienced and potentially key employees. The advertisement must intrigue and maintain the interest of a suitable candidate who would be attracted by the prospect of working for the business. This can mean that large display advertisements are required, often with images and an indication as to salary ranges and future prospects.

The increasing cost of media advertising in newspapers and magazines has caused a shift to online recruitment. More and more organisations are using online employment sites and special pages on their own websites as a means of attracting potential candidates.

There can be a great deal of competition for good candidates. Increasingly, in key job roles it is the candidate rather than the potential employer who can pick and choose. Organisations are also discovering that the proportion of key job roles being filled by internal and external recruitment is falling, and that recruitment consultancies are becoming particularly important for senior posts.

Interviewing

Face-to-face interviews are still popular with many businesses. They give the business a chance to meet qualified candidates, and the candidates can get a taste of the business. The interviewers can ensure that the candidates have the right kind of attitude, experience and characteristics for the business.

Businesses also use a number of other interviewing techniques:

- **telephone interviews** – an initial screening interview on the telephone is useful in helping the interviewer and the candidate to get a feel for whether there is a mutual interest in pursuing the application. It is a faster and more cost-effective way of creating a shortlist
- **computer interviews** – these are becoming more common. The potential candidate is asked to answer a series of multiple-choice questions online or to fill in a brief summary of their skills and education. Computer interviews can be used before shortlisting takes place
- **assessment websites** – these are particularly useful if the business is looking for individuals with keyboard and mouse skills. Responses can be timed and the candidates' computer proficiency assessed.

QUESTION TIME
16 minutes

Online recruitment site www.jobsite.co.uk believes that small and medium-sized businesses in Britain waste £69 million per year on poor recruitment decisions.

Jobsite favours: competency-based interviews; offering training to existing employees, so they can be more motivated and productive; and promoting internally, to use existing talent to its full potential. Businesses should also be more flexible, and communicate with their employees to help prevent them from leaving.

Finally, businesses should think carefully about where they advertise their vacancies. Small ads in national newspapers and using the Internet are ways of reaching the broadest possible selection of potential employees.

1 What is meant by 'competency-based interview'? *(2 marks)*

2 Explain the difference between internal recruitment and external recruitment. *(4 marks)*

3 Explain ONE advantage and ONE disadvantage of internal recruitment. *(4 marks)*

4 Discuss TWO reasons why a business may choose to advertise a job vacancy on the Internet, rather than in a national newspaper. *(6 marks)*

83

Remuneration

Wages and salaries

The term used to describe all types of pay is 'remuneration'. This is payment by the employer in return for the hours worked by employees. It is the most expensive part of most businesses' outgoings.

Depending on the type of job, an employee will be paid either a wage or a salary. Wages are usually based on the number of hours that have been worked in the previous week. Salaries, on the other hand, tend to be a twelfth of the annual payment to an employee. In other words, the employee is paid a twelfth of their total salary each month.

In both cases, payments are often made in **arrears**. The employees will have worked for either several days or several weeks before they are paid for their labour.

Payment methods

There are four usual ways in which employees are paid:

- **by cash** – usually paid on a Friday to part-time or casual workers on wages rather than salaries
- **by cheque** – either handed to the employer or posted
- **by credit transfer from a bank** – this is an example of **electronic data interchange**. Payments are guaranteed on a particular day of the week or month
- **by Bankers' Automated Clearing System (BACS)** – where money is transferred directly from a business's bank account straight into an employee's bank account.

Deductions

Employees do not receive all their wages or salaries. The money that is given to them has already had money deducted from it, including:

- income tax
- National Insurance
- pension contributions
- trade union subscriptions.

Wages and salaries are calculated using the PAYE – or Pay As You Earn – system. This means that employees pay their income tax and National Insurance as they earn their wages or salary.

Pay slips

Regardless of how an employee is paid, they will always receive a pay slip that summarises the payments made to them and any deductions that have been made. It usually includes:

- the hours worked
- the pay before tax and other deductions
- itemised deductions
- the pay after tax and other deductions
- how much income tax has been paid in this **tax year**
- how much National Insurance has been paid in this tax year.

Skills

The term 'human resources' is used because employees are seen as a valuable resource. The better the employee, the more valuable they become. There is a direct link between skills, experience, qualifications and pay. Employees with rare skills and good experience are often more difficult to attract and cost more.

A start-up business trying to find skilled and experienced employees needs to balance the risk of taking on someone with less experience and ability, against the greater cost of recruiting someone with more experience.

Older employees, particularly if they have been with the business for some years, will cost more, as they will have had a number of pay increases over time. However, pay is always connected with age. A start-up business needs to match or better the pay offered by more established businesses; otherwise it could not possibly attract experienced employees away from other businesses.

Time rates and piece rates

Most employees on wages are paid a 'time rate'. This means that their pay depends upon the number of hours they have worked. They will have been allocated an hourly rate of pay. Their pay before deductions is equal to their hourly rate of pay multiplied by the number of hours they have worked.

Rather than being paid for the number of hours they have worked, employees on 'piece rate' are paid for the number of items they have made, or tasks that they have completed, over a given period of time. Piece-rate workers (known as 'pieceworkers') tend to be paid when a batch of work is completed.

> **For example**
>
> An employee is paid 10p for every letter folded and put into an envelope. If they managed to do 1,000 of them, then they would receive £100.

Businesses now have to be very careful about setting piece rates, because they are expected to pay the **National Minimum Wage** to all employees.

Overtime

Overtime is additional pay that is given to employees for working over and above their normal working hours. Overtime payments are usually higher per hour than regular hourly pay.

> ### For example
>
> If an employee receives £7 per hour, they might receive 'time-and-a-half' for overtime, giving them £10.50 per overtime hour worked.

Bonuses

Bonuses are often paid to employees because they have achieved a goal or an objective set by the business, or because the business itself has achieved particular goals or objectives.

Bonuses are usually paid as a lump sum at a particular time of the year, perhaps just before Christmas or shortly before the end of the tax year. Alternatives to bonuses include holidays, cars or other non-financial rewards.

Commission

Commission is usually paid to employees who are on relatively low hourly rates of pay. Commission is usually a small percentage of the total value of sales made by that employee. Commission is added to the employee's basic pay.

> ### For example
>
> If an employee receives 2% commission, he or she will receive £2 in commission for every £100 of products or services sold.

⏩ **Bonuses in particular are seen as a way in which a business can reward employees for their contribution towards the business achieving its aims, objectives or targets. Bonuses are usually paid on a sliding scale, with more senior employees and managers receiving larger bonuses, to reflect their additional contributions during the year.**

QUESTION TIME
19 minutes

A business receives a rush order for £1,000 of products. The business knows that the materials used will cost £400, but in order to produce the products and sort out the order it will need ten of its employees to work 5 hours overtime each at £10 per hour. The business owner wonders whether it will make any money out of the rush order.

1 Define the term 'overtime'. *(2 marks)*

2 Why is the business willing to pay overtime to its employees? *(4 marks)*

3 Calculate the total cost of fulfilling the order. *(5 marks)*

4 Advise the business on whether it was appropriate or not to accept the order? *(8 marks)*

─── **KEY TERMS** ───

Arrears ▶ the payment is made after the work has been done.

Electronic data interchange ▶ a system that links the business directly to its bank in order to make automatic payments.

Tax year ▶ the period from 6 April one year to 5 April the following year.

National Minimum Wage ▶ the lowest legal hourly payment to employees, set by the government. It is dependent upon the age of the employee.

85

Monetary and other benefits

Performance-related pay

Performance-related pay – also known as 'merit pay' – is additional payments made to employees who manage to achieve specific goals. Usually these goals have been agreed in individual appraisals or in team meetings, or are announced to employees across the whole organisation.

Performance-related pay is similar to a bonus, but the payment is linked closely to actual achievements, such as:

- increased efficiency
- higher profits
- lower numbers of complaints
- dealing more quickly with customer queries.

Individual employees could be awarded performance-related pay because they have achieved certain goals, they are efficient and helpful, or they have a good record of attendance. The system rewards individual employees for meeting agreed goals, which could give them a higher rate of pay than others doing similar work who have not met the goals.

Appraisals

Many businesses link performance-related pay to appraisals – one-to-one interviews and discussions between an employee and a manager or supervisor. Appraisals review the employee's performance and form the basis for development and improvement or future training.

In an appraisal, each employee can be graded. For example:

- unacceptable (U)
- improvement needed (I)
- good (G)
- high achievement (H)
- outstanding (O).

If the employee can reach the outstanding category, then they will be awarded a 5–10% pay increase. Those in category U do not receive a pay increase – not even to keep pace with **inflation**.

Problems

Performance-related pay was the big new idea of the 1980s. By the early 1990s, nearly 60% of businesses had adopted it.

However, by the late 1990s, businesses were beginning to realise that it did not really achieve what it set out to do. Also, it was expensive to run and was causing unhealthy rivalry between employees. Nonetheless many businesses still use performance-related pay.

The main problems with performance-related pay are that:

- it is often not generous enough to encourage employees
- it is seen as being unfair
- it damages teamwork, as one person wants to take credit for success
- it is actually unlikely that money alone will **motivate** employees. According to government research, less than 10% of employees believe that performance-related pay is the best way of improving motivation at work.

Fringe benefits

As an alternative to extra pay or higher rates of pay, a business may instead offer a range of non-financial rewards, known as 'fringe benefits' or **incentives**. These include:

- **subsidised** meals and drinks
- free or subsidised travel
- free pick-up and drop-off to and from work

- free travel passes
- travel loan schemes
- company cars
- essential car users' allowances (employees provided with a company car and a company credit card for fuel)
- overseas travel and expenses for work
- refund of travel expenses
- discount on purchases made from the business
- loans and mortgages at reduced rates (typical for bank employees)
- health insurance.

Pensions

As well as the State Pension (paid for by National Insurance contributions), there are two other forms of pension:

- **non-contributory pensions** – the employer (not the employee) pays into the pension scheme
- **contributory pensions** – the employer and the employee both pay into the pension scheme.

Pensions that feature a contribution from an employer are a very attractive fringe benefit for an employee, as the pension will support the employee after they retire.

Generally there are two different types of pension scheme:

- company pension schemes
- personal pension schemes.

Company pension schemes usually include a contribution from the employer. The advantage of personal pension schemes is that the pension is related only to the employee. When they move job to a different business, the pension can move with them.

Inflation ▶ a general rise in prices. As costs rise to produce products or provide services, these contribute to pushing up prices, creating inflation.

Motivate ▶ to encourage, particularly making an employee happy with their work so they perform at their best.

Incentives ▶ any kind of reward or benefit to encourage an employee.

Subsidised ▶ partly paid for by the business or offered to employees at the price it costs the business to obtain it.

Gross pay

Gross pay is an employee's total pay before deductions. The monthly gross pay of an employee paid is:

$$\frac{\text{annual salary}}{12}$$

The weekly gross pay of an employee paid on an hourly basis is:

Hours worked × hourly pay rate + overtime hours × hourly overtime rate

Deductions

The two major deductions from gross pay are income tax and National Insurance.

The amount deducted depends on the person's gross pay. The higher the gross pay, the higher the deductions. Deductions may also include pension, donations to charity or trade union subscriptions (monthly payments).

Net pay

Net pay is the actual amount of money paid to the employee after deductions. The simple formula for calculating net pay is:

Gross pay − deductions

For example Net pay

Suppose an employee receives £28,000 per year. The employee is allowed to earn £4,000 tax-free. After that, the employee pays 22% income tax and 15% National Insurance. The way to work out the employee's monthly net pay is:

£28,000 − £4,000 = £24,000   £24,000 × 37% = £8,800

£24,000 − £8,800 = £15,200   £15,200 + £4,000 = £19,200

$$\frac{£19,200}{12} = £1,600 \text{ per month net pay}$$

▶▶ Banks and other financial institutions offer reduced-rate loans and mortgages as a fringe benefit to their employees, while other businesses may offer discounts on the products and services they sell.

Reduced-rate loans and mortgages are seen as a way of locking the employee into the business for the longer term. If they were to leave the business, then they would no longer be eligible for the reduced rates. Unless they found a similar deal elsewhere then, despite finding a better-paid job, they might actually be worse off.

The same can be said for pension schemes, although pensions are technically portable. This means that pension contributions made while working for one organisation can be transferred into a new pension fund with a new employer.

QUESTION TIME
21 minutes

QPC Limited, a customer contact centre, runs a staff incentive scheme. Initially they ran their bonus scheme based on annual financial targets. Now they have switched to a range of different goals, including revenue targets, break-even targets and personal targets based on each employee's own job role.

The new bonus scheme is designed to give employees a percentage of the available bonus, even if they do not achieve every target in each three-month period.

1 Explain the term 'incentive scheme'. *(2 marks)*

2 Explain the term 'bonus scheme'. *(2 marks)*

3 Give TWO reasons why businesses like QPC Limited run incentive schemes. *(4 marks)*

4 When QPC Limited ran the bonus scheme on annual financial targets, why might the financial targets not have been met? *(5 marks)*

5 In your opinion, was QPC Limited right to introduce a new incentive scheme that was not only based on financial targets? *(8 marks)*

87

Motivating staff

YOU WILL FIND OUT:
- what motivation is
- about the four key motivators

What is motivation?

Motivation is about creating a drive in employees to take action and to perform to the best of their ability. A motivated individual decides to pursue particular goals because they feel valued. Certain situations or circumstances may motivate employees; others may demotivate them.

A motivated employee can satisfy their own needs and goals, while also satisfying those of the business. Some people look for motivation in relationships that they have at work with their colleagues, such as a good team spirit. Employees like a sense of belonging, to feel part of a team, to be valued by their boss and to be seen as being important to the success of the business.

Some employees are motivated because they get a buzz out of the mental or physical challenge of what they are doing. Others are motivated because they realise that everything new that they do, or challenge that they manage to succeed in, helps them to develop.

Motivation does not come just from being paid or from having a secure job. That was how many

businesses and managers thought motivation worked in the past. It may work for a period of time, but after a while there is nothing for the employee to feel motivated about. Employers need to keep up their employees' levels of motivation, otherwise performance will drop and there will be problems. A positive attitude to work, a commitment to the business and a belief that their role is valued are essential to keep employees motivated.

The four key motivators

Certainly a part of motivating employees is to pay them a sufficient amount that suggests they are valued financially by the business. But in the long term, this is not enough in itself.

Small businesses may not have the skills, funds or back-up to use some of the more complicated and effective ways of motivating staff that larger, more experienced businesses use. But this does not mean that attempts to motivate staff in a start-up business will fail. They can use the four key motivators described here.

Job enlargement

Job enlargement refers to employees doing a range of different tasks rather than repetitive or boring ones. Employees like to have interesting and challenging jobs, but many of them will end up with monotonous work. If this situation continues, then no matter how much money an employee is being paid, they will not feel fulfilled or motivated. They will either look for another job or simply leave.

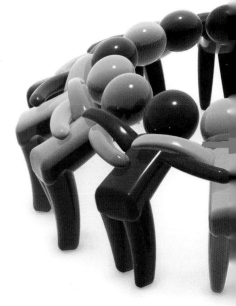

Responsibility and opportunities for self-development are key motivators in helping to ensure that employees continue to work to the best of their ability and in the interests of their employers.

Job design

Opportunities for job enlargement come down to good job design:

- An employee's job should require a wide range of different skills, so they can have variety in their work.
- They should be given whole jobs, not part of a job. In other words, they should be able to see something through to the end and get a sense of achievement by having completed it.
- They need to be given jobs that mean something. Above all, they need to be able to see why they are doing it.
- They need to be given a degree of freedom to decide the order of their work, so they can set their own priorities, within reason.

88

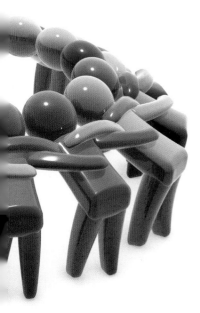

- They need feedback. They want to be recognised and praised if they have done a good job. This helps them feel valued and part of the whole business process.

Job enrichment

Small businesses want employees who can turn their hands to a wide variety of different jobs. In start-up businesses, job titles usually mean very little; everyone will be expected to help out if there is a job that needs doing, including the bosses. By allowing and encouraging employees to help out beyond what is strictly their role, their jobs are enriched – with greater variety, challenges and stimulation.

Job rotation

Another key way to ensure that employees remain motivated is to switch them around from one job to another. This is known as 'job rotation'. It might sound chaotic, but it has some very clear and tried-and-tested advantages:

- It stops employees from getting bored. They can learn new skills and they can see the business and its processes from a completely different angle.
- It helps them understand how everything fits together. Understanding what is involved in another job can prevent misunderstandings and arguments in the future.
- It means that employees pick up extra skills. This is a process known as 'multi-skilling'. When there are rush jobs, or absences due to illness or people leaving, the employees can quickly fill the gap and know what they are doing. This may not be a long-term solution if someone has left the business, but in the short term it can prevent the business from grinding to a halt.

> ⏩ The four key motivating methods – job enlargement, job design, job enrichment and job rotation – are all simple ways in which even a start-up business can benefit from thinking about employees' roles from the outset. Job enlargement refers to employees doing a range of different tasks rather than repetitive or boring ones. Enrichment tends to give them more responsibility. Rotation gives them a wider range of skills. Good job design can accomplish all these things at the beginning of an employee's working life with a business.

QUESTION TIME
26 minutes

1 Define the term 'job rotation'. *(2 marks)*

2 Explain the difference between job enlargement and job enrichment. *(4 marks)*

3 Select two different areas of good job design, and discuss how these can motivate employees. *(6 marks)*

4 What are the advantages to a business of a multi-skilled workforce? *(6 marks)*

5 A business has to choose between job enlargement and job enrichment as a way to motivate some skilled employees. Advise the business on which one should be chosen. *(8 marks)*

89

Benefits to the business

What indicates motivation?

There is a clear link between motivated employees and the performance of a business. Businesses that have motivated staff tend to perform far better than those that have bored and demotivated employees.

The table below suggests the kind of indicators of motivation that a business might notice among its staff.

The benefits of having motivated employees

Even a start-up business would notice that motivated employees can bring them far greater benefits than the negative behaviour of demotivated ones. Motivation affects productivity, quality, levels of waste, communication and the overall efficiency of the business.

MOTIVATED EMPLOYEE	DEMOTIVATED EMPLOYEE
Arrives early for work	Poor timekeeping
Because of workload, volunteers to do overtime	Higher than average level of sickness
Helps others with their jobs	Not really interested in getting involved
Takes responsibility	Always moaning and arguing
Provides support and encouragement	Avoids responsibility
Willing to do extra work	Does the minimum
Committed to targets and goals	Lots of errors and lots of waste
Good communications	Complains about targets and goals and does not aim to achieve them
Asks useful questions	Blames others or the system for faults and problems
Interested in self-development and team development	Not a team player, endures work and does not care about others
Enjoys work and time with colleagues	Does not enjoy time at work and does not mix with colleagues
Interested in the business, its future and their place in it	Believes the business needs them more than they need the business

Higher productivity

Motivated employees tend to work harder. They respond to greater work demands and, although they may be extremely busy, will make every effort to keep up to date and not to let the situation overwhelm them.

Higher productivity means employees putting in a harder working day, where they achieve more. They will feel a sense of satisfaction at having coped with the additional stresses and strains. This is beneficial to the business because more will have been done.

However, a business does need to be careful that this high rate of work does not continue for too long, otherwise it will exhaust and overwhelm the employees. At that point they will begin to make mistakes.

Fewer mistakes, better quality

Motivated employees take their job roles very seriously. They have an interest in doing high-quality work that is accurate and valuable to the business. If an employee does not feel motivated, they will have no interest in the quality of their work and they will not care, or even notice, that they may have made mistakes. Motivated employees always strive to maintain quality and to put mistakes right if they have made them. But more often than not, they will avoid mistakes by being careful and attentive to their work.

Maintaining high levels of quality and reducing mistakes keeps costs down for a business. Every customer complaint costs money and reputation. Every returned product also means extra costs and waste.

90

Better communication

Businesses need to encourage employees to communicate with one another and to communicate with their managers or supervisors. Demotivated employees tend not to bother communicating their problems or ideas. By encouraging employees to exchange ideas, make suggestions for improvements and give feedback on systems, policies and procedures, and whether they are working or not, the business can benefit.

Improved communication means that the business can move forward as a whole. Problems can be quickly identified and dealt with before they become serious issues. By encouraging employees to participate, perhaps by organising regular staff meetings, a business can learn from the experiences of employees who are actually dealing with situations on a day-to-day basis. Anything that can improve the efficiency of the business is advantageous. A secondary benefit is that if changes are made as a result of a suggestion by an employee, the employee will feel even more sure that their views and opinions are valued.

Coping with urgency and priority

For small businesses, predicting just how busy they will be and how many employees they will need can be very difficult. So there will often be situations where tasks have to be carried out immediately – and possibly in addition to regular work that employees need to complete.

Small businesses with a relatively low number of employees will rely on employees' goodwill in such circumstances. Motivated employees will not be putting on their coats five minutes before the end of working hours, ready to leave, if they see that there is something urgent that still needs to be done. Nor will they carry on with routine jobs, when something more pressing crops up. They will offer to help. A demotivated employee will not notice things like this and will not respond, no matter how urgent or important it is.

QUESTION TIME
16 minutes

1 Identify and explain TWO advantages of a motivated employee. *(4 marks)*

2 Identify and explain TWO disadvantages of a demotivated employee. *(4 marks)*

3 A small business will not have the same funds available as a large one in order to motivate staff. Should motivating employees still be important for small businesses? *(8 marks)*

> Employee productivity links directly with a business's profitability and efficiency. The more productive employees are, the fewer mistakes they make. The higher quality of their work contributes towards the success of the business.
>
> Low productivity, poor quality and frequent mistakes can be disastrous for start-up businesses, costing them money, losing them sales and perhaps leading to their failure.

Motivation methods used by small businesses

YOU WILL FIND OUT:

- about training
- about greater responsibility
- about financial rewards

Training

Offering training and development opportunities is a key way in which even small businesses can motivate their employees. It benefits both the employee and the employer.

Most jobs are becoming more and more complicated and need a broader range of skills. It is in the best interests of employers to train their employees to the highest possible standards, to help them do their jobs to the best of their ability. At the same time, offering training to employees reinforces the fact that they are valued by the business.

Untrained or badly trained employees make mistakes. They can become a liability, as customers and suppliers can be dissatisfied by the level of service or the communications they receive.

A business will usually carry out a process of training needs analysis, identifying the training requirements of its employees. This helps the business to identify which employees would benefit from particular types of training, and can also be seen as a reward for an employee's efforts and willingness to learn new things.

In a small business there are no huge training budgets and money is always tight. But training is often seen as a two-way investment. It improves the quality of the employees, by ensuring that they are up to date with the latest technology and ideas, and that they have acquired additional skills. At the same time, employees welcome the opportunity to learn new skills and broaden their expertise.

Greater responsibility

As we saw on pages 88–9, techniques such as job enlargement, job enrichment and job rotation can all contribute towards giving employees greater responsibility and decision-making power in their day-to-day tasks. The same can be said for encouraging teamwork. Natural leaders or experts usually emerge from teams, taking the lead in tasks that they feel particularly confident or competent to handle.

Encouraging employees to take on more responsibility allows them to broaden and improve their levels of skills and expertise, cope with more complex jobs, and take the strain off hard-pressed managers and supervisors. Again this is particularly important for small businesses with only a few employees, who may be constantly under pressure to perform more and more complicated tasks.

Small businesses often suffer from employee shortages, because they cannot necessarily predict which parts of their business will come under pressure as the business grows. There is often a time lag between increased workloads due to business growth and taking on extra employees. It takes time to find the right employee, even when the need to take on someone extra has been identified.

Again, rewarding existing employees with new, more senior positions is a great motivator. It also means that when the business is looking for additional employees, it can search for less experienced candidates, as the more senior

positions will have been taken up by employees who know what is involved and have been willing to take on the extra responsibility.

Financial rewards

Although financial rewards are not the whole answer to keeping employees motivated, linking financial rewards with performance and business success can work well. Like any business, a start-up will have set a series of objectives or targets, which it aims to reach and hopefully exceed. Employees will have played an important role in ensuring that these objectives or targets have been met, so a business should reward them for their contribution.

As we saw on pages 88–9, this can be done in a number of different ways, for example a broad-based bonus system, paid as a lump sum to all employees.

A more precise way is to link additional payments to individual performance, but this often means having to set up some kind of appraisal system, where individual targets and goals are compared to actual performance. This is not always possible for a start-up business, as setting up the appraisal system – let alone running it – takes too much time and effort.

Commission can also work as a means of rewarding employees, but it relies on each employee being in a selling role. Commission is paid as a percentage of the total value of sales that an employee has achieved. It is not a system that can be easily applied to those who do not make direct sales to customers, and could be a problem if they are rewarded on a different basis.

An increasingly popular way of rewarding employees financially is to make them shareholders of the start-up business. Instead of paying them cash, they are given a number of shares. This makes them part-owners of the business. From that point on, they have a direct interest in every aspect of the business, as the value of their shares and any dividends they may receive are directly linked to the success and profitability of the business. It can also help to retain employees, as part-ownership gives them a stronger bond with the company and they may view their job role in the longer term as a result.

As start-up businesses become more established, they will be able to bring in many of the systems and innovations used by larger, more established companies.

Paying bonuses is still one of the simplest financial rewards that a start-up business can offer. The business will simply set aside a certain amount of the profit made and distribute it among its employees. However, this means that highly motivated and key employees, who have worked consistently over the year, may be rewarded with precisely the same amount as an employee who has not been very useful or productive, which could lead to difficulties.

QUESTION TIME
29 minutes

According to Learn Direct Scotland, pay can be a demotivator. It believes that pay packets send a message to employees:

- If a business is paying less than the competition, then employees may be demotivated.
- If a business only pays more when employees threaten to leave, then it is rewarding disloyalty.
- If a business offers higher rates of pay to attract new employees, current employees will be angry.
- If a business uses its end-of-year profits as a basis for its bonuses, employees do not always see the link between their personal efforts throughout the year and the bonus they receive at the end of the year.

Source: adapted from www.learndirectscotland.com

1 Explain the term 'bonus'. *(2 marks)*

2 Identify TWO reasons why a business will train employees. *(2 marks)*

3 Why might employees who have been given more responsibility be motivated? *(3 marks)*

4 Identify and explain TWO reasons why employees may not be motivated by a bonus reward scheme. *(6 marks)*

5 Advise a small business on whether or not its bonus reward scheme should be based on individual performance. *(8 marks)*

6 Should a small business use financial rewards, including bonuses, as its only method of motivation? *(8 marks)*

93

Protecting staff through legislation

What is legislation?

Most businesses will have policies on how they handle employees, but employees also have specific rights and responsibilities that are enforceable by law. Legislation in this context means laws and regulations that impose minimum standards or requirements on a business in employer/employee relations.

The table on the right summarises the main employment issues and whether or not there are minimum legal requirements.

What are employers' legal responsibilities?

Regulations and legislation on equal pay, minimum wages, discrimination, employment rights, and health and safety are legal responsibilities of all employers, regardless of their size.

Many of the rules and regulations are Acts of Parliament. These laws have often been created to deal with – or outlaw – particular problems that employees have experienced in the past. Other laws, often referred to as 'regulations' or 'directives', are European Union laws. They apply to British businesses, as all countries that are EU members have to abide by them.

Most businesses have staff policies, which take the legislation into account as minimum standards. Staff policies outline the rights and responsibilities of employers and employees and aim to explain how particular situations will be handled by the business. Different policies will be more or less relevant to different people who work for a business. Some health and safety issues, for example, may relate only

EMPLOYMENT ISSUE	MINIMUM LEGAL REQUIREMENT	
	Yes	No
• Maternity/paternity/adoption	✓	
• Leave and absence	✓	
• Equal opportunities	✓	
• Working hours and overtime	✓	
• Health and safety	✓	
• Pay	✓	
• Dealing with harassment, victimisation and bullying	✓	
• Conduct and disciplinary action	✓	
• Rewards, benefits and expenses		✗
• Measures to improve performance or manage change		✗
• Use of company facilities, eg email, Internet and phone use		✗
• Training		✗
• Right of search		✗
• Patents and copyrights		✗
• Confidential information		✗
• Drugs and alcohol		✗

to people operating machinery or working with computers.

By setting up a policy and making sure that minimum standards are kept, a business reduces the chance that it will break one of the laws. This also helps to make employees more positive and productive, as they know they will not be discriminated against.

A start-up business has to consider:

- **Employment terms and conditions** – these include pay, contracts, working conditions, working hours, holiday pay and entitlements, and handling part-time and temporary workers.
- **Workplace disputes** – a business has to put policies in place to resolve problems. It needs to know what to do if an employee complains or misbehaves.
- **The rights of trade union members** – whether individuals have the right to join – or not to

join – a trade union, and what to do when trade union members take **industrial action**.
- **Handling overseas workers** – whether particular employees need permission to work in Britain, and how to handle references and pre-employment checks on candidates.
- **Families** – businesses need to be aware of pregnancy and maternity or paternity rights, adoption rights, parental leave and flexible working.
- **Redundancy** – a business has to be sure that it has a valid and legal reason for making them redundant. Redundancy occurs when an employee's job no longer exists, when the business decides to reduce the number of employees, or when the business is closing down or moving.
- **Discrimination** – is an important area. It includes discrimination on the grounds of disability, age,

94

Within two months of starting work for an employer, all employees are entitled to a written contract of employment. It has to include details of pay, working hours, holiday entitlements, sick pay arrangements, notice periods and information on disciplinary and grievance procedures. The contract of employment is an agreement between the employer and the employee. It outlines employer and employee rights and duties.

In effect, a contract of employment is made as soon as an individual accepts a job offer. From that point on, both sides are bound by its terms until it is ended, or until both sides agree to change it.

gender and equal pay. It also covers dealing with bullying at work.

- **Health and safety** – has become an important area, placing legal requirements on employers. There must be health and safety representatives, safety procedures, and methods of dealing with workplace stress, accidents at work and special health and safety hazards. It also includes drug testing and the monitoring of employees for drug or alcohol use.

KEY TERM

Industrial action ▶ this happens when there is a dispute in the workplace that has not been resolved. During industrial action, employees can refuse to work (i.e. can go on strike) or will only do their basic job, trade unions can ban overtime, or an employer can lock their employees out of the workplace.

QUESTION TIME
17 minutes

According to the Federation of Small Businesses, only 20% of small businesses in Britain feel confident about employment law. Many are worried about the complicated regulations and all the paperwork. This means that many have put off taking on employees.

As a result, many entrepreneurs decide to work on their own, and the number of small businesses (defined as those with nine or fewer employees) has fallen. This means that with a decreasing number of small businesses taking on employees, some potential jobs are never even created due to the complicated regulations and paperwork involved.

Source: adapted from www.fsb.org.uk

1 What is meant by the term 'legislation'? *(2 marks)*

2 Identify FOUR different employment issues that have minimum legal requirements. *(4 marks)*

3 Why might a small business be less confident about applying the different employment rules and regulations than a large business? *(5 marks)*

4 Discuss ONE advantage and ONE disadvantage of a small business offering better than minimum standards. *(6 marks)*

Equal pay, minimum wages and discrimination

Equal pay

Pay is a major aspect of a relationship between employers and employees. Setting the right rate of pay is necessary to attract and to retain employees. But pay rewards need to be fair. There are rules and regulations that aim to ensure that this is the case.

Equal Pay Act 1970

Under this Act, every employment contract includes an 'equality clause', which guarantees both sexes the same money for doing the same or broadly similar work, or work rated as equivalent by a **job evaluation** study.

The clause operates unless an employer can prove that pay variation between the sexes is reasonable and genuinely due to a material difference between their cases.

In 1983, the Equal Pay (Amendment) Regulations came into force. This gives a person a right to claim equal pay for work of 'equal value' to that of a person of the other gender in the same employment, where there is no existing job evaluation scheme, and where there is no person of the opposite sex engaged in 'like work'. The Equal Pay Act 1970 (Amendment) Regulations 2004 made equal value claims even clearer.

In terms of recruitment and selection, it is therefore illegal for an organisation to offer a job at one rate of pay to a person of one gender, and a similar job at a higher rate of pay to a person of the other gender.

Minimum wages

Most British employees have a legal right to a minimum level of pay, known as the 'National Minimum Wage'. The level is set by the government each year. The minimum pay is regardless of the size or type of business or the work that the employee does.

National Minimum Wage Act 1998

The minimum wage is a legal right that covers nearly all employees above compulsory school-leaving age. It sets the absolute minimum hourly rates for groups of employees in different age bands.

As of May 2009, the minimum wage for those aged over 22 is £5.73 per hour. For those aged 18 to 21 it is £4.77 per hour. For all workers under the age of 18 who are no longer of compulsory school age it is £3.53 per hour.

In terms of recruitment and selection this means that employers would not be able to advertise vacancies attracting hourly rates of less than the minimum wage.

Discrimination

Discrimination refers to situations when an employer treats one employee less favourably than others. It is illegal to discriminate on the grounds of:

- gender
- marital status
- pregnancy
- sexual orientation
- disability

- race
- colour
- ethnic background
- nationality
- religion or belief
- age.

Direct discrimination is when one employee is treated differently to others. Indirect discrimination is when the employer has a policy that disadvantages a group of people.

Sex Discrimination Act 1975 (and later amendments)

In terms of recruitment and selection, an organisation should not:

- appoint on the basis of gender, marital status or sexual orientation
- offer less favourable terms and conditions on the basis of gender.

The law covers a broad range of workers, including contract workers. It applies regardless of length of service in employment or the numbers of hours worked. It allows for employees to take a case to an employment tribunal. If the case is successful, they will receive compensation for any financial loss they have suffered. An award for injury to feelings can also be made.

Where an organisation can prove that specific requirements are necessary in the appointment of an employee, then what is known as 'genuine occupational qualifications' apply. These include:

- **physiology** – for example a male model to model men's clothes
- **privacy and decency** – for example when care assistants of

a particular gender deal only with clients of that gender

- **single-sex accommodation** – such as the crew of a submarine.

Race Relations Act 1976 (and later amendments)

It is unlawful for a person, in relation to employment by him or her at an establishment in Great Britain, to discriminate against another:

- in the arrangements he or she makes for the purpose of determining who should be offered that employment, or
- in the terms on which he or she offers that employment, or
- by refusing or deliberately omitting to offer that employment.

Under this law, 'racial discrimination' means treating a person less favourably than others on racial grounds – which means race, colour, nationality, or ethnic or national origins.

This law protects individuals against people's actions, not their opinions or beliefs.

Disability Discrimination Act 1995 and 2005

The Disability Discrimination Act applies to all employers during the recruitment and selection process.

Many employers have demonstrated that they have a positive policy towards employing disabled people. Employers that place advertisements in jobcentres and encourage disabled applicants will display a two ticks disability symbol on their advertisements. This means that the organisation has a commitment to employing disabled people and will give them a

guaranteed job interview, provided they meet the basic criteria of the person specification.

There are good reasons for an individual to declare their disability. Under the Act, employers are required to make reasonable adjustments to working conditions to enable disabled people to work for them. It is advisable for applicants to state their disability at the earliest possible stage, rather than waiting for a medical questionnaire to be completed.

Age discrimination is also unlawful in most situations, as is discrimination on the grounds of religion or beliefs.

The Human Rights Act 2000 has also had an impact. It particularly applies to the public sector and is designed to protect employees' rights to privacy. It also means that employees have the right to see any information that an employer may be holding about them.

KEY TERM

Job evaluation ▶ an independent review of a particular job role to determine exactly what is involved in it in terms of duties and responsibilities.

Businesses now need to be careful about using phrases such as 'highly experienced', 'mature' or 'enthusiastic', because they can be considered discriminatory.

Age discrimination now means that making an employee retire before they are 65 is unlawful. Employees have the right to request to work beyond 65. It is also illegal to discriminate by refusing to employ someone who is over 65 or to refuse to give employees who are close to retirement the same opportunities as younger employees.

1 What is meant by the term 'discrimination'? *(2 marks)*

2 Explain why a business would be breaking the law by paying a female employee more than a male employee for completing similar work. *(3 marks)*

3 Explain why a business would be breaking the law by hiring a male applicant for a job instead of the female applicant who was the better candidate. *(3 marks)*

4 Explain why a business would be breaking the law by employing a non-religious female applicant for a job instead of a religious female applicant who was the better candidate. *(3 marks)*

5 Identify and explain ONE advantage and ONE disadvantage to a business of age discrimination being banned. *(6 marks)*

97

Employment rights

New legislation and rights

New legislation and regulations have begun to help employers and employees get the most out of their relationship. Employers can make reasonable demands on their employees in exchange for the pay and benefits they give them; while employees are more protected now than they have ever been.

Successive waves of legislation and regulations have meant that employees have almost equal status in the eyes of the law, regardless of their employment contract status. However, there will often be a bias in favour of full-time, permanent positions as far as employers are concerned. These are the employees who have a long-term relationship with – and commitment to – their employers. Those in temporary positions have only a brief relationship with the employer, but the law now states that they must be treated as if they were permanent employees.

The laws are gradually allowing and encouraging individuals to seek work around their other commitments without losing rights and benefits. In the long term, it is in the interests of the whole country for the maximum number of people to be in employment. By equalising rights and responsibilities, regardless of the employment contract, legislation has encouraged many more people to seek and to keep work, rather than relying on state benefits.

Terms and conditions of service

An employee should be given a written set of terms and conditions of service at the earliest opportunity. These written details are often referred to as a 'statement of particulars'. This statement is usually included in a contract of employment.

The details in the statement of particulars' are specified under the Employment Rights Act 1996. This Act was amended by the Employment Act 2002. The law sets minimum terms and conditions of service, and even if the employer fails to include them, they are automatically incorporated. The employer can, of course, offer more generous terms than those set out by law.

The primary rights and duties of both employers and employees are included in the contract of employment. They fall into two categories:

* **express terms** – including pay, hours and holidays, which should be put in writing and handed to the employee within eight weeks of beginning work
* **implied terms** – which are not expressly stated, but are fairly obvious to both employer and employee. They would include statutory rights, such as equal pay and a duty of care.

Employer and employee rights and obligations

The law governs the very basic rights and responsibilities of employers and employees. For example, the employer must:

* provide a safe place of work
* ensure safe working methods
* provide appropriate training
* provide safe equipment.

Contracts of employment

An employee's rights at work will depend on their statutory rights and their contract of employment. The contract of employment is a legally binding document between the employer and the employee. Normally the contract of employment will refer to several other documents, which are often bound together in an employee handbook.

The contract of employment lays out the precise nature of the employee's job responsibilities and obligations, including:

* the total number of hours to be worked per week
* the starting and finishing times
* the number of paid days off
* details on sick leave, maternity leave and paternity leave
* rights in respect of pension schemes
* grievance procedures
* periods of notice to be worked
* details on resignation and termination.

The employer may also inform the employee about:

* company rules and regulations
* codes of behaviour
* dress codes
* the organisation's objectives – this can be an important part of ensuring that the relationship between employer and employee remains strong and that they are working towards the same goals.

An employee's contract of employment cannot take away rights they have by law. However, in many cases an employee's contract gives them greater rights than they have by law.

Statutory rights

Every employee has certain legal – or statutory – rights, regardless of the number of hours per week they work. An employee may only gain these statutory rights after they have worked for an employer for a certain length of time. Statutory rights of employees include:

- a written statement of terms of employment within two months of starting work
- an itemised pay slip from the very first day of work
- being paid at least the National Minimum Wage
- having no illegal deductions made from pay
- at least four weeks' paid holiday per year
- time off for trade union duties and activities
- being accompanied by a trade union representative to a disciplinary or grievance hearing
- being able to claim unfair dismissal, if they take part in official industrial action and are dismissed as a result
- paid time off to look for work, if they are being made redundant
- time off to study or train (for 16 to 17-year-olds)
- paid time off for antenatal care
- paid maternity leave and the right to return to work after maternity leave
- paid paternity leave
- paid adoption leave
- the right to ask for flexible working
- reasonable time off to look after dependents in an emergency
- a maximum 48-hour working week
- weekly and daily rest breaks (although there are special rules for those who work at night)
- protection against discrimination on grounds of sex, race, disability, sexual orientation, age, religion or belief
- the right to work until they are at least 65 years old
- notice of dismissal, provided they have worked for the employer for a month
- written reasons for dismissal from the employer
- being able to claim compensation if unfairly dismissed (this usually means that the employee must have worked for the organisation for at least a year)
- redundancy pay if they are made redundant, assuming that they have worked for the organisation for two years
- not being victimised or dismissed for 'blowing the whistle' on a matter of public concern in the workplace.

Part-time workers have the same pro-rata contractual rights as full-time workers. Fixed-term employees have the same contractual rights as comparable permanent employees. Employees may have additional contractual rights, which can usually be found in the contract of employment.

> ⏩ By allowing employees to balance their responsibilities and duties outside the workplace, an employer can generate conditions where the employee is fully focused on their work. Flexibility comes when the employer recognises that employees want non-standard contracts of employment, certainly in terms of working patterns.

QUESTION TIME
23 minutes

1 What is a contract of employment? *(2 marks)*

2 Identify FOUR details contained in a contract of employment. *(4 marks)*

3 What is the difference between expressed terms and implied terms in a contract of employment? *(4 marks)*

4 Identify FOUR legal rights that an employee is entitled to. *(4 marks)*

5 Suppose part-time employees who work for a small business three days a week are allowed a 30-minute lunch-break, while full-time employees are allowed one hour. Explain whether the business would be acting legally or illegally in these circumstances. *(4 marks)*

6 What advantage does a contract of employment provide to both the employer and employee? *(5 marks)*

99

Health and safety

The importance of health and safety

The Health and Safety at Work etc Act 1974 (also referred to as 'HASAW') requires employers to provide a healthy and risk-free (as far as is practicable) workplace for their employees. This means that the employer must assess any potential risks or hazards in the working environment that could have an impact on their employees.

Most employers will have a health and safety representative, who will have been given training and will have a working knowledge of HASAW. This representative will regularly inspect the working environment and report to the employer any particular hazards or problems that may have been uncovered. The employer then has a responsibility to deal with these issues.

From time to time a representative of the Health and Safety Executive, usually a local government employee, will inspect the working environment and carry out similar inspections to those carried out by the business's own health and safety representative. If the employer has not responded to potential hazards, then they could run the risk of the business being closed down until the situation has been dealt with. Normally the inspector will give the employer a limited period of time to deal with the situation before further action is taken.

It is therefore in the interests of both the employer and the employee that health and safety issues are raised and then dealt with as promptly as possible.

Health and safety requirements

There are many health and safety requirements in the workplace. These require the employer to provide a safe working environment and adequate welfare facilities. Specifically, employers must:

- ensure that entrances and exits are safe and clear
- ensure that equipment and systems are safe and serviced on a regular basis
- take steps to ensure that the handling of heavy objects and the storage of dangerous items is a priority
- provide instruction, training or supervision as required
- ensure that all accidents are rigorously investigated and their causes eliminated.

Health and safety law

HASAW requires an employer to provide a number of levels of protection for their employees. Before 1974, employees did not have legal safety protection in the workplace. The purpose of this Act is to provide a legal framework to promote, stimulate and encourage the highest possible standards of health and safety in the workplace.

Everyone has a responsibility to comply with the Act, including: employers; employees; trainees; the self-employed; manufacturers; suppliers; designers; and importers of equipment that will be used in the workplace.

Employers have a general duty to 'ensure so far as is reasonably practicable the health, safety and welfare at work of all their employees'. Employers are required to:

- provide and maintain safety equipment and safe systems of working
- make sure that materials are properly stored, handled, used and transported
- provide training, information, instruction and supervision
- ensure that employees are aware of instructions that may have been provided by manufacturers and suppliers
- provide a safe working environment
- provide a safe place of employment
- provide a written safety policy
- provide a written risk assessment
- ensure the safety of others, including the public
- have regular conversations with safety representatives.

In addition to this list, employers cannot ask employees to carry out tasks that could prove to be hazardous to them, particularly if they lack the necessary safety equipment to do the job. Employees must:

- be aware of their own health and safety and that of others
- be aware that their actions may be liable to legal action
- cooperate with employers
- not interfere with equipment or anything that has been provided in the interests of health and safety.

Inspectors

In order to ensure that employers comply with HASAW, local authorities have environmental health officers who can carry out inspections. The Health and Safety Executive also has inspectors, who may visit large manufacturing, construction and other industrial sites.

Environmental health officers and Health and Safety Executive inspectors can:

- enter premises without appointments at reasonable times
- investigate and examine premises and equipment
- take equipment apart and take samples of substances and equipment
- see any documents and take photocopies of them if necessary
- if they are barred from entry, ask the police to ensure they gain access
- ask employers and employees questions under caution
- seize any equipment or substances, if they feel there is an immediate danger from them.

Enforcement

If employers continue to avoid following the requirements of HASAW, they will face enforcement action. Two things may happen:

- they may be issued with a legal notice, requiring them to improve the situation within a set period of time or the notice will prohibit them from using equipment or unsafe practices immediately
- they could be prosecuted (as could employees) and face a fine or a prison term.

> It is the responsibility of employers to ensure that their employees know what hazards and risks they may face and how to deal with them. For this reason employers will arrange health and safety training during working hours. It is important for the organisation to make sure that all new employees – not just existing employees – receive this training.
>
> Even before an employee starts work, they may have an occupational health screening to test their fitness for the job. Some health screening is driven entirely by health and safety at work considerations.
>
> The main purpose of occupational health screening is to:
> - establish and maintain a healthy working environment
> - ensure the best physical and mental health in relation to work
> - adapt work to the capabilities of employees in relation to their physical and mental health.

QUESTION TIME
27 minutes

1 **Identify FOUR health and safety requirements of a business.** *(4 marks)*

2 **Explain why a business should ensure that entrances and exits to the business are safe and clear.** *(4 marks)*

3 **Explain why a business should ensure that employees receive the required training.** *(4 marks)*

4 **How might a local authority environmental health officer ensure that a business is following the required health and safety rules and regulations?** *(5 marks)*

5 **How might health screening avoid health and safety problems?** *(4 marks)*

6 **Identify and explain TWO problems that a business may face if the health and safety rules and regulations are broken.** *(6 marks)*

101

What have you learnt?

This section has focused on how businesses recruit, motivate and retain employees. We will cover this topic in more detail in Unit 2.

We have looked at:

- **recruitment** – why businesses need to recruit, how they recruit, and how they work out pay and other benefits for their employees
- **motivation** – how businesses aim to motivate staff and why this is important for all businesses, regardless of their size.
- **legislation** – how employees are protected by the law, the major areas being equal pay, minimum wages, discrimination, employment rights and health and safety.

Regardless of the size of the business, dealing with employees is an important task for business owners and managers. Employees are often the only people in a business who deal directly with customers or suppliers. Rules and regulations govern the way in which they have to be treated. These rules and regulations represent minimum standards – a good business will always exceed the minimum.

Hopefully you have done all of the 'Question time' exercises, so you will be starting to realise how the topic 'People in business' fits into the examination paper. You won't be expected to quote from any laws or regulations, but you will need to have a broad understanding of how they can affect small businesses and it would be wise to learn their names and dates.

Your teacher or tutor will be able to give you a copy of the 'Unit Revision Pack' from the *Teacher Support Pack*. This should help you to identify the main areas to focus on when you start your revision. It also includes a mock examination paper. The support pack material not only has information on this section, but also on the first three sections of this unit. You are unlikely to get a question that just revolves around the topic 'People in business' – there will be questions about recruitment, motivation and staff retention, but they will be mixed in with questions relating to other sections of this unit.

Integrated questions from Sections 1, 2, 3 and 4

Try these exam-style questions. They bring together the topics from Section 1 (Starting a business), Section 2 (Marketing), Section 3 (Finance) and Section 4 (People in business). The example below is not a real business situation.

ZERO HOURS CONTRACTS

Louise used to work a 35-hour week. One of the days was a Saturday, but she always took Monday off instead. She didn't mind – Saturday was busy and the time went quickly.

But everything changed three months ago, when another local company bought the shop.

A few days after they took over the shop, Louise was given a new contract of employment. It was explained to her as being really good and flexible – a zero hours contract. It does not say in the contract how many hours she has to work each week.

As the shop is very quiet in September and October, Louise's new employer rarely calls her in for duty. She has earned very little. She is at her wits' end and does not know how she is going to pay her next lot of personal bills.

QUESTIONS
47 minutes

1 Louise's new contract is known as a 'zero hours contract'. Define this term. *(2 marks)*

2 Is Louise's method of pay based on a time rate or piece rate? Explain. *(4 marks)*

3 Which advertising method is the local business likely to use to recruit new shop employees? *(4 marks)*

4 How would the use of a zero hours contract affect the local company's ability to recruit new staff? *(5 marks)*

5 Louise used to be paid £278.00 per week. Now she is paid £7.66 an hour and on average works around 19 hours a week. Calculate her weekly wage and explain whether she is better or worse off. *(5 marks)*

6 Explain ONE advantage to the local company of having a zero hours contract with employees. Suggest ONE disadvantage of this to employees like Louise. *(6 marks)*

7 Discuss how Louise's motivation may be affected by this new zero hours contract. *(6 marks)*

8 What would have been the reason for the local company taking over the business for which Louise works? *(6 marks)*

9 Advise the business on whether a zero hours contract should be maintained or not. *(9 marks)*

103

What is operations management?

YOU WILL FIND OUT:

- what operations management is
- what an operations manager does
- how operations management can make a business more effective

What is operations management?

Operations management can be described as the activities that produce and deliver products and services. All organisations use operations management, because they all produce products and services. Operations management is important, because it has an impact on the cost of producing products and services. This in turn affects revenue.

Operations management organises the whole process relating to:

- designing products and services
- buying components or services from suppliers
- processing those products and services
- selling the finished goods.

A large manufacturing organisation will use aspects of operations management in a wide variety of different, but closely related, managerial disciplines, including:

- manufacturing
- stock control
- the management of distribution systems
- human resources
- marketing
- administration and finance
- research and development.

Operations management used to be known as 'production management' and applied almost exclusively to the manufacturing sector. Many organisations still use that term. However, the management function has broadened to include many other aspects of the **supply chain** – not just production – so it is now common to use the term 'operations management' to describe activities in the manufacturing sector and increasingly in the service sector.

What does an operations manager do?

Given the wide range of different job roles and tasks in operations management, it is difficult to describe exactly what an operations manager actually does. Certainly they are responsible for a wide range of different functions, but the functions themselves are determined by the nature of the business – depending on whether it is a service-based industry or a manufacturing organisation. In smaller businesses, individuals who perform jobs such as accounting or marketing may be operations managers.

How can operations management make a business more effective?

Quality

Quality is the setting of minimum standards that either match or exceed the expectations of customers. Quality is usually at the top of the list of operations management objectives. A product or service must conform to the requirements – in terms of its quality and what it can do – that have been set down by the business. This is known as 'conformance' or 'conformity'.

The effect of good quality is that consumers will continue to purchase the products and services, bringing in revenue to the business.

Speed

The time taken between a customer asking for a product or service and receiving it is also important. The business must be able to respond quickly, as this is viewed positively by

---

For example **Key success factors**

In fashion retailing, customers want a broad range of styles, quality and colour. Some are willing to pay more for exclusive styles and premium quality. Retailers want reliable and speedy suppliers. There is a lot of competition, as it is easy to enter the fashion retail market (by simply buying stock from the large number of wholesalers and distributors), and some competitors will have strong buying power.

Key success factors for a fashion retailer are:

- to combine a customised service for consumers with a low-cost operation
- to be able to respond quickly to changes in styles and fashions
- to listen to customers
- to have low overheads and low labour costs.

customers and they are more likely to return to the business to purchase on another occasion. As a result, the business can probably charge slightly higher prices.

Fast manufacturing can also mean reduced costs, as fewer raw materials and components are in stock waiting to be used and greater automation also means reduced wage costs.

Speed can also affect profits in the service industry. For example, swiftly processing passengers through a terminal gate at an airport reduces the turnaround time of the aircraft.

Dependability

Dependability means providing products and services on time and delivering them when they were promised. Dependability can be the most important factor to customers when they are choosing a supplier.

Dependability has an impact on cost. It saves time and money (because less time has to be spent in dealing with customer complaints about late delivery of products or services), and gives the business a level of stability that allows it to become more efficient.

Flexibility

Flexibility is the notion of being able to change the operation in some way if required. This could mean product or service flexibility, volume flexibility or delivery flexibility.

Customers will expect the business to be relatively flexible, perhaps incorporating new ideas that customers have suggested or coping with unexpected changes in demand and still delivering products and services on time. Flexibility means being able to speed up production in response to new demands. It also saves time and money and helps maintain dependability, as the business can immediately respond to customer orders.

> As with almost any activity undertaken by a business, success or failure depends on the resources available to it. Resources must be spent on establishing good operations management. This is not strictly limited to financial resources (although these do play an important role in funding the necessary machinery, processes and training). The more important consideration is the actual use of the resources available to the business, in order to ensure that any initiatives introduced provide positive benefits. Other key resources include human resources and management, as both of these are vital in setting up the processes and maintaining them.

QUESTION TIME
16 minutes

1 Define the term 'operations management'. *(2 marks)*

2 Define the term 'quality'. *(2 marks)*

3 Explain the importance of quality to a business. *(3 marks)*

4 Explain the importance of speed to a business. *(3 marks)*

5 Why are flexibility and dependability important to the fashion industry? *(6 marks)*

105

Production methods

What methods of production are there?

Production is all about the creation of products and services to meet customer needs. Different products are made in different ways, using different methods of production.

Many of the production methods below are used more widely in manufacturing than in providing services, although services do use some of them.

Job production

In job production, each and every item is produced from start to finish before another product is begun. Job production usually only takes place when an order already exists for the product. In effect, the product is tailor-made to order.

Job production is one example of a production method used by services. Hairdressers and beauticians, for example, use job production, as they deal with one customer at a time. Clothes or cars that are made to the specific requirements of a single customer are also examples.

This is a technique that is not only used by **craftspeople**, but also for very large projects. A house-building project uses job production, for example, as does the building of a bridge or a section of a motorway. Each job is unique – from a meal in a restaurant that is cooked to order to a handmade piece of furniture.

Batch production

While job production handles only a single product at a time, batch production can deal with hundreds or thousands of very similar products, all made at the same time. They will use similar raw materials and components. Some parts may be different, such as a baker using different fillings for a batch of doughnuts.

The batches are made to order and the whole order is completed before the next batch is begun. Batch production tends to use machinery which can be set up for the specific batch. For example, a clothes manufacturer might set a machine to cut 1,000 size 12 skirt parts, but halfway through may change the material from black to blue.

Batch production can be used for both small and large batches. Specialist machines are used, and it is easy to change sizes and colours during the batch. Every time a new batch begins, the machines have to be reset. This is the only major problem, as the set-up time between batches may add to the costs of the business.

Flow production

Flow production is ideal for making **standardised products**. The product passes down an **assembly line**. At various stages, tasks are carried out to add to and finally complete the product. An ideal example would be car production.

Each employee working on the assembly line has a specialised job. This allows the business to benefit from a **division of labour**. Employees are skilled in their one role, making production fast and efficient. Flow production is always used in mass production of products like washing machines, cars and computers.

Process production

This is really a version of flow production, but instead of using an assembly line, production takes place in a plant (a factory), such as an oil refinery. The oil passes through a series of pipes and tanks and is gradually turned into petrol. The main difference is that in process production, the process has to be done in a particular order.

It is a very expensive production system, because it uses specialised machines. Very few employees work in the plant and the focus is on having an efficient and safe environment for the production.

Automation

Production technology has moved on very quickly and continues to develop. Computers and computer-controlled machines are gradually replacing employees on the production line. They can work 24 hours a day and only need to be reset when a new project starts. Time after time they can produce identical products far faster than humans can.

Lean production

The Japanese introduced the idea of lean production. It is an attempt to reduce the number of stages of production and minimise the number of raw materials, the amount of labour, the number of machines and the amount of factory space used.

Cell production

One way to achieve lean production is to switch to cell production. Production is broken down into various 'cells'. Each cell either makes

106

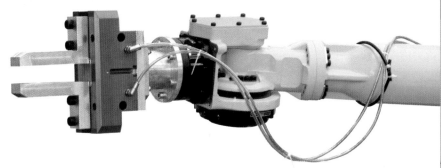

a whole product or carries out a process towards making the product. Employees usually work in a U-shape, with materials brought in at the top of the cell and worked on until they exit the other side of the U.

The Japanese have discovered that this a good way not only of speeding up production, but also of giving the employees in each cell more responsibility. This, in turn, improves the overall quality of the products made. The cell teams are fully responsible for all of their activities and allocate their own work.

Flexible production

The types of technology and production systems used by a business will depend on the type of market they serve. Businesses that make standardised products in large volume will probably use a flow production system, which could well be automated. However there are still many businesses that produce tailor-made products for each customer; while technology may be useful in improving the efficiency, each job is different and still requires the input of skilled employees.

Businesses look for the cost advantages that they can enjoy from making large-volume, standardised products, but with the flexibility to be able to produce different products for different markets. Smaller businesses tend to have flexibility in design and have the capacity to make one-off products for different customers, whereas larger businesses, with either robot-operated or automated production lines, do not tend to have this flexibility.

QUESTION TIME
18 minutes

1 Define the term 'division of labour'. *(2 marks)*

2 Identify which production method would be used to make a made-to-measure wedding dress and explain why. *(4 marks)*

3 Identify which production method would be used to make a range of shoes and explain why. *(4 marks)*

4 Identify which production method would be used to make cars and explain why. *(4 marks)*

5 How might a business introduce a batch production approach when previously it used job production? *(4 marks)*

107

▶▶ **Just-In-Time (JIT) production** is a philosophy developed in Japan. It emphasises the importance of deliveries in relation to the process of small lot-sizes (batches). The philosophy aims to reduce costs, work out the right level of production and eliminate waste.

'Kaizen' is a Japanese term which means continuous improvement. Little by little, the business moves towards improvements across the whole of its operations, each improvement building on the ones already achieved.

KEY TERMS

Assembly line ▶ the product itself moves around the factory on an assembly line, usually on a conveyor belt, stopping at each workstation.

Craftspeople ▶ individuals with specialist skills, such as carpenters, chefs or artists.

Standardised products ▶ identical products with no major differences.

Division of labour ▶ breaking down a complex task into a series of smaller tasks, so that employees can specialise and become faster and more efficient.

Technology and efficiency

Using technology in production

Robots

Robots are an important part of modern production technology. Robots on the production line are automatically controlled. Some are programmed by keying in instructions; others are taught to copy movements made by a human operator. New-generation robotics used on the production line can also check progress and pick up errors.

Modern factories use robots when employees can be replaced in repetitive work situations, where no real intelligence is required to carry out the tasks. Robots can also be used where the working conditions are dangerous or difficult for humans, for example if the materials used are heavy, or the conditions are hot or cramped.

While robots are expensive to purchase, programme and install, they become very economical to run once this initial investment has been made.

Automation

Many assembly lines have elements of automation, particularly in the car industry and in the production of pharmaceuticals.

Automated systems reduce labour costs, increase output and eliminate many health and safety problems. Automated systems can be as complex as required – from simple automated tests to fully automated production line systems. Many automated systems are modular, so they can be arranged to match the requirements of the business and the available space in the factory. Each module carries out a specific task, so it can be organised and placed at any point along the production line.

Once the system has been set up, the processes can be continually monitored. The equipment can be either automatic or semi-automatic. Semi-automatic equipment requires some employee input.

As the automated system simply repeats precisely the same actions at each point along the production line, it should not produce any defects.

EPOS

Many retailers have introduced electronic point of sale (EPOS) technology. This allows the business to monitor its sales and stock levels.

At the cash till, a laser scans the barcode of the product being sold. Not only do the product details appear on the cash register display, but the information is also passed on to a database holding the stock information. The new stock levels are updated in real time. The business can set automatic re-order levels, which are triggered when the stock falls below a certain level.

EDI

Electronic Data Interchange (EDI) is an Internet-based system that allows the business to create an integrated production process. It links the various parts of the business (such as factories, head office or branches) and the business's suppliers. As stock (such as components, raw materials or finished goods) is used or despatched by the business, the EDI system automatically triggers a re-order from suppliers. This is particularly useful for businesses that have adopted a **Just-In-Time (JIT)** production system.

Teleworking

New technologies have transformed the way in which businesses communicate with themselves, with their suppliers and with their customers. Laptops, the Internet, email and mobile phones allow work to be carried out and communication to be made almost anywhere in the world. This development has had an impact on the way in which some employees work. Many now have the capacity to work from home. This is known as 'teleworking'.

CAD CAM

There have been two major developments in design technology that have revolutionised the way in which products are created, tested and manufactured:

- **computer-aided design (CAD)** – uses three-dimensional technology to create drawings that can be viewed and altered with a single click of the mouse. They can be produced precisely and computer-tested, to ensure that they meet specific criteria.
- **computer-aided manufacture (CAM)** – as a continuation of the CAD system, businesses can also use CAM. This uses computer technology to plan and control the whole manufacturing process. The business can link up the CAD designs to the computer-controlled machines, to create an automated production process. The CAM system is very accurate. It is used by businesses to create specific products to meet the needs of different customers.

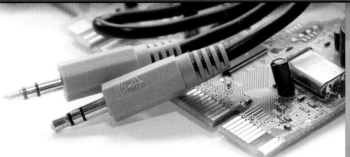

KEY TERM

Just-In-Time (JIT) ▶ a production system where a manufacturer only holds sufficient stock for its immediate needs. In effect, suppliers hold buffer stock for the manufacturer and deliver it on demand.

Efficiency and technological change

Technological change is a complex issue and it affects businesses in different ways. The table below summarises some of the key advantages and disadvantages:

Instant communication through email allows the immediate transfer of documents and images across the world.

Even meetings have been transformed by new communications technology. For example, videoconferencing uses the Internet to transfer real-time voices and images, so that meetings can take place with each person 'present' at the meeting in a different location. This reduces the need for expensive and time-consuming travel for face-to-face meetings and there are environmental advantages too.

ADVANTAGES OF TECHNOLOGICAL CHANGE	DISADVANTAGES OF TECHNOLOGICAL CHANGE
• Cost reduction – technology increases efficiency, speeds up design and manufacture, increases output and can be used instead of humans	• New risks – anything that has not been tried and tested could fail. A business committing itself to new technology may be prone to delays, breakdowns or other major problems
• New markets – using advanced technology such as the Internet, new markets can be opened up, extending a business's access to customers across the world	• Initial investment costs – new technology costs a considerable amount of money, not just for the initial purchase but for maintenance and for the training of employees. In five years' time the new technology may not be new at all and may have to be replaced
• Improved communication – this is quicker and easier and allows the rapid exchange of information	
• Better quality – new materials and new production processes bring more reliable and better quality products and greater choice	• Information overload – too much information could cause a business to have problems in its decision-making
• Employee benefits – robots and automated systems can take over boring tasks, giving employees more opportunity to come up with ideas and to focus on more interesting work. The workplace is also safer and cleaner	• Job losses – robots and automation mean fewer jobs, which creates problems for the wider society. In a business it may bring conflict between management and the workforce
	• Resistance to change – technology causes insecurity and challenges the traditional ways in which products and services are delivered. Some skills may no longer be required. Those affected may resist the implementation of the new technologies

QUESTION TIME
29 minutes

1 What is an electronic point of sale (EPOS) system? *(2 marks)*

2 Identify and explain ONE advantage of a supermarket using an EPOS system. *(3 marks)*

3 What is the difference between computer-aided design and computer-aided manufacture? *(4 marks)*

4 Identify and explain ONE reason why a business uses robots. *(3 marks)*

5 Which key technological development is appropriate to nearly all business, including new start-up businesses, and why? *(5 marks)*

6 Give TWO reasons why many large firms are willing to invest in new technology. *(6 marks)*

7 Give TWO reasons why a small business may not be willing to invest in new technology. *(6 marks)*

Quality issues

Quality and the customer

Quality means a certain specification or standard. Many people believe that notions of quality are always defined by the customer, as ultimately it is the customer who decides whether the quality standard of a particular product is worth the price being charged and how it compares to the quality and price being offered by competitors. In a highly competitive market, customers demand that a business's products are at least equal to, or better than, their competitors' in quality terms.

Quality does not just refer to the product itself. It can also refer to other factors, which together make the business and the product of a sufficiently high quality.

Quality can be a determining factor when a customer is choosing between a number of similar potential suppliers. The majority of businesses know this.

But there is always a minimum acceptable level of quality. This is often referred to as the product being 'fit for use' or 'fit for purpose'. Below this minimum quality standard, the majority of customers would be unwilling to purchase the product. There is always a trade-off between price and quality.

Customers will also expect a higher level of quality if the price charged for a product by a business is higher than the average price of products offered by competitors.

Quality can be a major factor in ensuring that customers make a purchasing decision in favour of the business, so quality is an important competitive factor. However, quality levels and the importance of quality depend on how competitive the market is, and to what extent quality plays a part in a purchasing decision.

Having a strong reputation for high-quality products is an advantage.

Maintaining quality

With quality usually being defined by the customer, businesses need to ensure that they maintain quality standards.

Most businesses rely on suppliers for raw materials, components and finished products. To ensure that minimum standards are maintained, they will impose quality standards on their suppliers. The larger the business, the more power it has to force its suppliers to conform to its notion of quality levels.

The maintenance of high-quality standards is vital to an organisation, whether it is producing products or providing services – and whether it is producing 10 units per week or 10 million. Unless systems that check quality and aim to reduce faults and wastage are implemented, then there is a danger that quality standards could drop as capacity increases.

Quality standards are part of an operational target. A business will expect that a certain number of products prove to be faulty, perhaps due to a component malfunction or a production mistake. An acceptable fault level could be up to 5%, but if capacity is increased, then measures need to be put in place to ensure that this maximum acceptable fault level is not exceeded.

110

For example Local v. national

A local shop cannot possibly compete with major stores on price grounds alone. It may offer identical products, but the corner shop can offer higher levels of customer service – and a better quality shopping experience.

Ombudsman ▶ an independent organisation that polices a specific industry and investigates complaints on behalf of customers; commonly known as a 'watchdog'.

After-sales service ▶ customer service after the sale; customers will expect support, advice and information on their product or service.

Quality and the law

In certain situations when businesses supply products and services to customers, quality standards may be set by legislation. For example:

- food products have to show sell-by dates and use-by dates and a list of exact ingredients and the sources of those ingredients
- electrical goods must be sold with a plug already fitted
- takeaway food must conform to various minimum health and safety quality standards.

To police the minimum quality standards, local authorities use Trading Standards Departments to periodically check businesses and ensure that minimum standards are being delivered. They also investigate complaints by customers with regard to quality issues.

Many industries themselves have their own trading standards, set by trade associations. These trading standards ensure that all registered businesses in that industry conform to the same levels of basic minimum quality. Some industries have an **ombudsman**, which is an industry regulator, to ensure that minimum quality standards are maintained. Some businesses also demand that their suppliers have obtained a British Standards Institute certification, which guarantees by law a minimum quality standard.

Good after-sales service

Many businesses recognise that quality requires them to meet customer expectations. Customers require their products to be of a consistently high level, over and above the actual reliability of the product itself. They require high-quality **after-sales service** and every aspect of their dealings with the business needs to be of a consistently high quality.

The problem that always faces businesses is that a customer's expectations of quality standards are always increasing. What may have been an acceptable level of quality in the past may no longer be acceptable to most customers now. Each time the business improves its quality standards, the expectations of the customer rise, so future expectations will be even higher.

 If a business, a product or a service is tainted with negative views on quality, then there could be severe implications for the business:

- The business will lose sales and reputation.
- It may have to discount the products.
- The poor quality image may impact on other products and services offered by the business.
- Retailers may be unwilling to stock the products.
- Customers would be less likely to make repeat purchases.
- If the business has to recall the products, then these will have to be repaired or replaced, leading to higher costs in labour and materials.

QUESTION TIME
25 minutes

1 Identify and explain TWO problems that a business faces when a product does not meet the minimum expected level of quality. *(4 marks)*

2 Why does a business in a competitive market have to ensure that the quality of its product is at the same level or even better than that of its competitors? *(3 marks)*

3 How can the quality of a product influence the price that is charged for it? *(4 marks)*

4 Identify and explain TWO strategies that a local hairdressing business could use to compete successfully against a well-known national chain of hairdressers. *(6 marks)*

5 Discuss whether or not a supplier to a national department store should respond positively to the quality standards requested of it for goods supplied. *(8 marks)*

111

The aims of customer service

YOU WILL FIND OUT:

● what customer service is

● about customer expectations

● about using market research

● about training employees

What is customer service?

Customer service – or 'customer relations' as it is also known – has three main aims:

- to identify customers who could be interested in the business's products or services
- to develop a relationship with those customers
- to try to hold onto those customers, in order to sell them products and services over a long period of time.

More broadly, customer service also involves:

- giving customers good service
- allowing customers to buy products in ways that suit them (for example online or using credit or instalments)
- making sure that customers have all the information they need
- supporting customers and reassuring them by answering any objections or queries
- closing sales efficiently and effectively
- following up sales with service and support
- contacting existing customers to achieve additional sales.

High-quality customer service means that customers will inevitably come back to make future purchases. Once a business has established quality assurance or quality standards for its products and services, it needs to focus on the maintenance, support and improvement of its customer service, to ensure that customer service expectations are met and exceeded – now and in the future.

Customer expectations

Customers demand reliable products and services that they can trust, at the price they want to pay, and for these to be available when and where they want them. These are basic customer expectations – but customers also expect far more than this.

The business needs to be aware of a customer's needs and expectations and provide products and services in such a way as to meet these demands – to provide customer satisfaction.

Customer needs and expectations are constantly changing. Awareness of new technology, consumer legislation and what competitors have to offer creates new demands. To satisfy customer expectations, it is vital for a business to be able to constantly improve its range of products and services and the ways in which they are sold and supported through after-sales service.

Customers trust driving instructors who have been trained by BSM or who are BSM-approved. This gives these instructors a distinct advantage over the competition, and goes a long way towards meeting customer expectations of the service.

Using market research

Many businesses use ongoing market research to find out about customer views and needs of products and services. Market research can help identify customers' expectations of the business's own products and services, as well as making vital comparisons with those of key competitors.

Market research in this respect tends to focus on **qualitative research** – research that focuses on the views and opinions of customers.

Qualitative research is different from **quantitative research**, which tends to look at broader facts and figures, usually related to sales

For example A quality organisation

The British School of Motoring (BSM) offers training for driving instructors, so that they can teach learner drivers essential driving skills in order to pass their driving tests. Over the years, the BSM has established itself as a good-quality organisation with an impressive driving test pass rate.

112

figures or numbers of customer complaints.

By investigating the views and attitudes of customers, provided the sample used is representative of the overall customer base, the business can both understand current attitudes and anticipate future expectations.

Training employees

In a large organisation, some departments may provide a range of services to other parts of the organisation. For example, the human resources department may provide personnel services to other departments, and the accounts department will pay employees in all departments and may deal with invoices from suppliers on behalf of the purchasing department. So a business has internal customers who receive a service from the business, as well as external customers.

It is therefore important that any customer service training done by the business includes the broadest possible range of employees – not just those who have contact with external customers, but also those who have internal customers too.

Traditionally, finished goods are inspected – or quality controlled – before they are sent out to customers. It may not be possible to inspect every single product, but a sample of products can be inspected. Some businesses use self-inspection by employees who have manufactured the product. This is an important and effective way of carrying out quality control, as it reinforces the importance of quality to all employees. This has become an important aspect of employee training, and at the same time gives employees additional responsibility and authority.

KEY TERMS

Qualitative research ▶ a market research method that seeks the views and attitudes of a relatively small sample of customers.

Quantitative research ▶ a market research method that uses statistical information to identify trends (usually linked to sales figures), market share and customer complaints figures.

QUESTION TIME
20 minutes

1 What are the THREE main aims of customer service (or customer relations)? *(3 marks)*

2 Identify and explain TWO aspects of customer relations. *(4 marks)*

3 Explain what is meant by the term 'customer expectations'. *(2 marks)*

4 What is the role of market research in enabling customer expectations to be met? *(5 marks)*

5 How does the British School of Motoring training benefit both the driving instructors and their customers? *(6 marks)*

113

Why is customer service important?

YOU WILL FIND OUT:

- about customer satisfaction
- about reputation
- about profits, health and safety and security
- about customers, the business and employees

Customer satisfaction

In today's business environment, customer service and customer satisfaction are key elements for success. To excel in today's competitive market place, organisations must create positive experiences for customers with every interaction. Customers are promised great service by advertising campaigns, so expectations are high. A business must always strive to exceed its customers' expectations.

Customer satisfaction has many key benefits, both to the business and to the customers. If a business can establish a reputation for high levels of customer service, then it can hope to ensure that customers are not merely satisfied, but delighted or even amazed at the level of service they receive from the business.

Benefits of good customer service

Businesses want to respond to customer needs. They also want to encourage new customers.

A good image

It is vital that the business has a good image as far as existing customers and potential customers are concerned. Businesses do not just offer customer services for the benefit of their customers; they know that good customer service – and hence a good image – will benefit them too.

Many businesses spend a huge amount of money on advertising, not only to tell customers about their products and services, but also to put across a positive and strong public image. They want customers to believe that their products and services are reliable, good value for money, safe, healthy and so on.

Increased sales

Good customer service leads to increased sales. Research shows that a 5% increase in customer loyalty can boost profits by between 25% and 85%. And satisfied clients lead to greater profitability and growth.

A business needs to generate enough money to:

- pay its staff (which is a benefit to the employees)
- buy equipment and stock (a benefit to the business, employees and customers)
- make a profit (which will benefit the owners of the organisation).

Repeat business

Another key benefit of effective customer service is that customers will be happy. If they are happy, they will continue to use the business, buy products and services from it and recommend it to friends and family. This is known as 'repeat business'.

Customer health and safety and security

Customers want a safe and secure shopping environment. There are laws to protect customers from hazards when they visit a business's premises, but many businesses take this more seriously than they are legally required to.

Customers cannot legally be exposed to dangers and hazards, such as slippery floors, fumes or trailing wires. Such hazards are monitored and dealt with by health and safety representatives in the business.

Cameras, security staff and specially trained shop-floor staff all assist this, in addition to stopping shoplifting.

For example Customer satisfaction

Marks & Spencer has a 'no quibble' refund policy. The Co-op tries to source Fairtrade products (these come from developing countries) as standard.

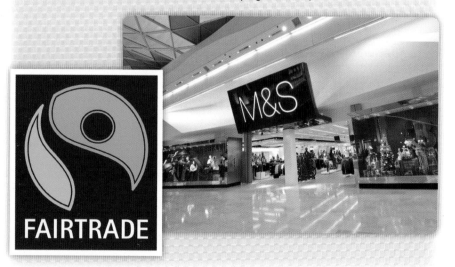

Disadvantages

Increased costs

Providing high levels of customer service is important but expensive. Employees have to be taken on to work in customer service. They are not actively selling products and services, although they may do so indirectly, if the customer is pleased with the way they have been treated. This all adds costs to the business, at a time when customers are demanding ever-increasing value for money.

Businesses have to have good reasons for charging more than their competitors. Aiming for a high level of customer service can be one of these reasons, although most customers will tend to buy from an organisation that offers products and services at the lowest possible price or that are at least competitively priced. This means that there is a constant temptation for businesses to reduce their customer service provision to save money and drive down their costs.

A bad reputation

As a business builds up its customer base, the hope is that it will begin to achieve a reputation for high-quality products, services, staff and customer service. A business stands and falls on its reputation. The last thing it wants is to be associated with poor service.

Unsatisfied customers can take their complaints to their local Trading Standards (run by local government to investigate customer complaints). Some of the worst examples can be seen on BBC *Watchdog*.

For businesses, good news travels fast, but bad news travels faster. If they provide poor service, or fail to sort out a problem, their reputation will suffer.

The effect of customer service on profits

One problem in providing customer service is how to measure its effectiveness and gauge its impact on the profitability of the business.

When setting up customer service provision, a business will set targets for dealing with customer complaints and problems. For example, it may have a recommended maximum waiting time for responding to customers' complaints, and may give instructions to staff about the exchange of products or refunds of money paid.

Now that businesses increasingly offer customer loyalty cards or store debit cards, they are able to track whether a customer service problem has led to a decrease in that customer's spending with the business, which could mean that they were not happy with the customer service. Or they could detect whether the customer was happy with the provision and continued to shop with the business.

> Every business is in competition with hundreds or thousands of others. Having a good level of customer service can give the business an advantage over the competition. This means that the business has to build up and maintain a reputation for excellent customer service.
>
> A dissatisfied customer is a lost customer. That customer will tell others about their bad experience, perhaps leading to more lost customers.

QUESTION TIME
24 minutes

1 Marks & Spencer has a 'no quibble' refund policy. What does this mean? *(2 marks)*

2 Give TWO benefits to the business of having a high level of customer service. *(4 marks)*

3 Give TWO disadvantages to a business of having a poor level of customer service. *(4 marks)*

4 Apart from price, identify and explain TWO other strategies that can be used by a business to ensure customer loyalty. *(6 marks)*

5 Should a small business focus on high levels of customer service? *(8 marks)*

115

Consumer protection

YOU WILL FIND OUT:

- what consumer protection is
- about customer care policies
- about awareness of consumer protection
- about consumer protection law

What is consumer protection?

Whenever a business sells a product or service to a customer, it is entering into a contract with that customer to provide that product or service. There have always been laws on contracts, but it is a relatively recent trend for there to be a comprehensive range of laws to protect consumers. This is known as 'statutory consumer protection'.

In the past, consumers who entered into contracts with businesses and found themselves at a serious disadvantage, discovered that the law was of little help. Many contracts were stacked too far in favour of the business. But now the key areas where there are contractual problems have been identified, and the gaps in existing law dealt with. Consumers are now protected by a range of laws and regulations (see the table below).

Customer care policies

Many customers are unaware of the terms of the contract they are entering into, and businesses do not often inform their customers about the contractual terms.

For example, many businesses do not provide any customer information on their policies on refunds, complaints or customer care.

Where and how information is provided depends very much on the size of the business. Larger businesses may have a website, although many do not provide customer information on their website; smaller businesses are more likely to provide customer care information by giving advice at point of sale. Most businesses also use printed material, such as leaflets and brochures, to some extent.

Customers need to have confidence in the products and services they buy and also in the business they are dealing with. Information about the business and its customer care policies should be readily available and easily accessible.

Awareness of consumer protection

Business awareness of consumer protection legislation is generally poor. Many businesses are unsure whether there is a specific body dealing with complaints for their business or industry. There is enormous confusion about the roles and responsibilities of various consumer protection agencies.

In a recent government survey, over half of businesses surveyed had never heard of some of the organisations involved in consumer protection and had no idea how to contact them. Overall, smaller businesses tend to be less aware than larger businesses.

It is important that businesses are familiar with consumer protection arrangements generally, not just with those bodies that are relevant to their own business. Employees also need to be aware. It is the responsibility of the business to inform their employees and keep them up to date with the legislation.

LAW	WHAT IT COVERS
Consumer Credit Act (1974)	• Controls debt collecting and credit reference agencies • Controls the way credit charges are shown • Provides safeguards to consumers who purchase goods and services on credit
Consumer Protection Act (1987)	• Prohibits the supply of goods that are not in accordance with the general safety requirement or that are unsafe • Prohibits misleading prices • Provides for the safety and protection of consumers by: – controlling consumer goods – making sure that consumer goods are safe – making sure that if they are unsafe, the retailer recalls them – ensuring that the supplier is responsible for damages arising out of defective goods – allowing for unsafe goods to be seized
Copyright, Designs and Patents Act (1988)	• Gives legal protection for designs • Makes it a criminal offence to counterfeit products or services • Controls the making, importing and distributing of copyrighted items
Copyright, etc. and Trade Marks (Offences and Enforcement) Act (2002)	• Gives legal protection for designs • Makes it a criminal offence to counterfeit products or services • Controls the making, importing and distributing of copyrighted items
European Communities Act (1972)	• Imposes safety restrictions on some products • Controls certain contracts

The Electronic Commerce (EC Directive) Regulations 2002 apply to businesses if they:

- sell goods or services to businesses or consumers via the Internet or email
- advertise on the Internet or by email
- provide electronic content for customers or provide access to a communication network.

The main purpose of the regulations is to establish the law as it applies to online selling and advertising. Customers using online services must be given clear information about the business and how to complete online transactions. If a business does not comply with the regulations, customers have the right to:

- cancel their order
- seek a court order
- sue for damages.

Consumer protection law

Consumer protection law in Great Britain comes not only from our own Parliament, but also from European Union directives or regulations. This is part of a process within the European Union to harmonise all aspects of business relations, so that businesses can enter into contracts across the continent in the knowledge that similar contractual terms apply.

The table below summarises the main British laws and regulations on consumer protection and briefly describes what they cover.

LAW	WHAT IT COVERS
Fair Trading Act (1973)	• Promotes fair trading and controls on suppliers and retailers who break the rules
Food and Environment Protection Act (1985)	• Protects consumers from the misuse of pesticides
Food Safety Act (1990)	• Prohibits the sale of unfit food • Controls the quality and standards of food, and the way it is described, labelled and advertised
Prices Act (1974 and 1975)	• Regulates the way in which prices are displayed • Provides protection and price information for consumers • Aims to promote fair trading
Sale and Supply of Goods Act (1994)	• Outlines the duties of sellers in the sale of goods • Outlines the rights of consumers
Sale of Goods Act (1979)	• Outlines the duties of sellers in the sale of goods • Outlines the rights of consumers
Sale of Goods (Amendment) Act (1995)	• Outlines the duties of sellers in the sale of goods • Outlines the rights of consumers in buying goods
Supply of Goods and Services Act (1982)	• As above, but covers services
Trade Descriptions Act (1968)	• Prevents the untrue description of products and services
Unfair Contract Terms Act (1977)	• Cancels unfair contract terms
Weights and Measures Act (1985)	• Regulates the weighing and measuring equipment used by businesses

QUESTION TIME
21 minutes

1 What is the purpose of consumer protection law? *(3 marks)*

2 A market stall owner sells a range of handbags under the name of a famous brand, knowing them to be fake. Explain why the law is being broken in this circumstance. *(3 marks)*

3 A customer buys a pair of shoes based on the description that they are made of leather. On getting them home, he realises that they are made of a synthetic material and not leather. Explain why the law is being broken in this circumstance. *(3 marks)*

4 A business knowingly sells meat pies that have become contaminated with chemicals during production and are unfit for human consumption. Explain why the law is being broken in this circumstance. *(3 marks)*

5 A supermarket customer purchases a box of cereal labelled as 750g but actually containing only 700g of the product. Explain why the law is being broken in this circumstance. *(3 marks)*

6 Identify and explain TWO consequences to a business of breaking consumer protection law. *(6 marks)*

117

Impact of ICT on customer service

The benefits to consumers of websites and e-commerce

Rather than having to visit dozens of shops to compare products, consumers can now do this with a few clicks of the mouse. If they discover the same product with the same availability at a lower price, they can negotiate lower prices from other suppliers too.

Comparing suppliers

There are many price comparison websites, which consumers can use to compare and select not only products and services, but also providers.

By comparing suppliers, consumers can:

- learn about the key features of the product or service being offered
- find out how this compares to other similar products or services
- make a price analysis
- compare delivery costs
- make an ongoing cost analysis – this means analysing the costs in real time, by continually looking at price changes

- make a risk assessment of the business – for example, has it got a good reputation? Many existing customers write reviews of the business, its products, services and reliability.

Immediate service

Using the Internet, customers will also be aware of the latest developments and be able to take advantage of immediate offers and sales, for example in airline ticketing.

Despite worries about online security, instant online sales and ordering facilities are a huge benefit to customers. The customer can secure a product or a service immediately, once they have established its availability.

It is now possible to:

- visit the retail store to check availability of products and then make a purchase online
- use an automated reservation system on the telephone, then visit the retail store for purchase
- use the online reservation system, then visit the retail store to make the purchase
- use the online reservation system, then complete the purchase online.

Many businesses use digital complaints services, so they can respond to complaints and queries far faster than they could using traditional methods, such as by post or through call centres. This is achieved by routing complaints through automated services to the relevant individual in the business who can make an immediate decision.

The benefits to businesses

Internet-based customer service

Businesses can now use customer call centres using Internet telephony (call charges are reduced, as conversations are carried out via the Internet through Broadband connections). Businesses can also set up interactive chat rooms. They can also create 24-hour-a-day, 7-day-a-week customer service support areas, which use Smart databases to help customers solve their own problems.

New, innovative customer service solutions are constantly being developed. For example, these allow instant communication via the Internet, giving the customer

For example E-commerce

In response to the increased competition from Internet-based competitors, traditional bricks-and-mortar-style organisations, such as Argos, have begun to make the transition to providing a mirror of their store service on the Internet. Customers can buy from the Internet and arrange for delivery, or they can order and reserve products for pick-up from one of the stores. This new market also requires customer service provision. As a result, comprehensive customer service provision has been established on the company's website (www.argos.co.uk). This also allows Argos to sell additional services, such as home IT support.

the ability to find a solution to their problem by selecting choices on an interactive website. Or customers can press selected buttons if they are contacted via the telephone.

Using scoring to choose suppliers

Businesses can look for a range of suppliers, using the Internet as their primary research tool.

Businesses use a scoring mechanism when they choose suppliers. It measures many factors, including:

- confidence
- the safety of the product
- its quality
- price
- ongoing support, if relevant.

Making supplier comparison decisions is said to bring down costs for businesses by between 7% and 8%. It can be a significantly larger margin for consumers.

Global and international markets

Businesses can use Internet marketing to branch out into new markets. They can offer their existing products to new customers, either in the country where they already operate or in other countries, perhaps where Internet connection is increasing.

It may be necessary to convert the way the business operates, designs its products, offers its services or markets them. Compared with traditional forms of marketing – including placing newspaper or magazine advertisements, renting billboards and running sales promotions in specific market places – Internet marketing is far more cost-effective.

In developing a new market, the first thing that needs to be done is to understand the new market and identify the opportunities. The business then needs to see if there is a fit in terms of its existing products and whether the new market can be served with them, or will require a new concept. The product is then tested and a suitable price is arrived at. It is then introduced into the market.

The additional consideration is whether the business will be able to provide an adequate level of customer service. If it can use ICT or Internet-based customer support, then many of these concerns can be overcome.

QUESTION TIME
27 minutes

1 Some potential customers will not order a product through a website due to worries about online security. What does this mean? *(2 marks)*

2 What is an advantage of online shopping for a customer? *(3 marks)*

3 Why can businesses like Amazon and CD-Wow! sell their products at a cheaper price through the Internet than book and music shops can? *(4 marks)*

4 What advantages does a website provide in dealing with complaints both for the customer and business? *(4 marks)*

5 How does the Internet enable a business to reach an international market? *(6 marks)*

6 Argos customers would originally have bought their products through its retail stores but can now also buy them online. Was Argos right to enter the online market? *(8 marks)*

119

What have you learnt?

In this last section of Unit 1, we have begun to explore operations management. Operations management is about organising the functions of the business so that it adopts the right way and the most efficient way of producing products or delivering services to its customers.

Operations management is a fast-moving aspect of business, as technology affects almost everything a business does – from the way it makes things, the way it collects and exchanges information, and the way it communicates with itself, its suppliers and its customers. We have looked at:

- different production methods used in manufacturing and providing services, noting how important it is for the business to operate efficiently. All businesses need to move with the times and adopt

new technologies as they can afford them. Above all, they need to maintain high-quality standards
- customer service – and recognised that even for start-up businesses, customer service is vital. It affects the way in which customers view the business and can contribute towards the business gaining a good reputation. All businesses need to be aware of the various laws that control how they deal with customers, setting out expected standards and ways of behaving
- how ICT and the Internet have affected customer service.

Hopefully you will have tried all of the 'Question time' exercises in this section, and you can see how operations management might apply to a wide range of different situations.

Your teacher or tutor will be able to give you a copy of the 'Unit Revision Pack' from the *Teacher Support Pack*. In it you will see the key areas to revise and you will have a chance to try a mock examination paper. The support pack also has information on all the other sections in this unit.

None of the questions on the exam paper will focus only on operations management. There will be questions on all of the other sections too.

Integrated questions from Sections 1–5

Try these exam-style questions. Now that we have finished the last section of Unit 1, you will find a mix of questions covering all five sections of the unit. This is not a real business situation.

HAMILTON COMPUTERS

Hamilton Computers assembles, installs and services IT systems for businesses in the Bedfordshire area. It has local, national and international competitors. The business is seeing a slowdown in sales and is worried about quality control.

Recent market research data has suggested that Hamilton Computers has a 9% defect rate compared to an industry standard of 6–7%. This may not seem much, but the business is aware that its computers have a growing reputation for not being as reliable as those of the competition.

The sales and marketing manager is sure that the slowdown in sales has nothing to do with the effectiveness of her sales force. She blames Production for the problems. As a result of the number of complaints from customers, the numbers of employees leaving the sales force is at an all-time high. After a stormy board meeting, the production director resigned and his assistant was promoted to temporary director.

Immediately the new temporary production director suggested that the factory should be closed for a week so that a complete reorganisation could be carried out. She argued for a £750,000 equipment investment and a training programme for all production staff. As importantly, she identified the fact that the business was using inferior but cheaper components from China, rather than components from South Korea, which was the source of most of the components that competitors were using. She felt that the cheaper components were one of the main reasons for the higher defect rate. She suggested that employees and managers from across the organisation be put into teams to investigate problems and suggest solutions.

The board was astounded by the wide-reaching suggestions and more than a little concerned about the potential costs.

1 What is meant by the term 'defect rate'? *(2 marks)*

2 Hamilton's defect rate of 9% is higher than the industry standard of 6–7%. What problems will the business face because of this? *(4 marks)*

3 How could the sales department and production departments have worked together to achieve customer satisfaction? *(6 marks)*

4 Why might Hamilton's current situation make it difficult to hire and retain employees? *(6 marks)*

5 How could quality be improved by organising staff across the business into teams to self-check work and to implement solutions to identified problems as they arise? *(6 marks)*

6 Should Hamilton Computers change to the South Korean suppliers or impose a minimum quality standard on their Chinese suppliers? *(8 marks)*

7 Advise the Hamilton Computers board on whether the £750,000 investment in equipment and the training programme should be implemented or not. *(9 marks)*

121

Written paper

Time allowed: 1 hour

The marks for each question are shown in brackets. The maximum mark for the paper is 60. You need to use good, clear English. Quality of written communication will be assessed in questions 1(c), 2(c) and 3(d).

QUESTION 1

Read Item A, then answer the questions that follow.
Total for this question: *15 marks*

Item A

Frankie, Jo and Will have been designing T-shirts since they did an art and design GCSE at school. So far, they have sold their T-shirts only to friends and family, but now they want to set up their own business and rent a small unit in the local area to turn into a mini-factory. They have saved up £15,000 between them, but they estimate that they will need double that just to get going.

1 (a) What is the most appropriate legal structure for the business? *(2 marks)*

(b) If the business were to approach a bank for additional funding, how might the bank be able to help it? *(4 marks)*

(c) Suggest the new business's probable aims and objectives and why setting these might be important for the future. *(9 marks)*

QUESTION 2

Read Item B, then answer the questions that follow.
Total for this question: *24 marks*

Item B

Sylvia creates handmade cards. On average, she sells 500 cards a month from March until December. This drops down to 250 cards for the other months of the year. This is mainly due to the fact that she sells them at a local market, which is open for only part of the year. She pays £80 a month to rent her stall at the market. Each of the cards costs her £1 to produce, and she sells them for £2.50 each.

Sylvia wants to increase her sales in the January to February period but she is unsure how to do this. Customers love her designs but she is thinking about reducing her costs to 50p but leaving her sale price at £2.50 per card to make more profit.

2 (a) Using Item B, calculate the total profit that Sylvia makes each year on her original figures. Show all your working-out clearly. *(7 marks)*

(b) Suggest, using the marketing mix, how Sylvia could increase her sales in the two quiet months. *(5 marks)*

(c) Suggest the production method that Sylvia could most effectively use. *(3 marks)*

(d) Sylvia's best friend, Cat, thinks it is a really bad idea to use poorer quality materials to make the cards. Sylvia just wants to make more money. Who is right and why? *(9 marks)*

QUESTION 3

Read Item C, then answer the questions that follow.
Total for this question: *21 marks*

Item C

Andy is a great fan of traditional wooden toys and for the past three years he has run a successful retail store in Worcester, called *Quality Novelty*. Andy is sure that the unique selection of products he sells, and the success of his store, would make an ideal franchise opportunity. He also wants to take on an experienced shop manager and an assistant, to free his own time so that he can pursue this idea.

3 (a) (i) How would you describe Andy's business idea, in terms of the products he sells? *(2 marks)*

(ii) Why might someone wanting to set up their own business be interested in a high-quality novelty franchise? *(5 marks)*

(b) Suggest TWO ways in which Andy could find the right potential candidates for his job vacancies. *(5 marks)*

(c) The alternative to setting up a franchise is for Andy to find the funding to set up the shops himself, and then recruit someone to run each store, paying them on a performance-related basis. Is this a workable way forward, and would the person running the store be sufficiently motivated? Above all, is it legal? *(9 marks)*

Introduction: Studying and the exam

What is the unit about?

Unit 2 builds on Unit 1 but focuses on the issues that businesses face as they grow. Unit 1 aimed to give you an understanding of businesses; Unit 2 extends your understanding and your application.

This unit is again split into five parts, each of which focuses on a different aspect of business expansion:

- The business organisation
- Marketing
- Finance
- People in business
- Operations management

Again, the unit headings, and the amplification (additional information and required coverage), exactly match the specification. Unlike in Unit 1, however, there is more business terminology in Unit 2, as well as some business mathematics. Unit 2 is a clear extension of Unit 1 but it requires you to think a little more deeply and to analyse and evaluate business options.

Why is it important?

There are hundreds of thousands of medium to large businesses in Britain. Some are household names that operate not just in Britain but across the world, while others are less well known, but at some stage they have all grown from relatively small beginnings. Growth is a difficult business itself, as businesses have to face new challenges and consider broader issues than they could ever have expected when they were small start-up concerns.

Unit 2 looks at the ways in which businesses expand and how this expansion might affect their legal structure, aims and objectives and their choice of location. It also looks at the marketing mix in some detail and at the necessary financial statements that businesses are required to create, analyse and understand. There are greater challenges in employing people and fixing on a sound and lasting organisational structure. And there are continuing concerns about how products and services are made or offered and what needs to be done in order to ensure that the business remains efficient and provides products and services of a consistent quality.

What is the assessment like?

The assessment for Unit 2 is a 1-hour written examination paper, worth 35% of the entire GCSE mark. There will be 60 marks available on the paper, equivalent to one mark per minute on average. All the questions in this book are based on that formula; in other words, if a question is worth 4 marks you should spend no more than 4 minutes on it, otherwise you will find that you will not have enough time to answer other questions that may be worth more marks. Timing is only one consideration, however. The quality of the answer is also very important. This is even more important for Unit 2, as greater emphasis is placed on assessment objectives 2 and 3.

ASSESSMENT OBJECTIVE	WHAT IT SAYS	HOW IMPORTANT IS IT?
AO1	Recall, select and communicate knowledge and understanding of concepts, issues and terminology.	10.5% of the marks for this unit and 30% of the overall GCSE.
AO2	Apply skills, knowledge and understanding in a variety of contexts and in planning and carrying out investigations and tasks.	12.25% of the marks for this unit and 35% of the overall GCSE.
AO3	Analyse and evaluate evidence, make reasoned judgements and make appropriate conclusions.	12.25% of the marks for this unit and 35% of the overall GCSE.

How do I get a good grade?

Examiners use a uniform marking system, which means that you will need 36 marks out of 60 to achieve a grade C, or 54 marks (90%) to achieve an A*. However, it is important to remember that whatever your mark for this paper, your final GCSE mark is gained across the three units.

Examiners are particularly interested in the *quality* of your answer. They have set three assessment objectives, as shown in the table above.

So we can see that Unit 2 is worth 35% of the GCSE. The examiners will also be interested in ensuring that you produce good-quality written English:

- Writing needs to be legible.
- Words must be spelt correctly.
- Punctuation and grammar should be accurate.

- Your meaning should be clear.
- You should use a style of writing that is appropriate.
- You should organise your information clearly, and use specialist words when needed.

Wherever you see this logo: you will find a section of text specifically designed to help you extend your understanding of a particular aspect of the specification. These sections will help you analyse and evaluate information in a manner required by the examiner for the assessment objective AO3.

Each of the double-page spreads has a set of questions on the right-hand side, all of which follow the mark-a-minute system. You should pay attention to the marks offered for each question. For example, if a question asks you for 'three advantages' but

offers six marks, that tells you it is not looking for just a three-word answer, but requires a little more depth. Similarly, it is important to provide explanations when required, or to show your working out when doing a calculation.

At the end of each section there is a revision guide with a set of integrated questions. The sections build up to this final spread, which takes questions from a broad area of the specification – not simply what you have just read. The deeper you get into the unit, the more likely you are to come across questions that require you to apply knowledge gained from other parts of the unit, just as you would in the exam. This is excellent practice for the exam, and it is a very good idea to get into the habit of answering all the questions you come across in the book.

How and why businesses grow

How businesses grow

There are several different ways of telling whether a business is growing, including:

- an increase in sales
- an increase in the amount of assets it owns and their value
- a growth in the business's **market share**
- employing more people
- making higher profits
- opening new markets at home or abroad.

Growth should give a business the chance to achieve its aims and objectives, but its aims and objectives may not be exactly the same as those of all the business's **stakeholders**.

> **For example**
>
> Employees (who are stakeholders) may view increased sales revenue very differently to the owners of the business. They may have to work far harder to achieve it, but may not receive any additional rewards for their hard work.

Why businesses grow

To survive

The main reason for growth is survival. To begin with, small businesses always have a disadvantage compared to their larger competitors, because their average costs are proportionately higher for the size of the business. The quickest way to redress this imbalance is to make more products or to provide more services. This means that the small business can then reduce its costs per product or service.

Unfortunately, quick growth in small businesses often draws them to the attention of larger businesses and puts them in danger of being bought. As the small business grows, this becomes less of a threat.

To reduce the risk of failure

A business can reduce the risk of failure by branching out into new markets, perhaps providing a wider range of products or services.

> **For example**
>
> If a small bookshop branched out into music and DVD sales, it would be less at risk if there were a fall in demand for books.

To expand their market

Businesses always want to be less dependent on a single market. This might mean the type of customer, the number of customers or the limited range of products and services that it offers. By finding different types of customer, or different types of products and services, it reduces the risk of that reliance.

To increase profits

Sometimes a business may find an investment opportunity that is too good to pass up. This might involve buying another small business. It will mean that the business will expand. It will hope to generate additional sales and profits by doing so.

To increase rewards

For all privately owned (private sector) businesses, increased profit means increased money for the owners. In the case of **shareholders** this will mean higher **dividends**. If the business is growing and doing particularly well, then the value of shares will increase, which is an additional benefit for the shareholders. The managers actually running the business will also receive rewards for growth – they will be able to command higher salaries as a result of their success.

To beat the competition

Most owners and directors are ambitious, and many of them want the status and power that come with a bigger business. By improving its market share, a business is taking sales away from its rivals. Ultimately this might mean that it can drive them out of business.

Why some businesses want to stay small

Just as there are very good reasons for a business wanting to become larger, some businesses never really want to expand. For example, the business owners may want to:

- **work on their own** – many small traders and partnerships just about cope with the level of work involved and do not want additional responsibilities. Sole traders, in particular, often want to work on their own – growing could mean having to take on a partner or employing people for the first time
- **remain independent** – growth usually means less control for the original owners of the business. To grow, they need investment – and investment is bought at the cost of losing independence
- **retire** – many owners of businesses are actually quite happy to retire

126

and sell the business off once it gets to a particular size

- **focus on a local market** – some businesses may only want to deal with the local or regional markets for their products and services
- **do what they do best** – some larger businesses actually break up, so that each part of the business can concentrate on what it does best. This is known as a 'demerger'.

> Government predictions in early 2009 suggest that the number of business failures will increase by 50% in 2009. The construction industry is the biggest loser, then business services, estate agencies and manufacturing.
>
> In 2008, there were around 21,900 business failures. This is expected to reach 32,300 in 2009, peaking at 32,400 in 2010. The predicted 2009/10 figures are the highest for nearly 20 years.

KEY TERMS

Market share ▶ the percentage of the total sales of a market that a business holds.

Stakeholders ▶ individuals or groups who are either directly or indirectly affected by the business or who affect the business.

Shareholders ▶ individuals or other businesses that have invested in a business by buying a part (or a share) of it.

Dividend ▶ a payment by which shareholders receive their share of a business's profits.

QUESTION TIME
25 minutes

According to Business Link, London alone has 50,000 female small business owners. The number of female role models and the flexibility of running your own business are believed to be the main reasons for the year-on-year increases in this number. Role models include Deborah Meaden from TV's Dragons' Den and Julie Pankhurst, the co-founder of Friends Reunited.

Even poor economic and trading conditions are not putting women off. Survival and success of these businesses seem to be based on the ability to react quickly to changes, loyal customers, high-quality products and services, as well as offering specialist products and services.

In business growth too, women seem to be leading the way, with over 50% of them claiming that they work to a highly structured business plan, compared to just over 30% of men. According to Business Link, most female business owners have clear revenue and profit targets, and use a wide range of business advice to stay ahead of the competition.

Making maximum use of business skills to achieve continued growth is vital at all times, and committed management is particularly important in making sure that small businesses survive in tough economic conditions.

Source: adapted from Business Link

1 Give THREE ways in which a business can grow. *(3 marks)*

2 Explain TWO reasons why a business will grow. *(4 marks)*

3 Why do some businesses, such as sole traders, not want to grow? *(6 marks)*

4 Why is survival the major priority in tough economic conditions? *(4 marks)*

5 In business terms, how could you describe someone like Julie Pankhurst? *(2 marks)*

6 What are the key areas to concentrate on to ensure the survival and success of a small business? *(6 marks)*

Methods of expansion

YOU WILL FIND OUT:

- about diversification
- about mergers and takeovers
- about joint ventures
- about horizontal and vertical integration

Diversification

Diversification takes place when a business decides to enter a new market, either an **allied** market (such as a coffee shop deciding to sell sandwiches) or something completely different (such as a coffee shop deciding to sell books).

The risk of being involved in just a single market is that if the market fails, then the whole business fails. By spreading risk across several different markets, a business is less likely to encounter problems. If one product or service fails, it can fall back on its other products and services.

For many businesses, diversifying might mean developing new products or services for new markets. The main problem is that the business may not have any expertise in that area. The simplest – and often quickest – way is to get involved with another business that does have the expertise. This can be done through:

- **a merger** – where two businesses agree to join together to create a new business
- **a takeover** – where one business buys control of another business
- **a joint venture** – where both businesses stay independent but decide to cooperate and pool their expertise in future projects.

Mergers

Mergers bring an expectation of higher sales and a larger market share. There may also be considerable savings to be made. For example, there is no need for two managing directors or two headquarters. Duplication usually mean **redundancies**, so employees may lose their jobs.

Takeovers

Takeovers occur when one business buys at least half the shares of another business. There are two types:

- **an agreed takeover** – the directors of the target business advise shareholders to sell their shares to the buyer, usually offering a higher price for the shares than the current market value
- **a hostile takeover** – the directors of the target business recommend that shareholders turn down the the other company's offer to buy the shares. The buying company makes a takeover bid by trying to buy as many shares as possible. It will probably have to pay a higher price for the shares than the market value, to encourage shareholders to sell their shares.

Joint ventures

Another way of getting involved in new areas or markets that could stimulate growth is by entering into a joint venture. Joint ventures involve two or more businesses. In effect, they create a new company. The businesses in the joint venture own all the shares between them. Usually the joint venture company will be set up to carry out a different type of work. It will use the skills and expertise, as well as the finance, from its **parent companies**.

Horizontal integration

Horizontal integration is when two businesses that make broadly the same products, or offer the same kind of services, join together through a merger, takeover or joint venture. For example: two car manufacturers joining together; or two chains of retail stores selling clothes joining together.

In the UK, if the combined market share of the new business will control more than 25% of the market, then the government, through the Competition Commission, will investigate the situation. They may rule that the merger or takeover is not in the interests of customers or consumers and will not allow it to take place.

For example The Tussauds Group

The Tussauds Group owns well-known tourist attractions, such as Chessington World of Adventures, Alton Towers and Madame Tussauds.

In 2006, the Tussauds Group bought the London Eye from British Airways. This is an example of horizontal integration and a takeover, as in effect the London Eye was a competitor for visitors to London.

> Conglomerate – or lateral – integration takes place when one business buys another business that has absolutely no connection to its current area of expertise or markets. Lateral integration is designed to diversify the portfolio of the parent group and to spread risks. However, mergers such as this are least likely to be successful.
>
> Types of lateral integration that are more likely to succeed are those where there are broad similarities between the two businesses, such as a car manufacturer buying a business that makes lorries or vans.

Vertical integration

Vertical integration takes place when a business joins with another business in the same chain of production. For example, a car manufacturer buying a car showroom; or a car manufacturer buying a business that finances loans to customers to buy cars.

Because vertical integration can occur at any point along the chain of production, there are two different types of vertical integration:

- **backward vertical integration** – when a business buys one of its suppliers, for example a chocolate manufacturer buying a business that owns cocoa plantations
- **forward vertical integration** – when the business buys one of its own customers, for example a brewery buying a pub.

Backward vertical integration

For the business, backward vertical integration offers closer links with its suppliers. It can get involved in product development, and control the quality and quantity of supplies better.

In 2005, the Tussauds Group was itself purchased by another business called Dubai International Capital. That business in turn is owned by Dubai Holdings, an enormous and diversified group that owns assets in technology, finance, education, tourism, energy and communication. The Tussauds Group is now part of a larger, worldwide entertainments group, known as Merlin Entertainments, which is second only in size to Disney. This is an example of forward vertical integration.

For the consumer, there is better coordination between the company and supplier, which could mean new product ideas. However, this could also lead to a reduction in the variety of products on offer.

Forward vertical integration

For the business, forward vertical integration means that the business can control competition in its own retail outlets. Its own products will have a prominent position in the outlets, and the business will have direct contact with its consumers. Problems arise when consumers get tired of seeing the same products and start to look elsewhere.

For the consumer, there are well-displayed products and they are served by expert staff. However, because the business now owns the retail outlets, it is unlikely that they will cut prices; in fact, prices may rise. Customers may be concerned to discover that the outlet only supplies the parent company's products, such as a brewery-owned pub.

--- **KEY TERMS** ---

Allied ▶ another market, product or service that has much in common with the type of work already being done by the business.

Redundancies ▶ this means the employee loses their job because it no longer exists.

Parent companies ▶ the companies that own all the shares of the joint venture business.

Portfolio ▶ the range of all of the business's assets and markets in which the parent group operates.

QUESTION TIME
28 minutes

1 What is meant by the term 'diversification'? *(2 marks)*

2 What are the major differences between a merger, a takeover and a joint venture? *(6 marks)*

3 What is the difference between an agreed takeover and a hostile takeover? *(4 marks)*

4 Why might a small business be vulnerable to a hostile takeover? *(4 marks)*

5 Explain how a confectionery manufacturer can grow by using horizontal integration, backward vertical integration and forward vertical integration. *(6 marks)*

6 What are ONE advantage and ONE disadvantage to a confectionery manufacturer of forward vertical integration? *(6 marks)*

129

Conflict between stakeholders as a business grows

Tensions between stakeholders

As a business grows, there will be changes in its relationships with its various stakeholders. Stakeholders are individuals or groups who are affected by the activities of the business in some way.

Typical key stakeholders are:

- the owners
- the managers and employees
- the customers
- the local community
- the business's suppliers
- the business's competitors.

There will always be tensions between stakeholders. Some will want something that will affect others in a negative way. For example, if shareholders want higher returns on their investments, then there is less money to reinvest in the business. There may also be a pressure to keep wages and salaries low. Prices could rise and suppliers will be offered less for their products and services.

Balancing the needs and demands of stakeholders is difficult for a business. Some stakeholders may accept slight changes or appreciate the position that the business is in, but others will find the situation unacceptable. The business will probably have to meet the needs of its most powerful stakeholders first, then try to sort out any problems with other stakeholders.

The owners

A business may be small at the start, but a sole trader may decide to become part of a partnership. Relationships within the partnership may change, as other people are brought into the decision-making process.

Eventually the owner may want to have **limited liability**. Becoming a private limited company is a way of achieving this, and it also brings with it the opportunity to bring in new skills and money to the business. At some point, the business may grow even further, and the creation of a public limited company (by selling shares publicly) can bring in additional funds. If a private limited company is going to become a public limited company, shareholders have to accept that they will lose some control over the business and will lose part of their share of the profits.

Shareholders are the owners of a business. They may not have very much influence on its day-to-day running, but they still have a relationship with it. If they owned enough shares, they could control it.

Managers and employees

A sole trader may begin a business with sole responsibility for management. If they decide to become a partnership or to set up a limited company, new people will take on part of the decision-making for the sole trader. The board of directors or the partners in a partnership determine the strategy of the business. They will expect managers to carry out the work on their behalf.

So the original managers of the business may now have layers of management between them and the actual job itself. This typically happens when there is a difference between the ownership and the control of the business.

Customers

Customers can benefit by a business getting larger, assuming that the business begins to enjoy **economies of scale**. The economies of scale will hopefully ensure that prices begin to fall. They may also mean that the level of service and the quality of work carried out by the business is either maintained or improved.

Smaller businesses, however, can be more flexible and more responsive to customers. They may be able to offer considerably lower prices and a more personalised service because, unlike a large business, they do not have the massive **overheads**.

The local community

The local community can be affected by changes in the size of a business.

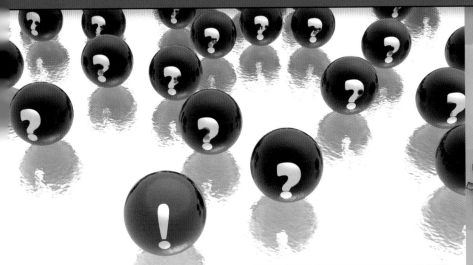

To begin with, there may be new employment in the area. There is also a knock-on effect, as local suppliers will receive more business from the growing organisation, generating even more jobs. On the positive side, this means that there will be more money in the local economy.

On the negative side, however, the local community may have to suffer additional transport movement in the area, as well as disruption, construction work and busier roads.

Suppliers

It is not just local suppliers that will benefit from a growth in the business. Any supplier that has an association with the expanding business should immediately benefit.

However, there may come a point when the business gets so large that it cuts out some of its suppliers and deals with its suppliers' suppliers directly. This is known as 'a purchasing economy of scale' – when the business is large enough to attract a big discount on a large order from a major supplier.

Competitors

Competitors will see an immediate effect as a business begins to grow. They will lose market share. If the competitor is growing in a growing market, then this is not such a serious risk. But if the market is not growing, and the competitor is increasing its sales, then someone somewhere in the industry is losing out.

The relationship between a major stakeholder and the business needs careful management. In the private sector, customers are usually willing purchasers of products and services. In the public sector (government or local authority-owned organisations), the relationship with customers or clients is very different. Some may be enthusiastic users of a public service; some will simply have no choice; while others may be reluctant to use the service.

— KEY TERMS —

Limited liability ▶ this means that the individual is only financially responsible up to the amount of money that they invested in a business. Their personal assets cannot be touched.

Economies of scale ▶ costs savings achieved by a business as a result of the larger number of products it produces or services it offers.

Overheads ▶ unavoidable expenses incurred by a business, such as rent and rates, which have to be paid regardless of the level of production.

QUESTION TIME
25 minutes

1 Define the term 'stakeholder'. *(2 marks)*

2 Identify and explain the expectations of THREE stakeholders in a business. *(6 marks)*

3 If the shareholders of a limited company are unhappy and want to sell their shares, which type of limited company offers the easiest route for the sale? *(3 marks)*

4 Identify and explain which stakeholders are affected by a loss-making business. *(6 marks)*

5 Why might a business find it difficult to satisfy the expectations of a manager, customer and owner all at the same time? *(8 marks)*

Deciding whether to become a limited company

Becoming a limited company

As we will see on pages 134–7, the options for sole traders and partnerships wanting to expand are to become either:

- a private limited company (which can use the letters 'Ltd' after its name), or
- a public limited company (PLC).

The table on the right shows what an expanding business needs to consider when it becomes a private limited company:

132

The accounts must be approved by the company's board of directors and signed before they are sent to Companies House. The balance sheet must be signed by a director. The directors' report, if one is required, must be signed by a director or the company secretary. If an auditors' report, special auditors' report or accountants' report is attached to the accounts, then it must state the names of the auditors or accountants and must be signed by them.

CONSIDERATION	EXPLANATION
Company name	The company name needs to end with the letters 'Ltd'.
Objections to the name	A company that is already registered can object to a new company's name, if it is too similar to its own. The Registrar of Companies at Companies House will decide whether this is the case, and can order the new company to change its name. Objections can be made at any time in the first 12 months. There are name-checking services that a business can use to find out whether there are similarly named businesses. The reason why a business cannot have the same name as an existing company – or a very similar name – is to avoid confusion and to stop the new business from pretending to be the existing business with that name.
Name changes	A company can change its name by a Special Resolution, which might alter the Memorandum or Articles of Association.
Company stationery	The company name, exactly as registered at Companies House, and the company number have to be shown, along with the registered office address. If the letterhead shows the names of the directors, it must list all of them.
Registered addresses	A company must have a valid address, not a mailbox number.
Company officers	A private limited company has to have a minimum of two officers; one must be the company secretary.
Who can be a director?	A director can be of any nationality and can be resident in or outside Britain. An individual or a corporate body can act as director of limited companies. It is up to the shareholders to appoint directors, but they cannot appoint anyone who has been disqualified from being a company director in the past by Companies House or the courts.
Who can be a company secretary?	All companies are required to have a company secretary. A secretary can be of any nationality and can be resident in or outside Britain. A corporate body may become a secretary of limited companies. A secretary is normally appointed by the company directors. For private limited companies, a company secretary does not require any qualification or previous knowledge.
Can directors and company secretaries be changed?	Yes, but Companies House must be told.
What does a director do?	The management of the business is undertaken on behalf of the shareholders by the directors. The directors have a duty to manage the affairs of the limited company for the benefit of all shareholders. They are expected to act in their company's best interests, even if these conflict with their own interests.

CONSIDERATION	EXPLANATION
Do directors have legal responsibilities?	Yes. They are responsible if things go wrong and they are responsible for making sure that Companies House gets all of the documents needed each year.
What are the responsibilities of the company secretary?	They are responsible for making sure that the forms are filed correctly with Companies House. They have to provide shareholders and auditors with notice of meetings. They send copies of resolutions (decisions that require a vote) to Companies House. They supply a copy of the accounts to every member of the company, every debenture holder (a lender or a creditor that has lent the business money) and every person who is entitled to receive notice of general meetings. They also have to keep and arrange for the safe keeping of minutes of directors' meetings and general meetings.
Do company secretaries have any powers?	Not really, but they can sign documents and agreements on behalf of the company.
Do company secretaries have any rights?	None under company law.
What are the Memorandum of Association and Articles of Association?	The Memorandum of Association details the powers of the company, the purpose for which it was formed (known as 'the objects') and the share capital of the company. The Articles of Association set out the arrangements relating to the regulation of the company in terms of the rights of its members and the authority of the directors. These two documents are printed and bound together as one document and referred to as the 'Memorandum and Articles of Association'.
What is share capital?	This is the capital of the company contributed – or to be contributed – by shareholders. The authorised share capital (also called the 'nominal capital') is the maximum capital that the company has available to issue. The amount of share capital stated in the Memorandum of Association is the company's 'authorised' capital. For example, the share capital of a company might be £1,000 divided into 1,000 shares of £1 each.
What is authorised capital?	This is the amount of capital with which the business started out. It is stated in the Memorandum of Association.
What is issued capital?	Issued capital is the value of the share issued to shareholders. The issued capital total cannot be greater than the amount of authorised capital.

1 **What type of businesses do Ltd and Plc stand for?** *(2 marks)*

2 **Define the term 'share capital'.** *(2 marks)*

3 **Why can't a company trade under the same name as an existing company?** *(3 marks)*

4 **What is the difference between a Memorandum of Association and Articles of Association?** *(4 marks)*

5 **What is the purpose of the company accounts being signed by the board of directors before being sent to Companies House?** *(3 marks)*

Private limited companies

Reasons to become a private limited company

If their business is expanding, sole traders and partnerships may consider changing the legal structure of the business into a private limited company, which entitles them to use the letters 'Ltd' after their company name. By doing this, they will be able to raise extra capital by selling parts – or shares – of the company and will be limiting their liabilities.

The key advantage of converting into a limited company is that all shareholders will benefit from the limited liability. If the business gets into financial trouble, then the shareholders only stand to lose the amount of money that they have invested in the business (by buying shares). This is also seen as a key advantage in attracting new investors.

The key reasons why many sole traders and small partnerships choose to become private limited companies are shown in the table below.

The process

The owners must first discover the true value – known as the 'nominal value' – of the business in order to divide it into shares. This is usually calculated by looking at how the business has performed in the past and what the business is reasonably expected to do in the future. Normally, this is done by an independent organisation, such as a bank.

Then the business needs to decide on the number of people and the percentage of shares that should be divided among the shareholders. Ownership needs to be very carefully worked out, as the shareholder with the largest share of the business has the greatest control over the business. The remaining shares can then be sold on to other businesses or family members or others, but they are not generally sold to members of the public (unlike the shares of a public limited company). By law, no more than 50 people can hold shares in a private limited company and

these people need to be 'desirable individuals'.

A board of directors also needs to be appointed by the business. The board will control the business. It will make decisions, and will determine the aims and objectives of the business. The board is elected by the shareholders. This means that an election needs to be held, with nominations and ballot papers, just like a general election.

As we saw in Unit 1 (pages 38–9), the business needs to complete documents and declarations:

- **a Memorandum of Association** – which has the company name, address, what it does, its liability and the amount and division of the shares
- **an Article of Association** – which details who has the shares, the qualifications and duties of the directors, the division of profit and how the business will be audited (how its accounts will be independently checked)

REASON	WHY?
Limited liability	A limited company is responsible for its own debts. Creditors can claim only the company's assets and not the assets of any of the officers or shareholders of the company. If the company becomes insolvent (has no money) and is forced to wind up (close down), only the property of the business can be used to help clear the debts. (A sole trader or a partnership is vulnerable to creditors and they may claim personal property to clear debts. If this is not enough, then the individual or partners can be made bankrupt.)
Tax benefits	Profits are taxed, but not at as high a rate as personal taxation
Raising finance	Finance can be raised by selling off issued shares. However, the value of the shares will depend on the performance of the business
Business continuity	The death or resignation of a director does not have an impact on the running of the business; it continues to trade as before. The shares of a dead shareholder are passed on to others, as detailed in the Memorandum and Articles of Association
Protecting the business name	Registration protects the name of the company. The law forbids any other business from using the name

- a statement of the nominal capital – the initial valuation of the business
- a list of directors – full names and addresses and other businesses they hold shares in or are associated with
- a declaration – that the business has put all the measures in place to satisfy the requirements of the Companies Act.

The business will then receive a Certificate of Incorporation. This means that the business can now operate with the letters 'Ltd' after its name. The limited company will need to send its annual accounts to Companies House each year. Anyone can look at these accounts for any reason (such as suppliers and potential investors, who will be interested to see how the business is doing and whether it is a safe and well-run business).

A registered company such as a private limited company only has limited liability (the shareholders cannot lose more than their original shareholdings). It must have a minimum of two shareholders and a maximum of 50. The business cannot offer shares or debentures to the public, and the transfer of shares is restricted. A private limited company is treated as a legal entity.

QUESTION TIME
25 minutes

Kevin is a window cleaner. He used to work for Molly Mops, a domestic and commercial cleaning business. He decided to start his own business, rather than continuing to work as an employee.

Kevin bought himself a van and a set of ladders. A friend painted his name and telephone number on the side of the van. He had to borrow £3,000 to buy the van, as he had no savings.

Kevin is very scared of trying to get new customers and avoids knocking on doors to ask people if they want their windows cleaned. Instead he waits for them to come up to him when he is doing someone else's windows.

He also subcontracts to Molly Mops and does pretty much the same work, but only gets paid half of what he was earning before.

He badly needs to take on another window cleaner so that he can do the jobs more quickly and expand. At the moment he can only manage to do about ten jobs a day, but would love to double that amount.

1 What are the implications of unlimited liability for Kevin? *(4 marks)*

2 What do you think is meant by the term 'subcontract'? *(3 marks)*

3 What is the difference between a private limited company and a public limited company? *(3 marks)*

4 Is Kevin's business a reasonable risk to a potential investor? Explain your reasons. *(6 marks)*

5 Advise Kevin on whether he should run the business as a sole tradership or a private limited company. *(9 marks)*

135

Public limited companies (PLCs)

What is a public limited company?

For a public limited company (PLC) to begin trading, it must have minimum **capital** of £50,000. Only two people are needed to sign the Memorandum of Association, but there must be at least seven shareholders.

Share trading

PLCs' shares are openly traded through a stock exchange. For example, British companies are traded on the London Stock Exchange, while American businesses use the American Stock Exchange.

If PLCs have a large amount of share capital, they can raise money by issuing shares. However, the vast number of shares issued can mean that smaller shareholders cannot exert a great deal of influence. Many shareholders of PLCs are criticised for appearing to be interested only in short-term profits.

The Alternative Investment Market

The London Stock Exchange tends not to allow new PLCs to trade their shares unless their share capital is worth several million pounds. But smaller PLCs can be listed on the Alternative Investment Market – a system designed to attract investors to new businesses without an established track record. The Alternative Investment Market is important to smaller PLCs, which do not have millions of pounds of share capital.

The board of directors

Decisions made by the board of directors are carried out by executive directors, but there are often non-executive directors on the board too. Non-executive directors may work only on a part-time basis. They are not managers of the company but are brought in for their particular expertise or knowledge.

In very large businesses, the directors and the managers will probably own very few shares. Shareholders outside the business will own most of the shares.

When business decisions are made at board level by directors and managers who do not own many shares, they may make decisions that the shareholders do not like. This can cause problems.

The AGM

A PLC must hold an annual general meeting (AGM). At this meeting the directors of the company present the **annual report** and the accounts to the shareholders. The shareholders then approve the accounts and appoint directors for the following year. The PLC needs to send a copy of the annual report and accounts to Companies House. They are housed with the Registrar of Companies so that they can be inspected by anyone with an interest in the business.

Shareholders do not have any real power in controlling the business from day to day. They could confront the directors at the AGM, or call an extraordinary (or emergency) general meeting (EGM) to demand an explanation, if the shareholders in question own at least 10% of the total number of shares. In extreme cases, they could vote the directors off the board. Ultimately, the only real power that shareholders have if they do not like the policy of the company is to sell their shares.

What are the liabilities?

As with private limited companies, investors in PLCs have limited liability. This means that they only stand to lose the money that they have invested in purchasing the shares. This is beneficial to potential shareholders and investors, as they know that if the company fails, they can only lose what they have invested.

If an individual or another business has a claim against the company, then limited liability means that they can only recover money from the assets of the business itself. They cannot turn to the managers or the shareholders personally to recover any money owed to them by the company.

What are the legal issues?

Just like a private limited company, a public limited company needs to be registered with the Registrar of Companies at Companies House. The following legal obligations are also required:

- The company's name needs to be clearly displayed outside all its offices and places of business.
- The company's name must be included on all stationery.
- The company's registered office address has to be shown on all stationery, including electronic business communications.
- All necessary registration documents need to be sent to the Registrar of Companies, completed and signed.
- Her Majesty's Revenue & Customs must be contacted for tax purposes and possibly for VAT purposes.

There are many advantages to operating a business as a PLC, and for registering the business on the Stock Exchange:

- **Equity capital** obtained from an initial public offering is considered a permanent form of capital, since there is no interest to be paid on the equity and it is not repayable (unlike debt).
- Equity capital from an initial public offering also allows a business to exploit its market opportunities straightaway, before the opportunity is lost as a result of a change in market.
- Funds generated by a public offering (offering the shares for sale on the Stock Exchange) are considered a relatively safe form of capital for a business.
- Becoming a PLC – or 'going public' – can allow the business the freedom and flexibility to raise capital as it needs to finance its growth and further development.

KEY TERMS

Capital ▶ the amount of money that a business has immediate access to.

Annual report ▶ a document that summarises the activities of a business in the previous financial year. It has a full financial report, including the balance sheet and profit-and-loss account. It details the company's assets, liabilities, earnings, profit or loss. It is presented at the annual general meeting for approval by shareholders.

Equity capital ▶ money that is raised by a business in exchange for a share of ownership.

QUESTION TIME
22 minutes

Fiona runs her father's organic vegetable business. Her father set up the business in the 1970s, first as a sole trader and then in partnership with his brother. Ten years ago, Fiona's father decided to make the partnership a private limited company.

Nearly all of the family works for the business, but Fiona, as the eldest and the one with the most business sense, is the managing director. Her father still owns some shares, but takes little interest in the business these days.

For many years they have been working with a chain of health food stores that is also a private limited company. Fiona is seriously considering merging with them to form a public limited company, although not all of her family are keen on the idea.

1 What do you think is meant by the term 'merging'? *(2 marks)*

2 Give and explain TWO reasons why Fiona wants the business to become a public limited company. *(6 marks)*

3 Why might members of Fiona's family be reluctant to create a public limited company? *(6 marks)*

4 Identify and explain THREE questions that Fiona might want to find answers to, in order to help her decide whether forming a public limited company with the health food stores is the right move for her family business or not. *(8 marks)*

137

Reasons for change

Why change aims and objectives?

As we saw in Unit 1 (pages 14–17):

- aims are basic statements about where the business wants to go or what it wants to achieve; they are its goals or statements of purpose
- objectives are the measurable targets of the business
- business objectives need to be SMART (Specific, Measurable, Attainable, Results-orientated, Time-specific), otherwise it is difficult to measure progress in achieving stated aims
- mission statements aim to wrap up the vision and the values of the business in a concise way, so that stakeholders – customers, managers, employees, suppliers and investors – can understand the business.

From survival to profit

If a start-up business has a considerable amount of investment behind it, then it may be in a position to have developed a mission statement, along with aims and objectives stating exactly what it aims to do. But many start-up businesses do not have clear aims and objectives. They just want to be able to survive the first few difficult months or years.

However, businesses may get to a point when they consider either writing a mission statement and sets of aims and objectives for the first time, or want to review them. Perhaps the business has already achieved its key aims and objectives. Or a start-up business may have survived the first year, which was its primary objective, and now it can turn its attention to making a profit. This may be its simple second-year objective.

A changing market

Some businesses may find that their competitive environment is changing and the market needs new products and services, perhaps supplied in a different way from what they originally anticipated. This may be as a result of new products and services being launched by competitors.

Less demand

Some businesses may find that their products and services are no longer required, or that there is less demand for them. This is particularly true as technology changes.

For example
From vinyl to MP3

A factory that used to press vinyl records would have seen demand virtually disappear. They may have switched over to producing CDs or DVDs, but now these are being replaced by downloads.

If there are changes in demand for products and services, then the business may have to alter its objectives by changing its sales targets or the amount of products it produces. These changes may not radically affect the mission statement of the business, but they will change the specific targets that a business aims to achieve.

Changing social objectives

Each different type of organisation will have a different set of objectives. For example, social enterprises, organisations in the public sector (like hospitals), charities and voluntary organisations do not aim to set profit or growth objectives. Their objectives are different to those of businesses.

Their central aims and objectives are usually determined by the purpose or the beliefs of the organisation. But this does not mean that they will not consider changing their objectives. For example, they may wish to focus on providing particular services to different or specific groups.

For example
A school's aims

A school does not seek to make a profit. Its aim may be to provide the best possible education for its pupils or students. It may also have objectives relating to attracting additional funding or replacing or updating buildings and facilities.

138

How a business decides

A business may start up in response to a specific business opportunity or because it has identified customers and already has expertise in particular products and services. It may have identified a problem it can solve; or found a gap or a niche in the market; or believed that the business would move in a particular direction.

However, experience may show that the business is develooping in a different way to that which it expected at the outset, perhaps because:

- new products have been developed
- sales have been made in different areas than were expected
- opportunities have arisen in international markets
- new technology has emerged to change the way the business operates
- the business is now sourcing its products, services and raw materials from different places
- the business has entered into a partnership with other businesses and organisations
- market share has grown quicker than expected

- the business has been approached by potential partners and is considering setting up franchises
- new opportunities have emerged for e-commerce that were not anticipated at the very beginning of the start-up process.

Some changes will have occurred because the business itself has moved in a different direction; others because the market, the competition or the customers have changed. Equally, the products and services themselves may have been transformed in response to these changes.

A business needs to decide whether it is content with trying to move in the same general direction that it anticipated at the beginning of its existence. If so, this may mean moving against the flow of change. However, if a business allows itself to go with the flow of change, then it needs to be sure that this direction will not lead it into difficulties.

Like many business decisions, changing fundamental aims and objectives is difficult and potentially dangerous – particularly if the business has no control over the direction in which it is going.

⏩ Breaking into new markets is a major reason why many aims and objectives are changed. Extra sales are always welcome, and businesses need to get the most out of their market. If a business does not increase its turnover every year, it is in fact shrinking. Businesses may change their aims and objectives to sell more to existing customers, or expand their customer base to sell to similar people, or they may try to find new channels to new markets.

QUESTION TIME
14 minutes

One of Nike's most famous mission statements was 'Crush Reebok'. Nike could have had a mission statement that said they wanted to be 'the best shoe company in the world with the best customer service'. Certainly Nike's mission statement was short, to the point – and not boring.

1 Nike's mission statement aimed to inspire and motivate everyone associated with the business. It had an unmistakable objective. But what did it lack? *(4 marks)*

2 Each mission statement should be different. Why should a business never try to write a statement similar to that of its closest competitor? *(4 marks)*

3 Why will Nike's mission statement change over time? *(6 marks)*

139

Changing aims and objectives as businesses grow

Becoming dominant

As they grow, businesses continue to position themselves so that they are ready for the future. They look at trends in the market and customer behaviour, and aim to grab as much market share as they can. If they can predict future developments, then there will be opportunities for future growth.

For example
IT Support

Many IT support businesses positioned themselves so that they could respond to the growth of home PC use. They have switched from being predominantly business-to-business services to business-to-consumer services.

Businesses may have seen major changes in sales by encouraging their customers to buy more frequently, or by getting their customers to 'trade up'. This means encouraging them to buy premium products and services that better suit their needs and also provide the business with a better profit.

Another alternative to encourage growth is for businesses to sell complementary products.

For example Hairdressing products

Hairdressers now have a broad range of haircare products in prominent positions beside the tills, providing additional sales, turnover and profit.

Becoming a dominant business in a particular market does not necessarily mean that the business is dominant everywhere. It may have local dominance in a town, city or region; or it may be selling to the majority of a particular type of customer. It may have enormous advantages over the competition and may, for example, have a **unique selling point** (or proposition) (USP).

If a business manages to achieve dominance, then it can be in a position to lead the way in terms of: setting price; quality of products and services; the way in which customers are dealt with; and how products and services are brought to the market.

It is difficult for competitors to challenge a business that is considered to be a **market leader**. Some seek to copy what the market leader is doing. These are known as '**market followers**'. Some may recognise that they cannot compete and will move out of that market. Others may try hard to dislodge the market leader, by cutting prices or offering better service or a broader range of products and services.

Once a business has become dominant, its purpose may change. Its aims and objectives may have been to become the dominant business. Now its new purpose is to retain that status.

International expansion

When a business starts up, its aims and objectives may be centred on its own home country and market. But some businesses may decide to expand into different countries, or opportunities may arise that tempt them into getting involved in new markets abroad. Now they need to refocus on the demands of their new customers – who may be very different from those they dealt with in the early days.

Selling and distributing products in overseas markets may mean finding partners, such as distributors or agents. Some businesses may enter into joint ventures with local businesses, while others may set up their own offices abroad.

To work effectively in an overseas market, a business needs to understand the legislation, culture and traditions. It also needs to remember that:

- different groups of people may be buying the products and services in different markets
- the products and services themselves may need to be adapted
- the way in which sales are made and customers are informed will be different
- everything needs to be expressed in the language of those customers.

140

For example Bicycles

In Britain, bicycles are generally seen as a leisure product. In countries as diverse as Holland and China they are seen as essential vehicles to take people to and from work. This means that the whole way in which bicycles are marketed abroad may be very different, as the purpose of the product is different.

New aims and objectives may have to be created, some of which will detail specific targets for different international markets. Initially, these aims and objectives may revolve around survival in the new market. After a year or so, the aims and objectives may be to produce a profit.

As the business becomes more complicated, setting separate aims and objectives for each new market may be essential. They can all still fit within the general mission statement or purpose of the business, but the precise aims, objectives and targets for each new market may be at a different stage. Over the years, as the business settles down in an overseas market, many of the aims and objectives can become the same at home and abroad.

A quick way of becoming a dominant business in a market, or expanding internationally, is to enter into joint ventures and partnerships with other businesses. Businesses that have available funds will opt for mergers and acquisitions as a quick way to expand:

- An acquisition occurs when one business buys another in order to control it.
- A merger takes place when two or more businesses join together and share control of the new, larger business.

QUESTION TIME
17 minutes

Halifax Fan Limited is based in Yorkshire and employs around 50 people. Recently it recognised that there might be sales opportunities in Asia. It entered into a joint venture with an Indian manufacturer after rejecting the idea of opening its own factory overseas. The business took the approach that it would be flexible with any partner, but it wanted to be clear about its own objectives.

1 Define the term 'joint venture'. *(2 marks)*

2 What would have been Halifax Fan Limited's objective prior to entering into its joint venture, and why? *(3 marks)*

3 Why was it important for the business to be clear about its key objectives? *(4 marks)*

4 The business has won a number of export contracts because of its Indian connection. Why might this have given it an edge over its competitors? *(6 marks)*

5 The business wanted to retain control and protect its investment. Why was this important? *(2 marks)*

141

KEY TERMS

Unique selling point (or proposition) ▶ something about the product or service (the price, the marketing, distribution or customer service) that sets the business apart from its competitors.

Market leader ▶ a business that is seen to be the most influential – or largest – business in the market.

Market follower ▶ a business that is prepared to follow the leaders in the market without challenging them.

Ethical and environmental issues

Social costs and benefits

Business activity brings a number of benefits, such as providing products and services, creating employment and contributing to the economy. However, there are also social costs, such as environmental damage.

A further complication is caused by new technologies, such as robotics or automation, or even by more widespread use of ICT. As businesses adopt new technologies, this creates unemployment, which is a social cost. But there may be better working conditions for the remaining employees, which is a social benefit.

Social benefits

Businesses:
- provide a range of products and services for all consumers, which would not otherwise be available
- create new ideas, inventions and information
- put money into the economy, both directly and indirectly, through wages and spending
- contribute to the wealth of the countries in which they operate
- support organisations, groups and charities through donations.

Social costs

However, businesses also:
- contribute to climate change or global warming by producing emissions
- create water pollution
- overuse chemicals or antibiotics in food production
- overuse resources that are difficult to replace, or use up resources that cannot be replaced
- contribute to congestion on roads and damage to roads

- carry out damaging activities that others may have to pay to put right
- push up prices through anti-competitive behaviour, so that the consumer suffers
- sell products or services that can have a negative impact on consumers.

Tackling social costs

There are generally four ways in which social costs can be tackled by society. Society can:
- make the practice a criminal offence, which has happened with many environmental and public health issues
- carry out investigations and bring charges against businesses whose products and services cause harm
- tax businesses that create social costs, and provide subsidies (give money to) businesses that provide social benefits
- provide the service itself.

Ethical and environmental aims

Many businesses recognise the importance of incorporating ethical and environmental aims and objectives in order to show that they are socially responsible. Businesses will aim to improve their environmental record, to make sure that their employees – and other businesses and groups that they deal with – are treated fairly, and that they support local communities.

Building ethical and environmental aims and objectives into the business brings enormous benefits. Customers are increasingly choosing businesses that are socially responsible to buy products and

services from, instead of basing their decision purely on cost. Investors are attracted to ethically responsible businesses. Employees are more motivated if they are treated fairly and allowed to develop. Customers, suppliers and other groups will trust the business, and they will enjoy better relations. The business can also save money, because being socially responsible and environmentally aware is actually cheaper than the costs of waste management.

Being greener

Businesses aim to address environmental problems by:
- replacing toxic substances with less harmful ones
- making their products multifunctional and reusable
- reducing their energy consumption
- making sure that many of their resources and materials are renewable and recyclable
- ensuring that employees receive environmental and health and safety training.

Community commitment

Businesses also like to stress their commitment to the community because it shows that they are socially responsible. The business can rely on the support of the local community. It can attract employees, and it can attract ethical investors and customers.

Businesses support local communities by:
- working with charities in particular areas
- sponsoring specific projects
- contributing to wider initiatives, such as literacy projects
- offering employment to disadvantaged groups.

142

For example
Fairtrade

The Fairtrade Mark can be awarded to products that have been certified by the Fairtrade Labelling Organisation. It means that the product conforms to standards that have improved the development of disadvantaged people in developing countries. Fairtrade sales are growing by around 20% per year and the Fairtrade Mark can bring benefits to both small and large businesses.

Social responsibility

Social responsibility needs to focus on:

- the market itself and how the business promotes itself, where it obtains supplies of products and services, and how its products and services are sold
- the employees, including the wages paid, working conditions and equal opportunities policies
- the community – whether the business is a good neighbour to its community and what the business puts back into the community
- the environment, including waste, use of resources and emissions
- human rights, which extends to ensuring that all suppliers are socially responsible.

In assessing whether it is socially responsible, a business needs to look at how far it goes beyond fulfilling its minimum legal obligations. Being socially responsible does not just mean staying within the law; it means being more socially responsible than is legally required. The United Nations has nine principles of social responsibility, focusing on human rights, labour and the environment.

QUESTION TIME
35 minutes

In 2007, the clothing chain Gap was linked with using children as young as 10, working up to 16 hours a day, to hand-embroider GapKids clothes in India. The business was condemned for exploiting children.

The business reacted by saying it would eradicate this practice and provided money to improve working conditions in India. It suspended orders with the textile workshops concerned.

Many people claimed that Gap had a responsibility and should have checked all the way back to where the cotton is produced in the fields.

1 Explain the difference between a social cost and a social benefit. *(4 marks)*

2 Identify TWO social costs and two social benefits. *(4 marks)*

3 The charity Save the Children believes that customers should be willing to pay more for products and services, and that cheap prices always mean exploited employees, probably including children. Is it reasonable for a business to expect customers to pay more because they are socially responsible? Explain your answer. *(6 marks)*

4 Some 60 million children work in India. How might Gap have checked that all of its suppliers were socially responsible? *(6 marks)*

5 Gap has provided money to improve working conditions in India. What strategies could Gap put in place for this to be achieved? *(6 marks)*

6 Do you consider Gap to be socially responsible by suspending orders with the Indian textile workshops? *(9 marks)*

How to choose a location

YOU WILL FIND OUT:

- about qualitative factors
- about push and pull factors
- about costs and benefits of locations
- about low-cost and multi-site locations

Qualitative factors

When deciding where to locate, businesses may focus primarily on the quantitative factors (the facts and figures). But views and attitudes – or qualitative factors – are also important factors. The appeal of any area and the quality of life it may offer are important considerations.

Equally, many overseas businesses have chosen to locate in Britain because English is the dominant business language in the world.

Other businesses may choose to locate in a particular area because it is already associated with that type of business or industry.

For example
High-tech locations

In the USA, film companies inevitably gravitate towards Los Angeles, as Hollywood is the film capital of the world. In Britain, the Thames Valley is associated with high-tech industries and is often referred to as 'Britain's Silicon Valley'.

Some locations appear to enhance the image of a business. For example, many businesses will have small offices in London for this reason, despite the fact that their main production facilities are elsewhere.

Push and pull factors

A push factor is a feature of a particular area that either makes it less attractive to a business or forces a business to consider relocating somewhere else. There are few advantages to a business in either locating there or remaining there. Typical push factors include:

- increased competition
- rising costs
- poor communications
- falling sales.

Pull factors, by contrast, attract a business to a particular area or convince them that they should remain there. Typical pull factors include:

- government incentives and grants
- lower labour costs
- good communications and infrastructure
- developing markets.

Costs and benefits of locations

Although location decisions are important to new businesses, they can also have a major impact on an established organisation. Usually at some point in a business's development it will have to consider relocation to a better location, which can offer it room to grow and a balance of positive quantitative and qualitative factors.

Relocation does bring problems (costs). For example:

- Some staff may not wish to move, so provision has to be made for them. This could include redundancy and compensation.
- The business will suffer disruption during the move, making it difficult to maintain a steady income.
- Customers need to be told about the location change, as do suppliers.

However, a good location can offer the business enormous benefits:

- New premises can mean that new systems, processes and management systems can be installed without many of the problems that would have been associated with trying to do this at the old location.
- The business can redefine itself, reassign roles, and streamline production and operations.
- An established business can take the opportunity to reinvent itself. It can take advantage of all of the benefits of the new location, while seeking to discard any problems it may have had in operating at its old premises.

Ideally, moving to a good location not only puts the business at the centre of its market, allows smoother distribution in and out, and brings with it its key personnel, but it also sets the business up in a situation where it can continue to enjoy these advantages for years to come.

Low-cost locations

Businesses tend to assume that after the costs of the move have been taken into account, they should be able to increase their efficiency and have a positive impact on their overall costs. In fact, the new location may have a drastic or major impact on the long-term profitability of the business. A business will therefore have to weigh up the cost factors and compare them to qualitative factors and other long-term issues before finally making a decision about moving.

This does not necessarily mean, however, that a business will always

144

seek to find the lowest-cost location. It may well be that a low-cost location does not really offer a solid platform for future expansion and success, compared to other locations.

Out of town

Supermarkets and other retail outlets some years ago took the very difficult decision that in order to expand, they had to move out of the high street. Not only was there insufficient space for them in the high street, but also the rents and rates were very expensive. Moving to out-of-town locations was a considerable risk, but ultimately it has proved to be more profitable for most of them.

Overseas

Shifting operations to an overseas location may appear financially attractive, but at a very basic level there may be language difficulties. Moving to an area where there are insufficiently trained staff may bring with it problems of ensuring quality of production or quality of raw materials and components.

Multi-site locations

There are many different challenges to managing a multi-site organisation:

- Communication can often be a significant problem, particularly if a communication structure is not put in place at the earliest opportunity. The use of ICT has certainly improved this situation, with the main office being able to access data generated by the subsidiary sites. In this way it can monitor progress and information,

such as sales figures or production totals.
- A structure needs to be created. This can be either formal or informal, but it needs to have clear reporting relationships.
- Standardised hours need to be established.
- Productivity levels and outcomes need to be mutually agreed.
- Goals, milestones and deadlines need to be clearly identified.
- Staff from the head office need to make both scheduled and unscheduled visits.
- Daily contact needs to be established via videoconferencing or conference calls.
- Remote sites need to be encouraged to communicate regularly with the main office to seek answers to specific problems.
- The whole business needs to be knitted together, by calling joint meetings, creating newsletters and generally encouraging cooperation and collaboration.

> ▶▶ Businesses that rapidly open in new locations may impress potential investors by their drive and sales growth. However, operating in different areas can often be as complicated as managing multiple brands of products or services.

QUESTION TIME
16 minutes

1 What problems will a business encounter when choosing to relocate? *(4 marks)*

2 Why might a small business be more concerned with location costs than best location? *(6 marks)*

3 How might a small business handle the extra pressures of two or more sites? *(6 marks)*

145

Factors influencing the location of a growing business

YOU WILL FIND OUT:
- about factors affecting location
- about multi-site locations

Factors affecting location

New businesses in particular are faced with a major and difficult decision as to where to locate. The location will have a massive impact on the business's costs and its access to customers and markets. These issues will ultimately affect its income and profitability.

Location decisions can be broadly split into quantitative and qualitative factors. The quantitative factors relate primarily to costs and revenues, whereas the qualitative factors focus on other issues that are not so easy to put a monetary value on, such as quality of life.

Many factors could affect a business's location decision. Some are outlined in the table below.

What are multi-site locations?

As an alternative to relocation, businesses often decide to establish additional locations as their primary strategy in achieving growth. The senior management of a business may then have the challenge of managing not only multiple offices, factories and sales teams, but also a number of individuals who may work from home.

Managing parts of the operation in different geographical locations requires the organisation to adapt its reporting procedures and processes, to ensure that the business continues to move in the same direction, with

FACTOR	EXPLANATION
Costs of the location	Costs of land or buildings can vary from area to area. Equally, additional costs, such as business rates, can vary. If the business is considering an international location, then lower-cost employees can make overseas locations more attractive.
Grants and incentives	Governments and local authorities may offer lower taxes or lower rents to attract businesses to locate in a particular region. Grants help draw businesses into an area.
Infrastructure	This incorporates the transport, energy and communications in a particular area. Good infrastructure will help push down costs of production, speed up distribution and make the business's operations easier.
The nature of the business	Some businesses that deal directly with consumers need to be close to their markets. Industries may need to be close to their raw materials. Service-based industries may not need to either be near their customers or their suppliers.
Market location	Some businesses need to be near their markets, either because they offer direct services or their products benefit from being close to their customer base by reducing distribution costs, etc.
Market access	A business needs to be assured that it can get its products and services into the market without incurring additional and unnecessary costs.
Exchange rates	Overseas businesses will usually quote prices in their own currency, but if they are selling into other countries the actual value of the sale can be affected by exchange rate fluctuations.
Political and economic stability	Political uncertainty and economic disruption can adversely affect businesses, particularly if they feel that it is unwise to invest at a particular point as the situation is uncertain.
Availability of resources	Primarily human resources, particularly potential employees who have a recognised level of qualifications, expertise or skills.
Company image	Certain areas have a degree of prestige attached to them and the business may wish to use this as a part of their overall corporate image.
Quality of life	This is a qualitative factor. It may be an important decision for the business to locate in an area that offers a good standard of living for employees and is an attractive and desirable location.
Ethical issues	Some businesses will continue to invest and expand in areas that they have long-standing associations with and where they have been employers for some years. Other businesses will avoid areas where wages are traditionally low, so that they are not seen to be exploiting the local workforce.

these separate divisions contributing in a timely manner. This is a particular concern if the business becomes a multinational operation, with separate parts of the organisation located in different countries.

While this means that there are particular complications, such as languages and different time zones, the challenges facing a business in operating across a whole country with numerous outlets or offices can be equally challenging.

 Business opportunities may mean a business shifting production or fulfilment (either making products and services available or handling customer service queries) to a new location. They may merge or acquire other businesses. The net result is that the business begins to operate from multiple work sites. The problem is maintaining a clear reporting relationship with the main headquarters. Inevitably, there are positive and negative factors to take into account.

EXAMPLE

Many British businesses locate their manufacturing in the Far East for these reasons.

There are development agencies all around Britain with a variety of incentives to attract businesses.

The proximity of a good road network or infrastructure projects can make areas attractive to businesses.

A retail outlet must be inside a large enough catchment area to draw in sufficient customers.

A retail outlet needs to be either in a high street location or a retail park, rather than a remote location.

Businesses located outside the European Union (EU) are required to pay a tax to import their products and services into the EU. Many overseas businesses (particularly the Japanese and Koreans) have set up production facilities in the EU for this reason.

A strong currency makes it difficult for home producers to export. It is cheaper for them to purchase products made abroad, which they then import.

Terrorist threats in certain countries have made businesses reluctant to locate or invest.

Businesses that focus on innovation often locate close to major universities to recruit the best graduates and use the best research facilities.

The supermarket chain Waitrose tends to locate in more affluent areas. Fashion designers may wish to be associated with London, Paris or Milan.

Although many businesses have relocated to more rural areas, inner cities are becoming more attractive. For example, there are inward investments (injections of cash into an area) in Cardiff, Newcastle and parts of London.

Businesses such as Cafédirect (Britain's largest Fairtrade hot drinks company) have long-standing associations with particular suppliers.

QUESTION TIME
25 minutes

1 What do you understand by the term 'market access'? *(4 marks)*

2 What is the difference between qualitative and quantitative location factors? *(4 marks)*

3 Identify and explain ONE location factor that is important to a business that exports its goods across the European market. *(3 marks)*

4 Identify and explain TWO location factors a business will consider when choosing where to site a new supermarket. *(6 marks)*

5 How might a business take ethical issues into account when choosing a location? *(4 marks)*

6 How might having multiple sites fulfil the goal to expand? *(4 marks)*

147

Issues relating to overseas location

YOU WILL FIND OUT:

- what a multinational is
- about reasons to become a multinational
- about advantages of multinationals
- about disadvantages of multinationals

What is a multinational?

A multinational organisation has its headquarters in one country and carries out operations in a range of other countries.

Multinationals are large organisations with enormous power and influence. They attract criticism but are sought as potential investors in countries around the world.

For example Multinationals

Household names such as Microsoft, Canon, Coca-Cola, McDonald's, Shell and Ford are all examples of successful multinationals.

Ford has manufacturing operations on six continents. They include assembly plants, engine plants, casting and aluminium plants. In Europe they have over 30 sites in nine different countries.

Reasons to become a multinational

There are many reasons why a business may decide to become a multinational organisation.

Location

As we saw on pages 40–3, the first steps towards overseas involvement can come from location decisions.

Access to raw materials

The business may also locate abroad to gain closer access to raw materials and components.

Lower costs overseas

A business might choose to become a multinational to benefit from the lower costs of operating overseas. It may also gain the advantage of less strict rules and regulations. For example, health and safety regulations overseas may be more lax. The business will also be able to tap into a new labour pool. This may be cheaper and more flexible.

Understanding the market

Being closer to overseas markets also helps businesses understand the market. They can appreciate customer requirements. If they are based in that country, they can respond to customer service issues with greater efficiency.

New market opportunities

The business will also be able to open up new market opportunities, particularly when its domestic market has become saturated and it is experiencing only slow growth. Operating abroad offers a brand new market and an opportunity for rapid growth. This may ultimately give the business greater economies of scale.

Overcoming protectionist barriers

Some countries and regions try to protect their domestic industries. China, for example, can be described as being protectionist. It puts up trade barriers to prevent its markets from being flooded with overseas products, affecting domestic businesses. To get round this, overseas businesses have entered into joint ventures with Chinese businesses, so that they can enjoy the benefits of the protectionist barriers.

Overcoming exchange-rate fluctuations

If a business is able to produce products in the country in which it sells them, then fluctuating exchange rates are no longer an issue.

Advantages of multinationals

Some countries are keen to attract multinational organisations because they bring benefits:

- They bring investment into the country. When a multinational business locates in a particular country it needs land and labour, and it will be spending money that will find its way into the local economy.
- Local people will be employed and existing resources can be exploited, with the possibility of attracting additional multinationals.
- Many argue that multinational companies not only bring with them new techniques and ideas, but they also improve the **human capital** in the host country. In other words, they train the local labour force and give it new skills.
- The multinational business also pays tax to the host government.
- Multinationals often invest in infrastructure to improve communications and road and rail networks. This also provides a valuable set of investments for the host country.

148

For example — Advantages

Japanese car manufacturers located in Britain to give them access to the EU and avoid trade barriers. As far as Britain is concerned, it has not only provided valuable employment opportunities, particularly in the North East, but it has also generally improved working practices and driven down the cost of vehicles, by bringing new competition into the market.

Disadvantages of multinationals

Some countries are suspicious of multinational companies and their motives, and there are costs associated with their establishment, including:

- Employment opportunities may not actually be as good as expected. If the business needs skilled workers, they may be overseas nationals, not locals.
- The relocation of the multinational to the host country may be temporary. They may only stay for the duration of a particular set of incentives, or until the tax advantages of moving elsewhere become too tempting.
- Employment prospects may be good in the early stages, particularly for construction workers. But if the business is using capital-intensive production facilities (which means that it has invested a large amount in assets),

then the longer-term employment prospects are actually quite poor.
- Weak or corrupt governments are susceptible to bribes and exploitation by powerful multinationals. Multinationals may target countries that they believe they can manipulate in order to get the best deal.
- Regulations may not be as rigorous in the host country. The business may cause significant pollution and environmental damage that they would not be allowed to cause in their own country. They may also dump waste products and have a long-term negative environmental impact on the country.
- The multinational may actually set up in the country specifically to sell products that are falling in popularity or that have been heavily regulated in their home country, such as tobacco products and certain types of drugs.

> Multinationals do not necessarily locate in underdeveloped countries in order to access a cheap workforce and cheap resources. Britain has been especially attractive for Japanese and Korean businesses. They have invested heavily in production facilities, especially in the vehicle market. This has mainly been to avoid the trade barriers that have been set up by the EU to discourage EU businesses and customers from purchasing products and services from outside the EU.

QUESTION TIME
33 minutes

A manufacturer has outgrown its factory near Manchester and faces a major location decision. The management has worked out that their average employees cost them £18 per hour and that to move to a new factory of sufficient size they will need to pay £125 per square metre per year in rent.

The finance director has just returned from a fact-finding trip abroad. He has discovered that the average cost of a Malaysian worker would be just £4 per hour and that a factory would cost just £25 per square metre per year. He proposes that they shut down the UK factory and shift production abroad.

1 Define the term 'multinational'. *(3 marks)*

2 Why do some businesses choose to become multinationals? *(6 marks)*

3 Identify and explain TWO advantages of operating as a multinational. *(6 marks)*

4 Identify and explain TWO disadvantages of operating as a multinational. *(6 marks)*

5 In the scenario above, is the finance director right? Are there any other factors that the business needs to take into account? *(12 marks)*

149

What have you learnt?

This section (The business organisation) is the first part of Unit 2 (Growing as a business). It builds on the work you did in Unit 1. It has covered how businesses expand, and how larger businesses may have different objectives to smaller ones.

We have looked at:

- expanding a business, along with the benefits and risks, and how this could lead to conflict between stakeholders
- the decisions behind businesses changing their legal structure. We have looked in more detail at private limited companies and, for the first time, at public limited companies
- how businesses might change their aims and objectives as they

grow, and incorporate ethical and environmental considerations to prove that they are socially responsible
- location – how location is important to growing businesses and what needs to be considered if a business is expanding overseas.

We hope that you have tried all of the 'Question time' exercises in this section. As you may have noticed, we have given 1 mark per minute for each of the questions. This is because like the Unit 1 exam paper, the Unit 2 paper is a one-hour exam and the maximum mark is 60. By getting used to the speed at which you will need to answer questions, this should mean that when you open the real exam paper, you won't panic.

You will not need to remember the legal process about incorporation (becoming a limited company), but you could encounter a question that relates directly to changes in the business organisation. Your teacher or tutor will be able to give you a copy of the 'Unit Revision Pack' from the *Teacher Support Pack*. This will give you further clues as to the areas to revise, as well as a mock examination paper.

Section 1 integrated questions

Try out these exam-style questions. They only relate to Section 1 (The business organisation), but in the real exam you should expect to see questions relating to other sections of the unit too. This is a real business situation.

150

LUSH

Lush is a handmade cosmetics business based in Britain, but now operating across the world. It has stores in most European countries and as far afield as Australia, Japan and the United States of America.

The business considers itself to be highly socially responsible. Its products are environmentally friendly. It is committed to only sourcing supplies from businesses that have never tested their products on animals and it supports a wide range of charities and other worthy causes. It makes donations to Animal Aid, to humanitarian groups in East Timor, and to environmental groups such as Dorset Wildlife Trust and the Stop Stansted Expansion Campaign.

QUESTIONS
40 minutes

1 Explain why Lush is considered to be a multinational. *(2 marks)*

2 What do you consider to be one of Lush's business objectives and why? *(3 marks)*

3 Why has Lush chosen to grow? *(4 marks)*

4 What locational factors would Lush have considered when choosing an overseas location? *(6 marks)*

5 One of Lush's products is known as the Charity Pot. All profits from the sale of this go to worthy causes. Why might an approach like this be a good way of showing that the business is socially responsible? *(6 marks)*

6 The business gives around 2% of its profits to charity and sources organic and Fairtrade ingredients. How might this approach affect the business's overall profits? *(6 marks)*

7 Lush began with start-up funds of less than £50,000. It now has a turnover of around £150 million per year, with over 600 shops and 1,200 employees. How might its aims and objectives have changed? *(4 marks)*

8 Some of Lush's stakeholders are not happy about its environmental and socially responsible approach. Advise the board on whether this approach should be continued or not. *(9 marks)*

151

Adoption and adaptation

YOU WILL FIND OUT:

● about the marketing mix

● what a product is

● about the customer adoption process

● about adapting products and services

● about modifying the marketing mix

The marketing mix

In Unit 1 we looked at the four interlinked components of the basic marketing mix:

• product (this includes services)
• price
• promotion
• place.

As businesses grow, they may need to review the balance of their marketing mix and alter it in response to market forces. Now we are going to look at each element of the marketing mix in turn and consider how it might need to change as a business grows.

What is a product?

A product (or service) is something that can be offered to the market in order to satisfy a need or a want. There are a number of different product types, including consumer goods, speciality products, raw materials, components and industrial services.

A basic product consists of a number of features:

• components and materials used
• usage
• performance
• features
• quality
• design
• reliability
• technical sophistication
• service
• technological advice
• maintenance and repair.

The customer adoption process

Customers 'adopt' a new product in a five-stage process:

• **awareness** – potential customers are informed about the product or service, either through promotion or by recommendation
• **interest** – potential customers now have an interest in buying it, as it may suit their needs
• **evaluation** – customers compare the product or service with other products and services already available, to decide whether to switch
• **trial** – customers now buy the product or service and try it out. If it does not meet their expectations, they will not buy it again; they may tell others that it is not as good or as useful as they had hoped
• **adoption** – having tried out the product or service, the customers are now pleased with its performance and other features and are happy to continue buying it. Hopefully for the business they will buy the product or service more regularly and recommend it to others.

Adapting products and services

Many start-up businesses will have targeted a niche market that was not being catered for by a larger business. Marketing and selling to a niche market often require a very different approach to marketing and selling in larger markets (also known as 'mass markets').

The products sold to a niche market are often tailor-made. There are likely to be fewer customers in a niche market, so they will want the product or service to be precisely what they require. Competition is low and high prices can be charged.

But there may come a point when a new business realises that:

• it misjudged the niche market – it is not as big as it appeared to be and the business has sold products and services to the bulk of that niche market
• the niche market may not be able to afford the products and services. Customers are happy to look elsewhere for more general products that nearly suit their needs
• the niche market is disappearing – it was only a passing trend or fashion and the products and services are no longer in demand
• major competitors have moved into the niche market and are squeezing the start-up business out of the market
• the niche market is actually larger than the business thought – and the types of products and services in demand are broader and more varied
• the niche market would be prepared to buy a range of additional products and services that the business does not currently offer. If the new business does not offer them now, then a larger competitor may enter the market and provide them to the customers.

As a result, the business will need to adapt the product or service.

Modifying the marketing mix

Products and services tend to follow a fairly predictable pattern in terms of sales over a period of time. Each time a product or service passes through a stage in its life, the business will have to revise the way in which it balances the marketing mix.

The business will try to improve sales by changing one or more of the elements of the marketing mix. This usually means modifying a product – to improve its quality, style, reliability, speed, packaging or taste – or restyling it to attract different types of customer.

When a business begins to offer a product or service for the first time, it is often a basic product. Once demand has increased, the business will offer different versions of the product and enhance customer service. Once demand has stabilised, it will continue to encourage sales, by bringing out different versions of the product to suit particular types of customer. Towards the end of a product's life, the business will take the weakest-selling versions off the market, just leaving the best-sellers.

For example Car restyling

Car manufacturers restyle their basic car models all the time. Food manufacturers do the same, constantly introducing new flavours, colours and ingredients. Manufacturers of household products also restyle constantly.

Each time they restyle, they are trying to attract a new group of buyers They are all still selling the same basic product; it has just been modified to attract additional sales.

QUESTION TIME
23 minutes

1 Identify **THREE** features related to a product. *(3 marks)*

2 What is the customer adoption process? *(2 marks)*

3 Choose **THREE** stages of the customer adoption process and explain them. *(6 marks)*

4 How might a business know when it is time to start considering bringing out special versions of a product or service for new customers? *(6 marks)*

5 The Apple iPod is a good example of product development, with new versions of essentially the same product being brought out on a regular basis. How might this approach have helped Apple's sales? *(6 marks)*

153

Product portfolio and mix

Product portfolio analysis

The term 'product portfolio' describes the products and product lines owned by the business, the business's desire to satisfy the needs of target markets, and its objectives.

A business will analyse its product portfolio to assess the market growth rate and a product's relative market share. Product portfolio analysis is a key activity in determining the direction and intensity of marketing strategies. It looks at the business opportunities as a product moves through its life cycle phases of introduction, growth, maturity and decline.

The Boston Matrix

The Boston Matrix was developed by the Boston Consulting Group to analyse products and businesses by market share and market growth.

In this matrix:

- 'cash cow' refers to a product of a business with high market share and low market growth
- 'dog' refers to a product of a business with low market share

and low growth
- 'wild cat' (also sometimes called 'problem child' or 'question mark') refers to a product of a business with low market share and high growth
- 'star' refers to a product of a business with high growth and high market share.

These phases are typically represented by an anti-clockwise movement around the Boston Matrix quadrants in the following order:

Starting from a market entry position as a 'wild cat'/'question mark'/'problem child' product, products are usually launched into high-growth markets, but suffer from a low market share.

To a 'star' position as sales and market share are increased. If the investment necessary to build sales and market share is successfully made, then the product's position will move towards the star position of high growth/high market share.

To a 'cash cow' position as the market growth rate slows and market leadership is achieved. As the impact of the product life cycle takes effect

and the market growth rate slows, the product will move from the 'star' position of high growth to the 'cash cow' position of low growth/high share.

Finally to a 'dog' position as investment is minimised, and the product ages and loses market share.

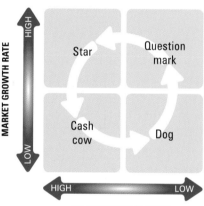

▲ **The anti-clockwise movement around the Boston Matrix**

At each position in the matrix there are a number of opportunities open to the business. For example, at the 'cash cow' stage, the options are:

- to invest to maintain market share
- to minimise investment in the product, maximise the cash returns and grow market dominance with other products.

Product mix and product line

'Product mix' is a marketing term used to describe a business's entire range of different products and product lines.

A 'product line' is a group of products that are closely related, either because they function in a similar manner, are sold to the same customer groups, or are marketed

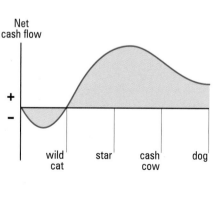

▲ **Link between the product life cycle and the Boston Matrix**

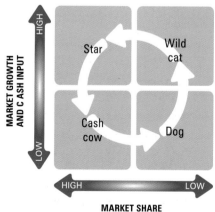

MARKET SHARE
AND CASH GENERATION

154

▶ The Ansoff Matrix examines the potential strategies available to a business in four areas, cross-referenced as new or existing markets and new or existing products. The matrix suggests the marketing strategies available to the business in each of four areas:

through similar distribution channels, or have similar pricing structures.

A business can alter its product line by using:

- **product line depth** – adding to the number of products in each product line
- **product line extension** – adding products to the product mix by bringing new products into an existing product line
- **product line filling** – plugging gaps in the existing product line to accommodate differing demands from customers
- **product line pricing** – a pricing strategy which features a series of steps in price between products in a product line. Normally the price differences are based on customers' perceptions of the products in terms of their features and benefits, as well competitors' prices
- **product line stretching** – extending the scope of the product line beyond what is currently on offer, perhaps taking the product into associated markets and applications.
- Market penetration – existing products into existing markets. The business seeks to increase its market share with the current product range. This is considered to be the least risky of all the options available. Existing customers are encouraged to buy more products and services, those

at present buying a competing brand are persuaded to switch, and non-buyers are convinced to begin to make purchases.
- **Market development** – existing products into new markets. Segments are targeted individually either through existing marketing and distribution channels or new ones are set up to service the new segments. As the business is moving into new markets, it needs to be aware of that the markets may be different and they may have different competitors.
- **Product development** – new products into existing markets. Assuming the business has sufficient resources, new products or developments in the existing products can be brought into the market. Provided the business has closely matched the new products with the requirements of its existing markets, risks are minimised. The major concern is how long it will take to develop the new products.
- **Diversification** – new products into new markets. This is the highest-risk strategy of all. There are two options available to the business: diversification, which relies on the business being able to use its existing product and market knowledge (production processes, distribution channels, etc.); and that the business departs from its existing product and market knowledge, by merging with (or taking over) a business operating in an unrelated area.

⏩ The alternative way of carrying out product portfolio analysis is to use the Ansoff Matrix. It takes a broader view and looks at the future possibilities open to the business.

QUESTION TIME
28 minutes

1 Define the term 'product portfolio'. *(2 marks)*

2 What is the Boston Matrix? *(2 marks)*

3 What is a product in the maturity stage of the product life cycle classed as in the Boston Matrix? *(2 marks)*

4 What is a product in the decline stage of the product life cycle classed as in the Boston Matrix? *(2 marks)*

5 Why is it a good idea for a business to carry out a product portfolio analysis? *(6 marks)*

6 Why might a business choose to expand its range of products and services? *(6 marks)*

7 Advise a business on whether a product that has been categorised as a 'question mark' using the Boston Matrix should be removed from the market or not. *(8 marks)*

155

Product life cycle

The product life cycle

The product life cycle is a widely accepted model that describes the stages through which a product or service passes – from its introduction to its decline and final removal from the market.

The stages of the life cycle

The key stages of the product life cycle are outlined in the following table:

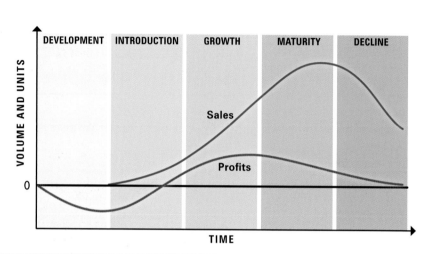

▲ The standard product life cycle graph, showing the phases of the life cycle and the association between profits and sales over the cycle

STAGE	EXPLANATION
Introduction/launch	In the birth or introduction stage, the business hopes to build product awareness and develop a market for the product. Significant amounts are spent on advertising and promotion to tell potential customers that the product is available.
Growth	In the growth stage of the product life cycle, the business seeks to build brand loyalty and increase market share. There is continued high spending on marketing to establish the product in the market.
Maturity	This is the third stage of the product life cycle. At maturity, the strong growth in sales slows down. Competition may appear with similar products. Marketing efforts now switch to defending market share while maximising profit. There is steady and continued support, with occasional promotions to maintain interest in the product.
Saturation	This stage of the product's life cycle is when competition has reached a stage which makes it difficult to keep the original product going. Indeed, it may be that the product is already growing stale. This 'saturation' period marks a slight downturn, which can be adjusted by a relaunch or a repackaging of the product; otherwise it will begin its inevitable slip into the decline stage.
Decline	This is the final stage of the standard product life cycle. As sales decline, the business has several options: • maintain the product, perhaps adding new features and finding new uses • try to reduce costs and continue to offer it, possibly to a loyal segment of the market • discontinue the product, selling off any remaining stock, or selling it to another business that is willing to continue the product. There may be little or no marketing support, although the business would wish to clear the stocks of the products before they cease production of it. At the decline stage, the business needs to carefully consider its policy towards the product or service. If the business decides to abandon it, then there may be other concerns about the turnover and profit of the business, especially if the product or service is not being replaced. If this happens, it will affect employees, suppliers and distributors.

⏩ The diagram at the top of the opposite page is a more complex view of the product life cycle. It illustrates the dangers often faced by product innovators in developing new product ideas. They can stand to lose potential sales as a result of the actions of competitors. The innovator has good sales until the competitors start moving into the market and begin taking sales away from them. After a time, there are so many competitors that the original business is squeezed out. Until the competitors enter the market, the innovator has a monopoly (that means it is the sole provider) in the market.

156

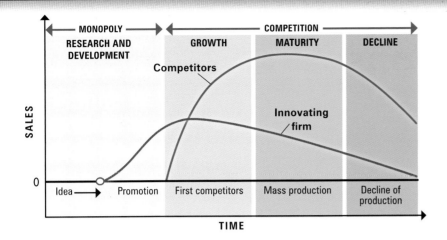

Product life cycle management

Businesses can identify different product life cycle patterns (see the set of graphs below). This gives them the opportunity to consider whether they can influence or manage the shape of the life cycle curve.

The ideas of the various shapes offer the following opportunities:

If the business has a range of different products and services, it will be able to decide where to use its resources. It will use its resources where it thinks they will benefit the most. Looking at the product life cycle, it is able to plan ahead and make those resource decisions.

Trying to match a new product and its likely product life cycle with an existing product may give the business some valuable insights into the potential trends in the future and how long the product might last.

The product life cycle is really useful when the business is creating a business plan. If it can identify the likely shape and length of the product life cycle, it might be able to work out the likely costs and income of the product over a period of time.

QUESTION TIME
20 minutes

1 What is a product life cycle? *(2 marks)*

2 What is the difference between the maturity and the decline stage of the product life cycle? *(4 marks)*

3 Identify a product that does not follow the traditional product life cycle and explain why. *(4 marks)*

4 What might a business do if the product life cycle shows very little growth of the product and sales begin to tail off? *(6 marks)*

5 How might a new business use product life cycles to help it? *(4 marks)*

157

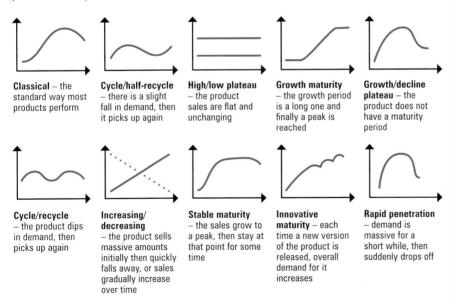

Classical – the standard way most products perform

Cycle/half-recycle – there is a slight fall in demand, then it picks up again

High/low plateau – the product sales are flat and unchanging

Growth maturity – the growth period is a long one and finally a peak is reached

Growth/decline plateau – the product does not have a maturity period

Cycle/recycle – the product dips in demand, then picks up again

Increasing/ decreasing – the product sells massive amounts initially then quickly falls away, or sales gradually increase over time

Stable maturity – the sales grow to a peak, then stay at that point for some time

Innovative maturity – each time a new version of the product is released, overall demand for it increases

Rapid penetration – demand is massive for a short while, then suddenly drops off

> ▶▶ A business will do everything in its power to maintain sales, particularly at the maturity stage, where sales are strongest. To reduce the risk that the product goes into decline, the business will continue to support it with advertising and promotion. It may give the product a facelift by changing a feature of it, such as its size, design or even its name.

Pricing decisions

Setting the price

Setting a price for products and services is one of the most difficult tasks facing a business. On the one hand it needs to take account of the costs that are incurred by the business; on the other hand it needs to consider the prices being charged by key competitors.

Another major problem for new businesses is that they are not well known, and nor are their products or services. They cannot usually compete on price, because they are not in a position to buy products in bulk from their suppliers at the same low prices as larger competitors. Also, it may cost them more to provide services, because they are not as efficient as larger competitors.

If a competitor was offering a similar product at the same price, then factors other than price – such as service, convenience and business reputation – may determine where customers buy their products and services. If the competitors were selling the same product for more, then the likelihood is that customers would make their buying decisions based purely on price.

As the small business begins to learn about the market, it will understand exactly how much it costs to buy or make a product or to provide a service. It will look for areas where it can save money. Any savings can either be passed on to customers to make the business more competitive, or used to maintain prices and give the business a bigger profit.

As a business gets larger, pricing decisions do not get any easier. The more competitive the market, the harder it is to come up with a pricing policy that works and will attract customers.

For example

Pricing strategy

A business may have a pricing policy of setting its prices so that they appear to be lower than they actually are, such as charging £9.99 instead of £10, so that they can say in their advertisements that their products are under £10. This could be a long-term pricing strategy.

A pricing tactic still using this psychological approach could be to drop the price temporarily to £9.49 or to temporarily increase it to £10.49. The business has still kept its basic approach and appears to be acting fairly in terms of price, as it has only stepped up or down by 50p.

Pricing strategies and tactics

Pricing plays an important role in the marketing mix. If the business makes the wrong decision on pricing, then it stands to lose customers. If it loses customers, it will lose revenue. This means reduced profits. There always has to be a balance between sales and revenue. A business cannot afford to sell products that make little or no money, even if it is selling tens of thousands of them. The revenue may look good, but the profits will be poor.

Pricing strategies are longer-

term approaches to price. Pricing strategies will be adopted so that the business can meet particular objectives, such as ensuring that there is a healthy demand for a new product, or that prices are set to take advantage of an increased demand.

Pricing tactics are part of pricing strategies, but tend to be used for a shorter period of time than pricing strategies – for maximum effect. Pricing tactics are either abandoned or changed as circumstances change.

158

Customer reaction

At the same time, businesses need to be aware of how customers may react to changes in the prices of the products and services they buy. Customers will have in mind what a product or service is worth to them. They will also have a reasonable idea of what competitors are charging. Few customers are so loyal that they are prepared to stick with a particular product or service regardless of its price. They will switch if there is a big difference in price.

Usually, customers will be happy to pay slightly more for a product or service if:

- it is exactly what they want
- they think that the quality of the product or service is better than that of the competition
- they need the product or service
- they have more available income to spend.

The problem is that many products are available from a wide variety of different sources. If the customer cannot find the right product or service at the right price, then they will simply go elsewhere. Customers will also go elsewhere if they cannot immediately get the product they

want from a particular supplier. They will be prepared to pay more for it if they can have it now from a competitor.

Although it is an important part of the marketing mix, price is linked to all the other elements of the marketing mix. Adopting a particular pricing strategy or pricing tactic alone is not enough to ensure success.

> Pricing competition tends to be short term and may temporarily increase a business's market share. But in the longer term, customers will come to expect lower prices. Eventually a business will get to a point where it cannot cut prices any further, or it will simply not make a profit. It then has to compete on a non-price basis.
>
> Businesses can compete on a non-price basis, by offering more convenience, better quality or additional services, such as home delivery, extended opening hours or customer loyalty cards.

QUESTION TIME
24 minutes

1 Why is it important that a business chooses the right price for its products? *(4 marks)*

2 Why might a small or new business find it difficult to price its products competitively in relation to competitors? *(4 marks)*

3 How might a business be able to compete on a non-price basis? *(4 marks)*

4 What might be meant by the term 'price-sensitive' as applied to customers? *(4 marks)*

5 If a business drops the price of its product, what is likely to happen to customer demand and why? *(4 marks)*

6 A business that sets the price that others copy in a market is known as a 'price leader'. Why might a business be happy to be a price taker? *(4 marks)*

159

Pricing strategies for growth

YOU WILL FIND OUT:

- about price skimming
- about price penetration
- about competitive pricing
- about loss leaders
- about cost plus pricing
- about influencing the pricing decision

Price skimming

Price skimming allows a business to set a high price for its products and services. This is a price that may only be acceptable to some of its customers. These customers are usually the ones who are most loyal and will buy the product or service regardless of its price. Usually, if the price is high, then the quantity sold is comparatively low. In theory, if the business were then to drop its price, the demand would pick up.

Price penetration

Penetration pricing is the opposite of price skimming. It is an aggressive pricing strategy. The business will set its prices deliberately low enough to attract as many customers as possible in the shortest period of time. The purpose of penetration pricing is to cause chaos to the pricing structure of competitors and take away market share from them. The business that has set these really low prices will quickly grab a large market share. At that point it will review its pricing policy and may then put prices back up, in the hope that the customers it has taken from the competitors will remain loyal to it.

Competitive pricing

Competitive pricing aims to match the changes and movements of prices charged by competitors for similar products and services offered in the market. The business will need to monitor the pricing of major competitors and bring its prices into line with theirs.

For example
Competitive pricing

Many of the major supermarkets use competitive pricing, trying to match the average price charged for the same product by other supermarkets. It is not always possible for the supermarkets to match temporary special prices, but they may still attempt to do this as part of a competitive pricing strategy.

Loss leaders

A loss leader is a product or service that is offered to customers at a major discount. Discounts will reduce the profits of the business in the short term, but the idea is that additional customers will be attracted and will become loyal customers. The hope is that by attracting new customers, they will also buy other products and services from the business that are not discounted, giving the business a chance to offset some of the profits it has lost by offering the loss leader in the first place.

Cost plus pricing

Cost plus pricing is one of the most common types of pricing policy. A business will simply add a certain percentage to its costs to decide the price of the produce or service it is selling. This type of pricing policy does not take into account any market conditions. Nor does it take account of what customers are prepared to pay or the prices charged by the competition.

For example
Competitive pricing

A business works out that it costs £10 to produce a particular product. It decides that its cost plus addition to those costs will be 20%. This will give it sufficient to cover any indirect costs and to make a profit. This means that the business can offer the product for sale at £12.

Similarly, if it produces a product costing £20, it will add £4 to the price using the same method.

Influencing the pricing decision

There are three key factors that affect the way in which a business usually finally settles on its pricing policy.

The costs

The pricing decision will need to include all costs – both direct and indirect – involved in making, buying, handling, distributing or providing a product or service, plus a reasonable percentage added to that total cost to give the business a profit.

The competition

A business will gradually become aware of the number of competitors in the market place. Some will be direct competitors, offering virtually the same (if not the very same) products and services; some will be offering the same products and

160

services at a lower price. A business may need to match these prices.

There will be competitors selling similar products or services that may not be as good, but customers may still choose them. Price changes may not be the way forward in this case. Instead, the business would need to focus on telling customers why they should be prepared to pay more for its products and services.

The customers

Customers are far more aware of options than many businesses believe. Customers remember past prices and have an idea as to what they believe is a fair or reasonable price. Customers will always tend to make a link between price and quality. They may also link price with other factors, such as convenience, fashion, trends and other issues that may make one product for some particular reason more desirable than another. As a result, they do not always go for the cheapest product.

An extreme form of pricing policy is known as 'predatory pricing'. The idea is to inflict financial damage on competitors, by forcing them to match ridiculously low prices, so that their profit margins are slashed. This is a short-term, very aggressive policy, which can be used to drive competitors out of a market. It has been used in many day-to-day products, such as baked beans, bread and tinned tomatoes. At one point in recent years, tins of baked beans were offered for as little as 6p – well below the cost price.

QUESTION TIME
26 minutes

Heather is a wedding planner. She does not have a fixed price for her wedding planning service, but simply adds 20% to the total costs of the bridal package chosen by her customers to cover her costs and to give her a profit. On average, customers spend £5,000 on their wedding, which means that Heather adds £1,000 to the costs.

A new competitor is operating in the area. They are offering a similar package, including their fee, for £4,999. Their advertising slogan is 'Your Wedding for Under £5,000'.

1 What is the difference between price skimming and price penetration? *(4 marks)*

2 Many national supermarkets will price a product as a loss leader. What does this mean? *(3 marks)*

3 A local florist uses competitive pricing. What does this mean? *(3 marks)*

4 In the scenario above, what is Heather's pricing policy? *(2 marks)*

5 What kind of pricing policy is being used by Heather's new competitor? *(2 marks)*

6 Suggest how Heather might change her pricing policy to remain competitive. *(6 marks)*

7 What factors will influence the final price that Heather decides on? *(6 marks)*

Creating a buzz

YOU WILL FIND OUT:

● what promotion is

● about AIDA

● why promotion is important for a growing business

What is promotion?

As we saw in Unit 1, promotion is any marketing communication activity that aims to inform, persuade or motivate customers or potential customers to buy or support a product or service.

The options open to start-up businesses are limited, largely because they lack the funds to pay for expensive promotional activities. However, at the same time they would probably not be in a position to take advantage of the positive impacts of their promotion, as demand might overwhelm them. Their initial focus might be on just supplying products or services to a local or regional area.

Promotions can be used to communicate with other businesses. These are known as 'business-to-business' (or 'b2b') promotions. Or promotions can be used to communicate with consumers. These are known as 'business-to-consumer' (or 'b2c') promotions.

Promotion does not necessarily have to achieve sales; it may simply aim to inform. This is often the objective of government advertising or advertising by charities.

It is important to realise that promotion is a major part of a chain of activities that begins with a business plan. Part of the business plan is the marketing plan, which details elements of the marketing mix. A part of this marketing plan is a promotional plan, without which even good products or services, at competitive prices and available in a wide range of outlets will never

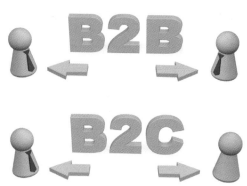

sell, because no one knows about them. A promotional plan will, therefore, focus on promotional objectives.

Promotion does not have to be carried out on a massive and expensive scale. It can focus in on a relatively small geographical area. For example, there would be little point in a British small sole trader promoting his or her product or service and receiving orders from China, when there is no reasonable prospect of servicing those customers. A small business may run advertisements or print leaflets that will just be seen in a single town or city.

Awareness, interest, desire, action (AIDA)

The four most common promotional objectives are awareness, interest, desire and action, known as AIDA:

A WARENESS – *a business uses advertising to gain awareness*

I INTEREST – *public relations or sponsorship generate interest*

D ESIRE – *interest is transformed into a commitment to buy the product or service*

A CTION – *customers are persuaded to take action and buy the product*

For example
Local sponsorship

A sole trader might sponsor a local sports team. They might then offer special deals for a limited period. Then they have to be able to sell when customers make enquiries about buying the product or service.

Grimshaw's *is proud to sponsor the*
Pulverton Darts Team

Come along on **tournament night** *and get*

15% OFF

at Grimshaw's when you present this voucher.

Only one voucher per customer.
Offer valid until 30th November.

162

Why is promotion important for a growing business?

As a business grows, it will be dealing with a broader range of customers, probably in a broader geographical area. Promotional techniques that it may have used on a limited scale when it was small might not work now. It will need to broaden the scope of promotional techniques that have worked for it in the past. Whatever the scale of the promotion, it all needs to fit together.

In raising awareness, interest, desire and action (AIDA) from customers, the business must be in a position to deliver – to match the demand it generates. The last thing it wants is to spend time, money and effort on promotion, then find it has to turn customers away because it has run out of stock or is too busy to provide the services.

As we will see on pages 164–5, there are many different types of promotional activity. There is a clear difference between them:

- **expensive and high-profile** – some promotional activities are designed to try to persuade and inform, to create an interest or a buzz about a product or a service. A typical example is advertising, which tries to be persuasive and have an immediate impact, is repetitive (so can be easily remembered) and is usually expensive
- **low-cost and less obvious** – the other type of promotional activity is less obvious. It can involve the packaging of the product or service, the brand name, the way in which it is displayed in a retail outlet, and supporting activities, like sponsorship and donations to charity that might be made by the business. These are relatively low-cost activities and may continue for long periods of time, even when there is no obvious advertising being done by the business.

Promotional activities such as advertising in the media are known as 'above-the-line' promotional activities. They include any kind of advertising – from television, radio, posters and billboards to the Internet. Above-the-line promotional activities focus on persuasion and impact.

Activities such as public relations, branding, merchandising, sales promotions, direct selling and packaging are all known as 'below-the-line' promotional activities. Below-the-line activities reinforce the more expensive above-the-line activities.

QUESTION TIME
16 minutes

Scaddings Plumbers is based in Bridport in Dorset. It is a family business, which has grown over the years and now has two generations of the family working in it. The business began as a sole trader and most of the work was generated by word of mouth.

Now the business is larger, it runs advertisements in local newspapers and distributes flyers around the area. The business also sponsors a children's football team in Bridport.

1 Why does Scaddings Plumbers promote its business? *(4 marks)*

2 Why might the business have changed the way in which it promotes itself? *(4 marks)*

3 What type of promotional activity is Scaddings' advertisement in the local newspaper? *(2 marks)*

4 What type of promotional activity is its sponsorship of the local football team? *(2 marks)*

5 Suggest another suitable promotional activity that Scaddings might find cost-effective. *(4 marks)*

163

Promotional activities to enable growth

YOU WILL FIND OUT:

● about advertising

● about sales promotions

● about sponsorship

● about direct marketing

Advertising

Advertising is a message paid for by a business, aiming to inform or influence individuals, and to convince people to take action. It is a general and impersonal message, even though it may be targeted at a small group of potential customers.

Advertising surrounds us – on the TV or radio, on the side of a bus, on a poster or even a logo on clothing. It aims to influence customers by informing them that a product or service exists and will satisfy their requirements. Advertising tries to persuade customers that they will receive benefits from buying the product or service. But it can only do this in the broadest sense. It aims to:

- increase overall demand
- create an image or change the image of a product or service
- make customers more loyal to that product or service
- protect or increase market share
- increase general awareness, interest, desire and action
- change peoples' views of the product or service.

A not-for-profit organisation (like a charity) would use emotion in its advertising in order to appeal to the audience to make donations.

Sales promotions

Sales promotions are any type of promotional activity, excluding advertising. They include:

- special offers
- price reductions
- competitions
- displays in stores
- discounts.

Sales promotions aim to encourage customers to buy the product by reminding them about it, either in the location where they normally buy it or to convince them that there is a reason to go to the outlet to buy the product. Sales promotions are also used to try to ensure that customers remain loyal.

For example Loyalty

A frequent purchaser of a particular product may be encouraged to collect tokens from the pack. A number of tokens can then be sent to the business and in return a free gift will be sent to the customer. This encourages customer loyalty. It also encourages additional purchases.

Sponsorship

Sponsorship involves giving financial support to an organisation, an individual, an activity or an event. Its purpose is to raise customer awareness of the sponsoring business, its products and its services; to create and improve the business's image; and to generate additional sales, as more people see its logo or product names.

For example Sponsorship

High-profile events such as the 2012 Olympic Games in London are heavily sponsored events. Sponsors will donate millions of pounds to the Games.

We see examples of sponsorship everywhere. For example on the television, with businesses such as Harvey's The Furniture Store sponsoring *Coronation Street* and Iceland sponsoring *I'm A Celebrity, Get Me Out Of Here!* And nearly every football team from the Premiership to the Sunday amateur leagues has a shirt sponsor.

Direct marketing

Direct marketing is an increasingly broad area of promotional activity. It involves selling, supplying or promoting products and services direct to the consumer. Many businesses use direct marketing, as it can target specific types of customer. The main types of direct marketing are as follows.

Direct mail

Direct mail is used by many charities and financial services organisations. They will compile or buy databases of individuals' names and addresses, and contact people direct with personalised mail.

Direct mail that does not offer products or services relevant to particular individuals is known as 'junk mail'. This is a particular problem for people who find themselves on such computer databases. It is even more of a problem for those with email addresses, who can receive hundreds of spam emails each year. Individuals will find themselves on direct mail or spam mail databases after having filled in their details for a competition, or registered their product or service with the provider, or registered on a website.

Mail order

Even with the Internet having an enormous impact on opportunities to make direct sales to customers, traditional mail order, through catalogues, is still very popular.

`For example`
`Mail order`

Prime examples of companies that use mail order are Littlewoods, Freemans and Marisota. One of the most successful mail order catalogue companies is Next, although it also has retail outlets. Sometimes, local agents will deliver catalogues and take orders, such as Avon and Betterware.

Telemarketing

Call centres up and down the country, and around the world, make calls to potential customers, using names and telephone numbers acquired from databases. Telemarketing is used extensively by charities, mobile phone businesses and financial services organisations.

Direct response advertising

Businesses run advertisements in magazines and newspapers, promoting their products and services and urging customers to contact them direct to make a purchase. This can be done by telephone, on the Internet or by filling in a coupon and posting it off to the business.

⏩ Telemarketing is also known as 'direct selling'. It aims to streamline the distribution channels between the business and the consumer, by cutting out parts of the distribution chain like wholesalers or retailers. It allows the business to deal directly with the consumer. In this way it can offer better prices and achieve a higher profit. The technology is very sophisticated; it can log how often a customer has been contacted, the number of orders, the length of conversations and personal details, so that a relationship can be built up between the business and the customer over time.

QUESTION TIME
21 minutes

In 2007, the radio station Xfm celebrated its tenth birthday. It decided to put on ten concerts, featuring some of the biggest acts in music.

Tickets for the concerts were only available to winners of competitions that were run on air. The winners gave their mobile phone numbers to the radio station and then they were sent a pair of mobile tickets direct to their phone on the day of the concert. Their mobile ticket was then scanned via a wireless network to a ticket database. This gave them access to the exclusive venue. It also meant that there were no paper tickets that could be resold. Nothing had to be checked manually, and everything was simple and efficient.

1. Explain the type of promotion used by Xfm. *(2 marks)*

2. Why might this type of promotion have been particularly effective for a business such as Xfm? *(4 marks)*

3. The Xfm concerts would have been funded through sponsorship deals. What is a sponsorship deal and why are businesses willing to do this? *(6 marks)*

4. Xfm is considering using direct mail to target specific groups in order to increase its audience figures. Advise the business on the suitability of this promotion method. *(9 marks)*

Selecting the promotional mix

YOU WILL FIND OUT:
● about promotion
● about promotional mix
● about promotional budgets

Promotion

Promotion is an important part of the marketing mix. As we have seen, promotion incorporates a number of different marketing techniques, including advertising, **personal selling**, public relations and sales promotion. It involves any communications with customers and potential customers.

There are several factors which influence the selection of promotional methods:

- promotional objectives
- cultural and legal restrictions
- the support the business gives to the promotional effort
- how the market is developing
- how the products and services are distributed
- suitable ways to get the message across
- activities of competitors.

Promotional mix

The four traditional components of promotion are:

- advertising
- personal selling
- public relations
- sales promotion.

The term 'promotional mix' describes a combination of two or more of these elements.

In addition to these, other techniques are now increasingly added to the overall promotional mix. The additional components include:

- branding
- corporate image

- customer service
- direct marketing
- exhibitions
- internal marketing (ensuring that all managers and employees in the business understand the features and benefits of the products and services)
- merchandising or point-of-sale materials (posters, cards, leaflets and display boxes in a retail outlet)
- packaging
- sponsorship
- email/Internet
- word of mouth.

Promotional budget

A promotional budget is the total amount of financial resources that a business allocates to its promotions over a period of time.

A business uses a number of different methods to allocate or estimate its promotional budget, as detailed in the table below.

--- KEY TERM ---

Personal selling ▶ any form of oral communication with a potential buyer.

METHOD	DESCRIPTION
Affordable approach	The business calculates its costs and expenses and works out the profit it would like to make. Any money that is left over can then be used for the promotional budget.
Objective and task approach	This approach looks at the objectives of the promotion and calculates the money that is required to meet them.
Competitive approach	This budgeting technique looks at what the competitors are spending and requires the business to spend as much, if not more, than the competitors.
Percentage of sales approach	Based on either actual or predicted sales figures, an agreed percentage per sale is allocated to advertising.
Historical approach	This approach is based on what has been spent in the past. It does not take into account what may (or may not) need to be spent, and may often lead to the business spending more than is necessary.
Experiment and testing approach	The business has no clear idea what it needs to spend. It therefore tries out different forms of promotion, finds out what is effective, and then works out its budget to see if it can afford a broader promotional campaign.

166

The way in which a business chooses to promote its products or services, and the amount of money it wishes to spend, may well depend on just how competitive the markets are in which it operates.

Where there are few competitors, customers will have very little choice, so less money will need to be spent on persuading customers to make a purchase.

If the product is in short supply, there will also be little reason for the business to promote the product (such was the case with the Nintendo Wii in the run-up to Christmas 2007). Where there are several products available and supply exceeds demand, promotional spending may well need to be comparatively high.

Finally, promotional spending and choice will depend on the stage that the product has reached in its life cycle. In the early stages, products and services need considerable support. At the very least the product or service needs to be announced to customers and they need to be persuaded to try it. Each time there is a change in the product or service, a promotion may be necessary to inform customers of these changes. Even when a product has reached maturity, it still needs a degree of continued support, to ensure that sales remain high. If sales dip, the business needs to make a key decision as to whether or not to relaunch the product or to let it just fade away.

QUESTION TIME
30 minutes

In 2006, online advertising spending broke through the £2 billion barrier, while television revenues fell and newspaper spending barely moved. Commercial radio revenues were down by 3%, national newspapers saw a rise of just 0.2% and television advertising fell by 4.7%. The £2 billion represents 11.4% of total British advertising revenue. Britain has 31 million Internet users. It is a huge growth area.

The bulk of online advertising spending comes from search advertising, worth £1.2 billion or 57.8% of the online market. Search advertising involves paying the owners of search engines to ensure that when keywords are used in the search, particular websites appear at the top of the list. Also, direct links appear beside the search results. It has been found that the majority of people using search engines only ever look at the first four or five results.

167

1 Identify and explain TWO factors that would have influenced a business's choice to use online advertising as a promotional method. *(4 marks)*

2 How might packaging, one of the additional components of the promotional mix, help to promote a product? *(3 marks)*

3 Define the term 'promotional budget'. *(2 marks)*

4 Identify and explain TWO factors that would influence the promotional budget that a business allocates to online advertising. *(6 marks)*

5 Why might traditional forms of advertising be losing out to online advertising? *(9 marks)*

6 Why might online advertising be attractive to small businesses? *(6 marks)*

In the right place at the right time

YOU WILL FIND OUT:

● about place

● about distribution

● about distribution systems

Place

Place is the final part of the marketing mix. It is all about the availability of products and services in the right place at the right time. It includes the physical location where the products or services can be purchased and the timing of their availability to customers.

Businesses spend a lot of time considering the best ways to ensure that their products and services reach their potential customers. They may well need to convince retail outlets to stock the products. They will also have to consider how to physically transport products from their factory, warehouse, importer or supplier to retailers, wholesalers and distributors.

Trying to persuade other businesses to stock products is never simple. In retail outlets, in particular, shelf space is always limited and it is probably full of products supplied by the business's competitors. A retailer will be taking a risk by cutting down the shelf space of products it knows it can sell in order to make room for a product that may not sell.

Another consideration is the type of product involved. Different distribution channels will need to be used if the product is enormous (like a tractor), if it is delicate and perishable (like strawberries), or if it has a short period of popularity (like a CD single).

Distribution

'Distribution' is the physical movement of products and services from the producer to the end user. A distribution channel ends when an individual or a business buys a product or service without intending to resell it.

Part of the distribution channel involves storage and transport companies. They are all parts of the distribution process, helping to get the product or service to the consumer.

A business needs to work out how best to organise its distribution channel so that it is efficient and effective:

- Will the distribution channel be effective in getting products and services to the consumer when the consumer needs them?
- Can the business distribute the products or services itself? If not, who else does it need to involve?
- If the products or services need to get to a mass market, does the business need to involve many other businesses to help it distribute them? (This becomes even more complicated if they are distributing in different countries.)
- How much help and cooperation will the business need from those in the distribution channel? Will parts of the channel hold stock, or will the product be delivered only as and when it is required for sale?

Distribution systems

A business has several different options when setting up its distribution system for its products and services.

Direct distribution

Some businesses can do their own distribution. This is known as a 'direct channel'. Products and services are delivered straight to the consumer, without anyone else being involved in the distribution channel at all.

Indirect distribution

Indirect distribution, on the other hand, means having at least one other partner in the distribution chain. For example, a business may manufacture a product and then transport it to a wholesaler, who in turn will transport part of that order to a number of retailers. The retailers deal directly with the consumer.

Indirect distribution can be quite complicated, as can be seen in the table on the opposite page.

For example Buying music

If you want to buy your favourite singer or band's latest single, you don't need to go into a specialist store. You can pick up the same product in a supermarket or in a multiple (a chain of stores), such as WH Smith. You don't even need to go into a shop: you can download it. With singles, it is all about immediate sales. Record companies know that most outlets will send CDs back or discount them if they do not sell straight away.

POSSIBLE INDIRECT DISTRIBUTION CHANNELS		
For consumer goods	*For business to business*	*For services*
Producer → consumer or door-to-door	Producer → user	Producer → consumer
Producer → retailer → consumer	Producer → industrial distributor → user	Producer → agent → consumer
Producer → wholesaler → retailer → consumer	Producer → industrial distributor → reseller → user	
Producer → agent → retailer → consumer	Producer → agent → user	
	Producer → agent → industrial distributor → user	

Multiple distribution

The third option is to use multiple (or several different) distribution channels. For example:

It may be possible for a business to distribute direct to some of its customers, but other customers may be more difficult to provide for directly, particularly if they live in other countries or are an entirely different market.

Some businesses may use direct distribution when they deal with other businesses, as the orders will be larger and probably more frequent. In this case, it is financially worthwhile

for the business to handle the distribution itself.

However, the business may also be selling to consumers who purchase the products or services infrequently. So the business may well use distributors or retailers to handle this side of its distribution.

Many businesses, as they become larger, will offer a broader range of products and services. Some may be easy to distribute in the ways that they have always distributed them, but others may present more difficult distribution challenges.

For example Music distribution

In the past, record companies distributed direct to music stores, to supermarket chains, or to distributors which then supplied individual, smaller music stores. This was a multiple distribution system. Now they also distribute via online downloads, such as those available from the iStore.

At no point did the record companies distribute direct to the consumer. They have always used other businesses in their distribution channels. But technology and the ways in which people buy music have changed the make-up of their multiple distribution channels.

A business will carry out distribution research to discover the most effective way of getting its products and services to consumers. It will look at the costs of each method of distribution and will always try to find a cheaper, more efficient and more profitable way of getting its products to its consumers in the most reliable manner.

QUESTION TIME
20 minutes

1 Define the term 'distribution'. *(2 marks)*

2 What are the key differences between direct and indirect distribution channels? *(4 marks)*

3 What is meant by the term 'multiple distribution channel'? *(2 marks)*

4 Give an example of a type of business that would use a multiple distribution channel and briefly explain why it would use this method. *(6 marks)*

5 What is the purpose of distribution research? *(6 marks)*

169

Distribution channels and growth

YOU WILL FIND OUT:

● about retailers and wholesalers

● about telesales

● about mail order

● about Internet sales

Retailers and wholesalers

For many years, manufacturers of products tended to use wholesalers or distributors to hold stock. The wholesalers or distributors then sold to retailers. Only the retailers had direct contact with the consumer.

With improved communications and more reliable transport systems, many large businesses, such as supermarkets, no longer need to buy from wholesalers. They buy direct from manufacturers. The manufacturers deliver the products to one or more of the supermarket's warehouses. From here the rest of the distribution is carried out by the supermarket chain itself.

This may be a perfectly workable system for large businesses, but it is not a practical solution for smaller businesses. They simply cannot afford to purchase the minimum amount of stock required by the manufacturer. They have to buy their stock from wholesalers. This is a more expensive way of buying products for the retailer, as the wholesalers need to make their profit out of each sale.

Some manufacturers, or service providers, are also retailers themselves.

Telesales

Telephone marketing – or telesales – accounts for around 20–25% of all direct marketing sales. The majority of those sales are in the business-to-business market. Businesses make telephone calls direct to potential businesses and consumers, but they also use freephone numbers (0800) or reduced-rate numbers (0845) to encourage customers to call them.

Telephone marketing can give a business the ability to talk directly to targeted customers. But many customers find these 'junk phone calls' to be very annoying. In fact, in the USA there is a national 'do not call' registry (rather like Britain's own Telephone Preference Service), and businesses can be fined if they call someone who has registered that they do not want to receive telesales calls.

As a result, telesales are shifting to direct mail, direct response TV and Internet promotions to prompt customers to call them.

Mail order

Mail order can be used as a distribution channel by a wide variety of different businesses. Depending

on their individual requirements, businesses may choose to:

- focus on business customers, by mailing out regularly updated brochures and catalogues
- focus on consumers, again providing them with regularly updated copies of their latest catalogues and backing this up with seasonal promotions and sales
- offer specialist products either to businesses or to consumers, such as DIY products
- offer a broader range of products and services
- use mail order as a direct distribution channel, as they are the manufacturers of the product or service and sell their products only through their own catalogues
- use mail order in addition to their other distribution channel
- effectively operate as mail order retailers, handling a wide range of different products and services from a number of different suppliers.

For example `Mail order`

Examples of businesses that use mail order as an additional distribution channel are Lush and Next. Each company only sells their own branded products.

Businesses such as Argos, Dixons, Comet and Tesco Direct use mail order services and websites as additional distribution channels to their traditional retail outlets.

Internet sales

Internet sales offer businesses of any size the opportunity to deal directly with other businesses or consumers in a more efficient and effective way than any other distribution system – provided that their potential customers are aware of their existence, of course.

Having a visible presence on the Internet is even more difficult than attempting to compete with other local, regional or national businesses. There are simply millions of different businesses. An Internet business is reliant upon promoting its website's address and providing ways in which the customer can easily find the website. Even when this has been achieved, it needs to convince the customer that placing an order with them is a safe and reliable option. It is incredibly difficult for a customer to make any judgement about a business simply by looking at its website. A professional-looking website does not necessarily mean that the business itself is professional.

However, Internet sales offer even the smallest business enormous opportunities. Success relies largely on recommendation and on building a reputation that it is reliable, trustworthy and honest, and that any information given to the business is secure – especially payment details.

Internet sales offer small businesses the opportunity to expand very quickly and also to penetrate markets that small businesses could never have dreamed of operating in only a few years ago. If the website becomes well known and the products and services are in demand, then even a small business has the opportunity to make sales all around the world.

Actually fulfilling those orders does present something of a problem. Products may have to be shipped overseas and customers will expect a contact point that will work for them, regardless of differences in time zones. All of these issues add layers of complication, despite the fact that the sales may be welcome. As a result, as sales begin to establish in different countries, businesses will set up mirror operations (copies of the operations they have set up elsewhere) so that products and services can literally be delivered closer to the market that is generating the sales, rather than trying to deal with them from a remote location.

Many mass producers want to sell their products in bulk. This means it is difficult for them to sell to smaller businesses. Wholesalers – often referred to as 'bulk breakers' – come into the equation. They place large orders with the producers, hold the stock, and then sell the stock in smaller quantities to smaller retailers, who can then sell on to consumers.

QUESTION TIME
33 minutes

1 Explain the difference between a retailer and a wholesaler. *(4 marks)*

2 Name THREE retailers. *(3 marks)*

3 Double-glazing businesses make use of telephone marketing. What is an advantage and a disadvantage of this method? *(6 marks)*

4 What might be the benefits to a business of dealing directly with its consumers? *(6 marks)*

5 What might be the disadvantages for a manufacturer of dealing direct with its consumers? *(6 marks)*

6 Are Internet sales advantageous to small businesses? *(8 marks)*

Selecting distribution channels

YOU WILL FIND OUT:

- about traditional and modern channels
- about choosing the right channel
- what questions to ask
- what works best

Traditional and modern channels

Manufacturers, in particular, still tend to use a traditional distribution channel. They use wholesalers and distributors as the main way of ensuring that their products receive the widest possible distribution to retailers, who can then sell them on to consumers.

This system can also be used by many services. For example, insurance companies and mortgage companies use banks, building societies and financial advisors to sell their services on their behalf.

For many businesses, this is still the most appropriate way to distribute their products or services, as it has worked for them or for their industry for many years.

For example

Banks have their own range of products and services, such as bank accounts, savings schemes and mortgages. They may also sell financial services on behalf of other businesses.

Not all businesses need to use wholesalers or distributors, choosing instead to distribute across their whole network of retail outlets themselves. They take large orders from manufacturers, and deal with the rest of the distribution through to the consumer. This is very much how large retail chains operate.

The alternative is to deal directly with the consumer – via the Internet, through telesales or through mail-order catalogues. Some businesses also have their own retail outlets.

Choosing the right channel

There are four types of distribution channel:

- **short** – important for perishable products
- **long** – often used for products that are manufactured overseas and pass through distributors and wholesalers
- **direct** – the manufacturer or primary provider of the service deals directly with the customer
- **indirect** – the manufacturer uses wholesalers, distributors or retailers in their supply chain.

There are three main considerations when a business wants to find out the ideal channel of distribution for its products and services.

Speed of processing

The first is whether the product needs to get to the consumer quickly. If it does, then the most efficient and rapid distribution channel needs to be found. This is a typical concern of food producers, because food products are perishable. In other words, they spoil and are worthless if they are not sold within a specified period of time. The food needs to be harvested, cleaned, processed, packaged and then shipped to wholesalers or retailers, so that it can be sold on to the consumer quickly.

Transporting heavy goods

The second consideration is whether the business makes large or heavy products. These can be expensive to transport. Ideally, they should move from the manufacturer directly to the consumer, or the business customer. This is particularly true of cars, vans, tractors, machinery and large pieces of equipment. The manufacturers will either deal directly with the buyer, or they will have a chain of distributors (for example vehicle showrooms) that hold stock for them and then sell directly to the customer.

Handling and storage

The third consideration is whether the products are non-perishable (this means they will not spoil if they are held in stock for some time). These can have relatively long chains of distribution. They need to be strong enough to cope with a great deal of handling and periods in storage.

For example

A toy company may design a new toy, but choose to have it manufactured in China. The toy then needs to be transported across the world to the toy company, or their distributors and wholesalers around the world. The product is then sold to retailers, who then sell it on to consumers.

172

What questions to ask

When a business begins to consider the distribution channel, it needs to ask itself a number of questions:

- **Who are our customers?** If it is dealing with large businesses and retailers, it can probably deal with these customers direct, through a short distribution channel.

  If most of its customers are retailers and consumers, then wholesalers and distributors need to be used, so a longer distribution channel may be necessary.
- **What are our customers' needs?** If the customer will need support and assistance after they have bought the product or service, then a short distribution channel – probably direct – is the best solution. But if little can go wrong with the product or service, and there will not be frequent questions, then a longer distribution channel would work.
- **Where are our customers and where could they buy the product or service?** If customers are in a relatively small geographical area, then retailers are probably the best option. However, if customers are scattered around the country, then a direct selling channel is probably the only way to provide for their needs.
- **Should any particular qualities of the product or service be considered?** Is the product perishable or non-perishable? Small or large? Perishable products need short distribution channels, as do large products. Smaller, non-perishable products can be handled by a longer channel.

What works best?

Long or short, direct or indirect channels all have benefits and disadvantages. A business will find it difficult to select the ideal channel, particularly in the beginning. It will have to test different channels and see which one works best.

For example, dealing directly with the customer (a direct channel) does give a business control and the ability to provide direct customer service, but it can be expensive, particularly if customers make small orders and are spread around the country.

Using another business in the distribution channel (an indirect channel) adds costs and they may only choose to carry the most popular products on offer. However, distributors or wholesalers can be important when customers are scattered and perhaps buy only in small quantities.

A business will find no ideal solution, but will seek to find the one with the most benefits and the least problems.

The market itself is also a consideration when looking at the distribution channel. Mass-market products that are sold in their millions are usually sold via wholesalers and large retailers. The wholesalers and large retailers buy the products in enormous numbers and effectively deal with the rest of the distribution themselves. Because these orders are so large and important, it is not worth the manufacturer's time in dealing direct with smaller retailers, who will only place relatively tiny orders.

QUESTION TIME
18 minutes

1 Why do perishable items have a short channel of distribution? *(2 marks)*

2 Why does a business prefer to keep the channel of distribution as short as possible? *(6 marks)*

3 What type of business is a cash and carry, and where does it fit into a distribution channel? *(4 marks)*

4 Why is it necessary for a business that offers services to have a distribution channel at all? Why don't they deal direct with their consumers? *(6 marks)*

173

What have you learnt?

Marketing was the second section of Unit 2 (Growing as a business). The information in this section has built on many of the concepts that were introduced in Unit 1. The focus is now, however, on a growing business.

The elements of the marketing mix need to be reviewed as a business grows. Some may still be appropriate to the business, but others will have to be amended in the light of experience, changes in the market or changes in the range of products and services offered by the business.

We have looked in turn at each of the four key elements of the marketing mix:

- **product** – product becomes more complicated when a business starts to broaden out and has a blend of old and new goods or services to offer its customers
- **price** – price and pricing policy can be vitally important. A business needs to get this right. It must decide how it is going to set its prices and how responsive they need to be to the market and to the competition

- **promotion** – as a business grows, promotion opportunities develop. The business may now have bigger marketing budgets, but the money still needs to be spent wisely. The business needs to reach the target market, get over the right message and stress the advantages to customers and consumers of buying the business's products and services, rather than those of competitors
- **place** – while a small business may have been content with dealing directly with consumers direct on a relatively small scale, this may no longer be an option as they grow. They may need to involve other businesses to help them get their products and services to their customers. Alternatively, they may decide to step up their own distribution operation and then distribute direct, setting up their own telesales, mail order or Internet services.

The 'Question time' exercises in this section should have given you a reasonable idea of the kind

of follow-on questions that you will find in the Unit 2 exam paper. Once again, the questions are allocated on the basis of 1 mark a minute. The main focus is on trying to recognise appropriate parts of the marketing mix that would suit a growing business. These may be different from those that would work for a start-up business.

Your teacher or tutor will be able to give you a copy of the 'Unit Revision Pack' from the *Teacher Support Pack*. This will give you more clues about areas to revise and a chance to try a full mock examination paper. As this is the second section of Unit 2, the following questions are not only about marketing, but also about the growing business organisation.

Integrated questions from Sections 1 and 2

Try these exam-style questions. They relate to both this section on marketing and Section 1 (The business organisation). The real exam will contain questions that relate to all five parts of Unit 2. This is a real business situation.

THE GREEN GARDENER

The Green Gardener is a family-run mail order company based in East Anglia. It was established in the 1990s and specialises in the natural control of garden pests. The owners, John and Annie Manners, have used mail order catalogues since the beginning. The business also offers a helpline, which is available seven days a week from dawn until dusk during the growing season. The business also has a website from which products can be purchased using secure online payments.

Source: adapted from www.greengardener.co.uk

QUESTIONS
30 minutes

1 Why might the Green Gardener be considered to be operating in a niche market? *(3 marks)*

2 Give a benefit and a drawback of the Green Gardener operating in a niche market? *(6 marks)*

3 In what stage of the product life cycle would the Green Gardener have been in the 1990s, and how would this influence the promotion method chosen? *(6 marks)*

4 John and Annie's son, Jonathan, runs the website and is closely involved in the day-to-day running of the business. What might be the appropriate legal structure for this business? Explain your reasons. *(9 marks)*

5 Why might the business have chosen to sell by mail order and via the website only, and not through other distribution channels? *(6 marks)*

Raising money for growth

YOU WILL FIND OUT:

- why a business needs cash
- why a business plan is important
- about becoming a PLC
- about funding growth

Why does a business need cash?

A business not only needs money to finance growth, but also for its day-to-day activities. There is a big difference between cash and profit:

- **Cash** is needed for a business to pay its bills. Cash needs to come into the business on a regular basis, as the business itself will have to find money every day, every week or every month to pay its bills. Cash is often referred to as 'working capital' – this is immediately available money for a business to pay its bills.
- **Profit** is the difference between a business's earnings and the sum of its costs. A business can be profitable but still short of cash.

A business can survive for a short period if it does not make any sales or if it fails to make a profit. But if it does not have cash, then it cannot survive.

Why is a business plan important?

Regardless of the size of the business, a business plan is essential, as it shows how the business intends to develop. A business plan is therefore vital when a business is looking for funding. It assists potential investors or lenders in understanding the objectives and goals of the business. It tells them where the money is going to be invested and how it will benefit both the business and them.

Potential providers of finance will want to see that the business owners are investing their own money in the business. This means not only investing their own cash, but also reinvesting any profits in the business. The owner should also show that they are prepared to use their own assets to guarantee loans. After all, if they are not prepared to risk their own money, why should a lender or an investor?

Money will always attract money, so a business plan should also show that the business has the backing of investors and banks. The more backers the business has, the easier it is to attract new investors.

A business plan should be realistic. It needs to highlight any potential financial difficulties and to show that the business can implement effective cash-flow controls. This is the case for both small and large businesses, but the stakes are higher for larger businesses.

Becoming a PLC

Until a business takes the leap to become a public limited company (PLC), it will have financing challenges.

Businesses that are not PLCs are not quoted on the Stock Exchange. This means that their shares are not freely available for sale to the public and it is difficult for them to create more shares that could be sold to attract additional investment, because ownership of many of these businesses is limited to a handful of shareholders.

Once they are larger, businesses need to prepare and publish financial information. This can be extremely useful when trying to raise finance. While small businesses are often seen as a risk by banks, larger businesses with a track record are looked on more favourably. Lenders and investors can make an informed decision by looking at the financial information provided to them by the business. They look at the risks involved, and then decide whether their money would be relatively safe.

176

Funding growth

Lenders are often unwilling to increase the size of loans without additional security. They want to know that the business has assets that they could seize if the business is unable to pay back the loan. Smaller businesses tend not to have too many valuable assets, but larger businesses may have acquired buildings, equipment and machinery. The more assets a business has, the more security it can offer to potential lenders.

As businesses begin to grow, it is extremely difficult for them to finance their own growth with their own cash. But as they become larger, their ability to fund their own growth becomes greater, simply because they are making more profit from a larger amount of money.

Apart from using its own profits to fund growth, a business can:

- **borrow money** – the problem with borrowing money is that it increases the debt of the business and nearly always means that borrowed money is secured on the business's assets (such as property or machinery). In addition, interest payment and capital repayments (the loan itself) will have to be made

- **create more shares** – to attract more investors. However, new shareholders (or equity investors) look at the investment opportunity and weigh up success or failure, just like existing shareholders. They hope to see the value of their shares increase over time and will expect to share a proportion of the profits through a dividend.

Whichever way the business chooses to go, it will try to avoid having too high a debt. But at the same time it does not want to issue so many shares that the original owners effectively lose control of the business. A balance needs to be found – and this is not always easy to achieve.

QUESTION TIME
20 minutes

1 **Define the term 'profit'.** *(2 marks)*

2 **Why might a profitable business experience cash-flow problems?** *(4 marks)*

3 **Why does a business not want high levels of debt?** *(4 marks)*

4 **How can a business plan be of use in securing funding from an investor?** *(4 marks)*

5 **Why is it more difficult for a small business to raise additional finance than a larger one?** *(6 marks)*

177

For a business to be able to grow its sales and profits, it needs to create a reserve of cash, so that when it has to pay out more money than it is making, it can continue to trade. This is all a part of managing the overall cash flow. To make a profit, the business will often have to produce products and services before it has actually been paid for them. If the business does not have enough money to do this, including paying its employees and suppliers, then it cannot survive in the long term.

Sources of finance

Retained profits

When a business makes a profit (this is the difference between its income and its costs), it has to decide what to do with this money. Shareholders and owners may expect to receive a proportion of it, but not necessarily all of it. 'Retained profit' is money that a business makes but does not spend or pay out as dividends – money that it decides to keep.

This money is then available to the business to help it expand. The business can develop new products, buy new machinery or property, or use it to help get over temporary cash-flow problems. Retained profit can also be useful if the business thinks it might go through a rough patch in the near future.

The problem with retained profit is deciding what level of profit to distribute to owners and shareholders – to continue to reward them for their investment – and what to keep for the longer-term needs of the business.

New share issue

The issuing of new shares is often referred to as raising 'equity capital'. These are new ordinary shares that are issued by a business. They entitle the new shareholders to any profit that the business chooses to distribute. This is the money available after the business has retained some profit and after it has paid those who hold a **debenture** or **preference shares**.

If a public limited company (PLC) wants to raise extra money, it can issue new shares. For businesses whose shares are traded on the Stock Exchange, the value of the share is equal to its **market value**. A privately owned company has very little share trading; its shares are not available to the public.

A PLC can sell the new shares to its existing shareholders in what is known as a 'rights issue'. Shareholders are offered new shares in proportion to the number of shares they already have.

When a business first offers shares, the original owners risk losing some control of their own business. Having made the investment, the new investors will want to have a say in the running of the business – to protect their money.

Any new investor will have an interest in ensuring that the business is a success – that it continues to grow, that it is profitable, and that overall the business increases in value. Raising equity capital, however, is quite costly and time-consuming. The investors will want some influence, they will monitor decisions being made and, above all, the original owner's share of the business will be diluted.

Loans

A loan is money borrowed by a business from a bank or finance provider for a fixed period of time, usually between three and ten years. It has a repayment schedule. The borrower pays interest on the loan, but does not pay the lender a percentage of its profits or give it a share in the business.

Many loans have very strict terms and conditions and are not very flexible. Having to find the monthly repayment can often cause cash-flow problems. In many cases, loans are also secured against business assets. Lenders often expect a charge to be paid if the business pays back the loan early.

178

Mortgages

A mortgage is a loan usually taken out to buy a property. It is usually for 15 years or more. Many businesses opt for a commercial mortgage, because the repayments are usually no bigger than what they would be paying in rent.

It means that the business owns the property, so they can sub-let (or rent out) any space they are not using to another business. Also, as the business grows, they may be able to add to the building and avoid having to relocate.

On the downside, the business usually has to come up with a large deposit. Also, if the interest rate is not fixed, then repayments can go up if the interest rate increases. And it means that the business is fully responsible for the building, so it will have to be maintained and kept secure.

—— KEY TERMS ——

Debenture ▶ a loan that is set against the business's assets. The lender receives a fixed rate of interest and the entire sum is paid back to them by a particular date. They are not shareholders.

Preference shares ▶ are owned by shareholders who receive a fixed dividend. The dividend is regardless of the amount of profit the business actually makes. Owners of preference shares cannot usually vote at shareholders' meetings.

Market value ▶ the price an investor is prepared to pay for shares.

Selling off assets

A fixed asset is something that is not directly used up in the production of the products or services. It includes vehicles, land, buildings, machinery, and fixtures and fittings. As a business grows, it will acquire a number of fixed assets.

If a business finds that it is not using a fixed asset, it may choose to sell it to raise money. However, the business needs to be sure that by selling the asset, it will not be making a problem for itself in the future when it may need to buy that same asset again.

▶▶ If a business is suffering from financial difficulties, it can choose to sell off one or more of its fixed assets to receive an injection of cash that it may desperately need. The value of the asset, however, depends on what another business is prepared to pay for it. Older machinery may not be worth anything like the value that the business originally paid for it.

A business can often negotiate special terms with the buyer of an asset. For example, it can sell the asset and then rent (or lease) it back from the business it has sold it to. In this way, the business loses ownership of the asset, but still has the asset available to use, although it will cost it money each month for the rent or lease.

QUESTION TIME
26 minutes

In 2008, the property development company Barratt Homes attempted to reduce its debts by selling assets. It sold off a shopping centre in Wrexham for nearly £80 million, a supermarket development in Chesterfield for £30 million and a number of other assets. It was forced to do this because it had debts of £1.65 billion.

Source: adapted from www.barratthomes.co.uk

1 Barratt did not want to use its retained profit to reduce its debts. What is retained profit? *(2 marks)*

2 Some of Barratt's debt would have been in loans and mortgages. What is the difference between a loan and a mortgage? *(4 marks)*

3 What might happen to Barratt if it could not sell its fixed assets? *(4 marks)*

4 Who might have insisted that Barratt sell off some of its fixed assets and why? *(4 marks)*

5 Barratt said that the reason for the sale would be to reduce group borrowings. What might this mean? *(4 marks)*

6 Was Barratt right to sell off some of its assets to reduce its group borrowings? *(8 marks)*

179

Profit and loss accounts and balance sheets

What is a profit and loss account?

A profit and loss account, sometimes called an 'income statement', is a summary of a business's financial transactions over a period of time (usually 12 months). The profit and loss account shows the 'bottom line' – in other words, whether the business is actually making a profit or a loss.

A profit and loss account tells the business owners, shareholders and potential investors just how well the business is performing. Most of the information shown on the profit and loss account is used by Her Majesty's Revenue & Customs (HMRC) to work out the tax liability of the business.

If a business is a limited company or a partnership whose members are limited companies, it must produce a profit and loss account for every financial year that it operates.

For sole traders or most partnerships, there is no need to do this – in effect, when they complete a tax return form, they are giving HMRC a version of the profit and loss account. However, it is advisable to produce a profit and loss account in any case, as potential lenders will want to see at least three years of accounts.

What does a profit and loss account show?

Companies are expected to present their profit and loss accounts in a certain format. Typically, a profit and loss account shows the revenues received by the business and its costs involved in generating that revenue.

The simple equation takes costs from revenues to reveal the profit (or loss).

Terms used on a profit and loss account are:

- **'gross profit'** – income minus cost of sales
- **'operating profit'** – gross profit minus any expenses
- **'net profit'** – the business's total revenue minus its total expenses.

A profit and loss account compares the current year and the past year. This enables shareholders and potential investors to compare the performance of the business. Negative figures are shown in brackets. Each item may have notes attached to it to explain the details behind the figures. It is also common practice for the top half of the profit and loss account to deal with gross profit, and for the bottom half to deal with net profit.

A number of associated calculations can be made from a profit and loss account. The profit and loss account is one of the two most important financial statements for a business. The other is the balance sheet.

What is a balance sheet?

A balance sheet only gives a snapshot of what the business owns, or is owed, at a particular point in time. Balance sheets tend to have a date, stating exactly when all the calculations were made.

The balance sheet is important, as it shows how the business is being funded and how those funds are being used. Of particular importance is the list of assets owned by the business and the list of liabilities (what it owes to other organisations). The balance sheet gets its name because the total value of all the assets must always be equal to – or must balance – the total value of all the liabilities. This means that the business has to account for every asset that it has and every liability that it has.

A business uses its balance sheet for three different purposes:

- for simple reporting purposes, as an integral part of annual accounts. In producing formal accounts such as a balance sheet, the business can monitor its own performance
- to help itself, investors, creditors and shareholders to assess the worth of the business. If the business wishes to raise finance, investors or lenders will want to see three years' worth of accounts
- as a tool to analyse and improve how the business operates. Customers offering large contracts will want to see audited (independently checked) accounts.

Limited companies and limited liability partnerships must produce a balance sheet as part of their annual accounts. (This is not necessary for a sole trader or an ordinary partnership.) They submit the annual accounts to Companies House, HMRC and shareholders. There are strict deadlines for submitting the accounts.

180

There is a strong relationship between the profit and loss account and the balance sheet.

The profit and loss account is a summary of the business's transactions. The net result of these transactions will show a profit or a loss.

The balance sheet does not show day-to-day transactions or the current profitability. But its figures do relate to the current state of the business. It shows any profits that have not been paid out as dividends and notes them as 'retained profits'. Under current assets, it shows available money (as cash or money in the bank) determined by the income and spending that has been shown on the profit and loss account.

What does a balance sheet show?

As a minimum, a balance sheet shows:

- **fixed assets** – what the business owns
- **current assets** – what cash the business has or is owed in the short term
- **current liabilities** – what the business owes in the short term
- **long-term liabilities** – what the business owes over a longer period.

Fixed assets

Fixed assets include:

- **tangible assets** – land, office equipment, machinery, buildings and other items. The value of tangible assets is shown as their resale value or their depreciated value
- **intangible assets** – including trademarks, long-term investments, patents, goodwill and even website domain names.

Current assets

Current assets are short term. They change from day to day. But as far as the balance sheet is concerned, this was the value of those current assets on the day that the balance sheet was prepared. They include:

- current stock
- work in progress
- cash in the safe or at the bank
- money owed by customers
- prepayments (money that has been paid for products or services that have not yet been received by the end of the accounting period)
- short-term investments.

Current liabilities

These are liabilities that fall due within the next financial year. Current liabilities include:

- tax payable within the year
- VAT payable within the year
- National Insurance payable within the year
- overdrafts
- short-term loans
- money owed to suppliers.

Long-term liabilities

Long-term liabilities include:

- loans that are due to be repaid after a year
- capital (share capital)
- reserves (retained profits after dividends).

QUESTION TIME
29 minutes

1 What does a profit-and-loss account show? *(6 marks)*

2 Identify TWO stakeholders that have an interest in the profit-and-loss account and explain why. *(6 marks)*

3 Why might a balance sheet be referred to as a 'snapshot'? *(4 marks)*

4 What does a balance sheet show? *(6 marks)*

5 What are the differences between tangible and intangible assets? *(4 marks)*

6 Why might a potential buyer of a business wish to analyse its balance sheet? *(3 marks)*

181

Components of financial statements

The purposes of a profit and loss account

A profit and loss account can be used for a number of different purposes:

- It can show a business's performance compared to previous years.
- The level of profit can be compared to the business's budgeted profit levels.
- It can assist in obtaining loans, by showing that the business has paid back the loan in the past and will be capable of paying back the loan in the future.
- As far as operational considerations are concerned, it allows the owners of the business and the managers to plan for the future.

Components of a balance sheet

The balance sheet is a 'snapshot' of the business's position at a given point in time. It is designed merely to show what the business owns and what it owes on the particular date when the balance sheet was prepared.

The balance sheet does not show day-to-day transactions, nor does it show current profitability. Its figures do, however, relate to the current state of the business. A balance sheet shows:

- **retained profits** – any profits that have not been paid out as dividends
- **current assets** – available money (cash or money in the bank) determined by the income and spending that has been shown on the profit and loss account.

Ratio analysis

Ratio analysis is an accounting procedure to compare one set of figures with another.

For example

Company A has sales revenue of £120,000 and Company B has sales revenue of £60,000. Using ratio analysis, we could see that Company A has twice as much sales revenue as Company B. Therefore the ratio is 2:1.

We can also use ratio analysis to help us see whether a business is in a successful period, compared to another period of time. For example, we could look at the current situation compared to the situation a year ago.

Ratios are particularly useful for comparing:

- the trends in a business's results over a period of years
- the results of one business with those of another similar business
- the performance of one business with the industry average performance.

There are a number of different ratios, all of which reveal different things about the business's performance.

Liquidity ratio

There are two ways of calculating the liquidity (the ability to pay debts when they fall due) of the business: the current ratio and the liquid capital ratio. Liquidity ratios are designed to look at the short-term financial health of a business. They look at the working capital to see whether it is sufficient and whether it is being managed correctly. If a business has too little working capital, it may not be able to pay off its short-term debts; if it has too much, it may not be making the best use of this financial resource.

Current ratio

The current ratio – also known as the 'working capital ratio' – is shown as a ratio of the business's current assets compared to its current liabilities. The formula is:

$$\text{Current ratio} = \frac{\text{current assets}}{\text{current liabilities}}$$

For example

If a business had current assets of £100,000 and current liabilities of £20,000, this could be expressed as 5:1, as the current assets outweigh the current liabilities by five.

Ideally, a business should have around £1.50 of assets for every £1 of debt. So the ideal ratio is 1.5:1. If a business has a ratio of less than 1:1, then it does not have sufficient current assets to pay its current liabilities (its short-term debts).

Liquid capital ratio

The liquid capital ratio – also known as the 'quick ratio' or 'acid test' – also looks at current assets and liabilities, but (unlike the current ratio) it does not include stock. The reason for this is that stock, although it is a current asset, is the hardest asset to turn into ready cash. It may simply take too long to sell, or may be valued at a particular price but worth less because it is old. This means that the acid test compares cash and payments due from debtors with the short-term debt of the business. The formula is:

Liquid = current assets – stock
capital ratio   current liabilities

The ideal ratio is 1:1. Anything less than this and the business will have problems in paying off its current liabilities (its short-term debts).

Profitability ratio

For businesses in the private sector – whether they are private or public limited companies – the primary objective is to produce a profit. It is therefore important to examine exactly how the profit has been made. Profitability ratios allow comparisons to be made between businesses. They tend to provide a percentage figure, rather than a ratio as such.

Gross profit margin ratio

The gross profit margin ratio examines the relationship between profits before allowing for overhead costs. The formula is:

Gross profit = gross profit × 100
margin   turnover

For example

If a business had a gross profit of £6,000 from sales (turnover) of £10,000, then the gross profit margin
= £6,000 × 100 = 60%
   £10,000
In other words, for every £1 of sales, the business has achieved 60p of gross profit. While this may appear to be a particularly good profit margin, none of the overheads have yet been taken into account.

A business could increase its gross profit margin by increasing its sales revenue while keeping its costs down, or by reducing its costs while trying to maintain the same sales revenue.

Net profit margin ratio

The net profit margin ratio is different to the gross profit margin ratio because it looks at profits after overhead expenses have been deducted. The formula is:

Net profit = net profit × 100
margin   sales

For example

A business has £10,000 of sales and a gross profit of £6,000. However, its overheads are £5,000. To work out the net profit, we must take the £5,000 from the £6,000, leaving us with £1,000. We now divide the £1,000 by the £10,000 and multiply this by 100 to give us our net profit margin. In this example it is just 10%.

This means that for every £1 of sales, the business has achieved 10p of net profit. This proves that expenses need to be kept down or reduced, while sales revenue has to remain static or be increased.

The profit and loss account is used to calculate the level of profit that has been made by a business. It includes the following calculations and information:

CALCULATION	PROFIT AND LOSS ACCOUNT ITEM
	Revenue (total sales)
Minus	Cost of sales
Equals	Gross profit
Minus	Overheads
Equals	Operating or trading profit
Plus	One-off items
Equals	Pre-tax profits
Minus	Tax
Equals	Profit after tax
Minus	Dividend payments
Equals	Retained profit

This data is usually presented in the form of a comparison between the current year and the previous year, so that straightforward comparisons between performances can be made.

QUESTION TIME
27 minutes

1 A business achieved £950,000 in revenue and its cost of sales was £725,000. The business overheads were £75,000. Calculate the gross profit and the operating profit. *(6 marks)*

2 A business has a turnover of £1.2 million in 2008 and a gross profit of £400,000. In 2009, it has a turnover of £1.5 million and a gross profit of £300,000. Work out the gross profit margin for BOTH years and comment on your findings. *(6 marks)*

3 A business has current assets of £450,000 and current liabilities of £112,000. Work out the current ratio and comment on what you find. *(6 marks)*

4 Should the financial performance be the only measure of success of the business? *(9 marks)*

183

Interpreting data on financial statements

Assessing performance

It is possible to use a balance sheet rather than a profit and loss account to assess how well a business is performing. Several measures can be used.

One thing to look for on the balance sheet is the level of stock. If the level of stock has risen from one period to another, then there could be problems. Looking at the profit and loss account can identify these stock levels. If sales have not increased, there could be a problem because the stock is just sitting there, unused and unsold. This may affect the business's cash flow.

Credit control can be examined by looking at the amount that debtors owe the business. If the amount owed is growing faster than sales, then there could be a severe problem with cash flow in the near future.

It is important for businesses to have a good payment record if they might wish to extend their credit with their suppliers in the future. Making early payments to suppliers may attract a discount, but the money paid out will affect the cash flow.

It is also possible to see on a balance sheet how much a business is borrowing to finance its operations. New businesses tend to borrow heavily. The more a business relies on loans, the more difficult it becomes to borrow more money.

Comparing profitability and efficiency from year to year is a useful measure of the business's performance. It gives the owners, shareholders or potential investors an indication as to the progress of the business – or lack of it.

Shareholders and potential investors will look for gradual improvements. They may be suspicious of huge changes (either good or bad). They will want to see a general upward trend to show stability and sensible management and decision-making.

Views of stakeholders

Many different stakeholders use accounts information as detailed in the table below (continued on the opposite page).

STAKEHOLDER GROUP	WHAT ARE THEY LOOKING FOR AND WHY?
Shareholders and potential investors	They are primarily concerned with the risks they may be taking in investing and the possibility of getting a financial return on their investment. They need information to decide whether the business is a good investment. They will look to see whether the business will pay out dividends and how efficient the management of the business is. The key information they are looking for on the profit and loss account and the balance sheet is: • information related to growth, as shown by sales • the profitability of the business, showing its overall level of profit and profit margins • the current investments of the business – the cash value of its investments and the assets it owns • the market value of the business, as reflected in its share price • how all these measures compare to similar competitors or other investment opportunities.
Directors, managers and employees	Anyone employed directly by the business is interested in its stability and continuing profitability. This even extends into retirement – when employees retire, they want to know that their pension funds are safe and that they will receive their retirement benefits. Individuals at any level in the organisation will be looking to receive at least a competitive rate for their pay and benefits. So employees will be looking at: • the business's revenue and profit growth • how much the business is investing • the numbers of individuals employed, their wages and salary costs • the valuation of the business pension scheme and how much the company is putting into the pension scheme.
Suppliers	Suppliers are likely to be trade creditors. Their primary concern is whether the business is able to pay its short-term debts to them. In other words, they will be looking at the short-term liquidity of their customer's business. They will look at financial statements for information on: • cash flow – which will show the key income and expenditure of the business and its relevant balances • how much working capital (current assets to pay current liabilities) the business has, and how this is managed • what the payment policies are in terms of prioritising the payment of invoices.

184

A business's income relies on the business's level of activity. To some extent so do costs. Income is sales revenue. It therefore depends upon the production of products or the providing of services at increased levels to attract additional sales revenue.

Additional activities mean that there are additional direct costs and semi-variable costs (expenses that have both fixed cost and variable cost components, like electricity). These are associated precisely with the activity levels that generate sales revenue or income.

The other area is fixed costs, such as overheads. These fixed cost figures remain static regardless of the level of activity, the direct costs or the sales revenue.

In the following example, the relationship between costs and income – and therefore profit – is linked, regardless of the level of activity involved.

In this example we have three different sales revenue totals, but all of them have produced the same profit level. Fixed costs have increased over the period by £10,000, while direct costs have fluctuated between £120,000 and £140,000. So we can see that the close relationship between incomes at different activity levels is directly influenced by associated and non-associated costs.

YEAR	FIXED COSTS (£)	DIRECT COSTS (INCLUDING SEMI-VARIABLE COSTS) (£)	SALES REVENUE (£)	GROSS PROFIT (£)
2008	100,000	125,000	285,000	60,000
2009	100,000	120,000	280,000	60,000
2010	110,000	140,000	310,000	60,000

STAKEHOLDER GROUP	WHAT ARE THEY LOOKING FOR AND WHY? (continued)
Customers	Customers could include direct consumers, who purchase from the business, or other businesses. They will be looking for information on: • the development of new products • sales figures and growth • whether the business is investing in itself and increasing capacity.
Lenders	Any individual or organisation that lends money wants to know whether the loan can be paid back when it is due, and whether the business can keep up interest payments. Lenders will look at: • the business's cash flow • the security of any assets against which lending has been secured • the short-term, medium-term and long-term investment requirements of the business.
Government	Several government agencies or departments take an active interest in the financial information of a business. For example, local government requires businesses to pay local taxes and rates, and Her Majesty's Revenue & Customs handles Value Added Tax and collects Corporation Tax.

QUESTION TIME
16 minutes

1 Why will shareholders and investors look for gradual growth, rather than rapid growth? *(4 marks)*

2 Why might suppliers be interested in the financial information of a business? *(6 marks)*

3 Why might it be important for customers to know how well a business is doing? *(6 marks)*

185

What have you learnt?

Finance was the third section of Unit 2 (Growing as a Business). The purpose was to look at the sources of finance available to a large business, as compared to the finance for a small or start-up business that we studied in Unit 1. We have looked at:

- finance for large businesses and the main methods that large businesses use to raise funds
- the advantages and disadvantages of each source of finance
- profit and loss accounts and balance sheets – their purpose and how they are useful to stakeholders in assessing the performance of a business
- the various items you might find on a profit and loss account or a balance sheet

- how to interpret the information on financial statements and what it tells us about the business.

In this section we have looked at simplified versions of financial statements. In the examination you will be expected to be able to analyse their content. Luckily, you will not have to remember any of the formulae or ratios. The examiner will put them in the exam paper if you need to use them.

The 'Question time' exercises will have given you a clue as to the type of questions that you can expect to find in the Unit 2 exam paper. The calculations in particular should be fairly straightforward. They are a good way to pick up marks. Again, the questions were based on the mark-a-minute system, so do not spend more time than is necessary.

If you need to, come back to a question at the end if you are struggling with it.

Your teacher or tutor will be able to give you a copy of the 'Unit Revision Pack' from the *Teacher Support Pack*. In it you will find a list of things that you should revise and a mock exam paper.

Section 3 integrated questions

Try out these exam-style questions. They now cover the first three sections of Unit 2. In the real exam, questions are likely to cover all five sections of Unit 2 – not just these three. This is a real business situation.

186

SANGTON LIMITED

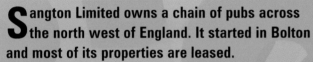

Sangton Limited owns a chain of pubs across the north west of England. It started in Bolton and most of its properties are leased.

The business needed a commercial loan of £700,000 to transform a building from a shop/restaurant into a brand new cafe bar. It borrowed the money from the Co-operative Bank. The business was expected to put together a full financial forecast and a business plan to help convince the finance providers.

Source: adapted from Business Link

187

QUESTIONS
41 minutes

1 What is a commercial loan? *(2 marks)*

2 Why did Sangton Limited have to produce a forecast and a business plan? *(4 marks)*

3 Although the business arranged to borrow £700,000, the project took longer than anticipated. The cash flow from the rest of the business grew, so it only ended up borrowing £600,000. What source of finance did the business use instead of the balance of £100,000? Explain your answer. *(6 marks)*

4 Should Sangton Limited have issued new shares to raise the required funds for the cafe bar, rather than obtaining a loan? Explain your answer. *(9 marks)*

5 Identify and explain ONE current asset owned by Sangton Limited. *(3 marks)*

6 Explain whether the commercial loan would be considered a current liability or a long-term liability. *(4 marks)*

7 What type of legal structure does the business have and what advantages might this structure have given it? *(5 marks)*

8 Suggest what kind of promotions the business might use to publicise its 800-seat, late-night cafe bar. *(8 marks)*

Reorganising the structure

YOU WILL FIND OUT:

● about spreading the workload

● about organisation charts and trees

● about hierarchies

Spreading the workload

A difficult part of settling on the organisational structure of a business is to adequately spread the workload that will be placed on individual employees or groups of employees.

Many businesses allocate sufficient employees (or additional employees as necessary) in areas that directly generate sales revenue. But they usually keep employee levels relatively low in areas that cost money but do not generate income, such as administration. This can often be a false economy, as unequal workloads put unnecessary and unworkable pressure on certain parts of the business and can cause systems to break down and communication channels to fail. It can ultimately result in higher than average **labour turnover**.

For very small businesses, responsibilities for particular jobs or routine duties are usually blurred. However, if a business has job descriptions, then there will be a clear indication as to the responsibilities and duties assigned to each employee.

Job allocation involves assigning duties and responsibilities to specific job roles or to teams, departments, sections or groups of employees.

The range of duties and responsibilities allocated to each job role will have a bearing on the workload involved. The more duties and responsibilities assigned to a role, the heavier the potential workload for that individual.

Organisation charts

The traditional way of visualising the organisational structure of a business is to create an organisation chart, which illustrates:

- each of the departments and how they are broken down
- the levels of responsibility of managers, by showing different managers who have the same level of responsibility at the same level in the chart. This can also show how departments and their managers work with one another
- the lines of communication within the business, showing how information passes up and down the organisation (from senior management down and then back up to the senior management via the layers of management).

Organisation trees

The West Yorkshire Fire and Rescue Service organisation chart below is a simplified organisation tree. It shows five individuals answering directly to the Chief Executive, all with the same level of responsibility for one or more management areas of the organisation, such as Human Resources or Training and Development. Underneath this senior management group, there will be managers responsible for each geographical area and each fire station, and beneath them will be the firefighters and other support staff.

As you can see from the illustration opposite, organisation trees often look like pyramids. There are only a handful of individuals at the top, but there are more and more managers, supervisors and employees as you move down the tree. Those employees at the bottom report, through successive layers of management, to the senior managers. This is known as a **hierarchy**.

By organising the business in a strict order, it is possible to identify and place individual managers and employees in areas of specialism.

KEY TERMS

Labour turnover ▶ a measurement (usually as a percentage) of the number of employees joining and leaving a business. The higher the percentage, the higher the turnover of employees in that period.

Hierarchy ▶ the arrangement of the levels of authority in a business, with successively more authority and responsibility further up the hierarchy.

EXAMPLE OF AN ORGANISATION CHART
SOURCE: WWW.WESTYORKSFIRE.GOV.UK

Organisation chart: FIRE AUTHORITY → CHIEF FIRE OFFICER/CHIEF EXECUTIVE → ASSISTANT CHIEF OFFICER/DIRECTOR OF FIRE SAFETY & COMMUNITY RELATIONS; DEPUTY CHIEF OFFICER/DIRECTOR OF OPERATIONS; CHIEF FINANCE OFFICER; DIRECTOR OF CORPORATE RESOURCES; ASSISTANT CHIEF OFFICER/DIRECTOR OF HUMAN RESOURCES. Lower level: SENIOR FIRE SAFETY MANAGER; AREA MANAGER COMMUNITY SAFETY; AREA MANAGER/SENIOR OPERATIONS COMMAND OFFICER; AREA MANAGER/SENIOR OPERATIONS POLICY & PLANNING OFFICER; SENIOR CORPORATE RESOURCES MANAGER; HUMAN RESOURCES MANAGER; AREA MANAGER/SENIOR TRAINING & DEVELOPMENT OFFICER.

EXAMPLE OF AN ORGANISATION TREE

SOURCE: WWW.EMERALDINSIGHT.COM

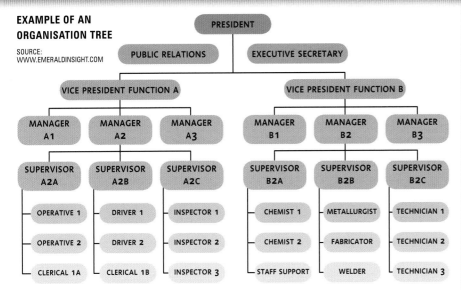

Hierarchies

A hierarchical organisational structure looks like a pyramid. Power, responsibility and authority are concentrated at the top and decisions flow from the top down. Structures with multiple layers of management are very hierarchical – each layer of management hangs onto its authority and responsibility, making sure that it is always part of any decision-making process. Information passes through each level, both up and down.

An increased number of employees in a particular department means that more managers or supervisors have to be created or promoted in order to manage their activities. Adding additional employees to an existing department will, without additional management support, eventually lead to enormous inefficiencies.

For example

Anything to do with marketing – for example, public relations and advertising – would normally be part of the marketing and sales department. The production department would have a works manager, someone with responsibility for quality, designers and those involved in purchasing raw materials and components for the production lines.

The ways in which businesses are organised are determined by the nature of the work involved. Some departments are functional (actively involved in doing the business's work), while the rest are in support roles, such as administration.

QUESTION TIME
22 minutes

1 Why might a business need to reorganise its structure? *(6 marks)*

2 What is meant by the term 'de-layer'? *(2 marks)*

3 What is meant by the term 'hierarchy'? *(2 marks)*

4 What is meant by the terms 'chain of command' and 'span of control'? Why are they different? *(6 marks)*

5 What is the benefit of producing an organisational chart? *(6 marks)*

Certain managers in the structure can resist decisions made by senior management; perhaps ideas are watered down, ignored or deliberately misunderstood so that they will fail. Equally, useful information coming to them from lower down the organisation can be withheld. The feeling is that information, or the possession of it, is more important than the good or bad it might do to the business as a whole.

Difficulties such as these are a good reason why many businesses have chosen to 'de-layer', cutting out layers of middle management and pushing responsibility and decision-making further down the organisational structure.

De-layering means that managers have a wider span of control, an increased workload and more stress. Also there may be problems for employees, as management jobs will be lost through redundancy.

189

Types of organisational structure

Flat structures

A flat organisational structure is a type of hierarchical structure – it looks like a pyramid – but it has fewer layers. A hierarchical structure can often be 'de-layered' – that means having layers removed – to create a flat structure. This process allows decisions to be made more quickly and efficiently, because layers are able to communicate more easily with one another. The organisation can become less bureaucratic. (A bureaucratic organisation has sets of regulations to control activity.)

It is a simple structure, often used by organisations operating from a single site. The directors and other major decision-makers are more available for consultation with employees, who often feel more a part of the process. This encourages motivation, particularly among junior managers, who are likely to be given more responsibility through delegation from the senior management level of the structure.

Chains of command

The chain of command in an organisation is typically associated with a business that has a hierarchical structure. The chain of command is the formal line of communication, beginning with the board of directors or managing director, who then passes instructions down to departmental managers, who pass them on to section heads, who in turn pass them on to individual employees.

This chain of command is typical in a pyramid-shaped organisation, where more individuals have to be informed of decisions and instructions as you move down the pyramid. The chain of command of the board of directors or the managing director encompasses every individual underneath it in the hierarchical structure. The chain of command of a section head is the immediate employees who work under that individual's supervision.

The chain of command is closely associated with the span of control.

Spans of control

The span of control comprises the number of subordinates for whom a manager has direct responsibility. The ideal number frequently quoted is between five and nine individuals under the control of one manager.

Beyond this number, it becomes increasingly difficult to react or respond to individuals' specific needs. In this case, additional levels of hierarchy would need to be inserted both above and below each manager, to reduce the span of control to a manageable level. Too wide a span of control can mean that the manager is overloaded with work, has little time to make decisions and cannot control the activities of their employees.

The wider the span of control, the more it enables managers to develop clear objectives and goals. They can also delegate tasks more effectively and can carefully select and train their employees. The managers and employees all have greater responsibility (as there are fewer layers of management) and they are therefore more motivated.

Some situations are ideal for wider spans of control. For example, when:

- the work is relatively routine
- there are well-trained employees working for the manager
- there are supervisors or team managers to support the manager
- there are similar jobs that can be done by the employees, so the manager can switch them around to cope with heavier workloads
- the employees are happy to take on work without close supervision.

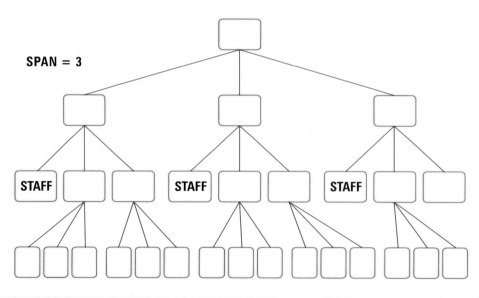

SPAN = 3

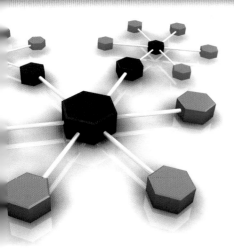

The key advantages of wide spans of control are:

- fewer layers of management, so decisions and communications are quicker
- less wages and salaries to be paid to managers overall, as there are fewer of them.

The key advantages of narrow spans of control are:

- quick communications between the manager and employees
- easier to control employees, as there are fewer of them
- feedback from employees can be quickly used
- the manager does not have to be as skilled as a manager with a wider span of control.

In 1916, Henri Fayol, a French industrialist, wrote that many of the root causes of industrial failure were down to management and personnel.

Fayol was a 'top-down' theorist, who believed that change must begin with the board of directors or the managing director. Fayol also identified some rules, which he considered management should follow. He wrote that an individual who specialises would become more skilled, efficient and effective. He also considered that the manager should have the ultimate accountability for the employees.

QUESTION TIME
30 minutes

The diagram below shows an organisational structure and the spans of control.

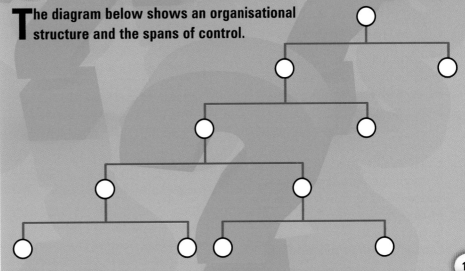

1 In the diagram above, what is the span of control for all of the managers in the organisation? *(2 marks)*

2 Why might a narrow span of control in a business mean that the organisational structure is tall and narrow? *(4 marks)*

3 Identify and explain TWO advantages of a narrow span of control. *(6 marks)*

4 What kind of span of control would you expect to see in a flat organisation and why? *(6 marks)*

5 Identify and explain TWO advantages of a wide span of control. *(6 marks)*

6 What benefits can a business gain through de-layering? *(6 marks)*

191

Centralised and decentralised structures

Centralisation and decentralisation

Centralisation means making the decision-making processes more concentrated in one place in an organisation.

Decentralisation involves a gradual dispersal of decision-making control across an organisation. The purpose of decentralising is to encourage flexibility and to assist faster decision-making. This, in turn, means faster response times.

Integral to the dispersal of decision-making is the movement of power and authority from the higher levels of management – or from a single headquarters unit – to various divisions, branches, departments or subsidiaries of the organisation. Decentralisation means delegation, as responsibility and power are passed to lower-level management.

Decentralisation is also strongly associated with the concept of empowerment. This gives front-line staff the power, authority and responsibility to make immediate decisions themselves, without always referring to senior management.

For example Tesco

An example of a decentralised structure is the supermarket chain Tesco. Each Tesco store has a store manager who is able to make decisions about their store and is responsible to a regional manager.

ADVANTAGES OF CENTRALISED STRUCTURES
- Senior managers enjoy greater control over the organisation
- The use of standardised procedures can result in cost savings
- Decisions can be made to benefit the organisation as a whole, whereas a decision made by a departmental manager may benefit their department but disadvantage other departments
- The organisation can benefit from the decision-making of experienced senior managers

Some organisations may decide that a combination of centralised and decentralised management is more effective. For example, functional areas, such as accounting and purchasing, may be centralised to save costs, but recruitment may be decentralised, as units away from head office may have very specific staffing needs.

Vertical decentralisation
Some organisations implement vertical decentralisation. This means that they hand the power down the hierarchy of their organisation. Vertical decentralisation increases the contribution to decision-making of those at the bottom of the organisation chart.

Horizontal decentralisation
Horizontal decentralisation spreads responsibility across the organisation. A business might decide to use this for the implementation of new technology across the whole business. This implementation would be the sole responsibility of technology specialists.

ADVANTAGES OF DECENTRALISED STRUCTURES
- Senior managers have time to concentrate on the most important decisions (as the other decisions can be taken by people lower down the organisational structure)
- Decision-making is a form of empowerment. Empowerment can increase motivation and therefore mean that staff output increases
- People lower down the chain have a greater understanding of the environment they work in and the people (customers and colleagues) with whom they interact. Their knowledge, skills and experience may enable them to make more effective decisions than senior managers
- Empowerment enables departments and their employees to respond faster to changes and new challenges, whereas it may take senior managers longer to appreciate that business needs have changed

Empowerment

An empowered individual is one who is allowed to control their own contribution within the organisation. They are given the authority and responsibility to complete tasks and attain targets without the direct intervention of management.

The benefits of empowerment to an organisation are that it reduces the importance of repetitive administration and the number of managers required at the various levels of the structure. Streamlining management levels often increases the effectiveness of communication.

For an employee, empowerment increases their creativity and initiative, as well as their commitment to the organisation, by allowing them to work with autonomy.

Autonomy

Autonomy is a measure of an individual's independence in their job role. An autonomous individual has a degree of control over what they do, the order in which they do it, and the processes involved in carrying it out.

Autonomy also suggests that the individual may have a greater influence over their own working environment. Truly autonomous workers, therefore, are those who are enabled by alternative work arrangements (such as the ability to decide how often they need to be at their desks) or a form of remote working, such as telecommuting (also known as 'teleworking').

▶▶ Delegation involves the active use of the skills and experience of employees in subordinate positions. An individual considered suitable to perform a particular task is given the authority to carry it out.

Delegation means that the manager needs to support and monitor the progress and, once the task is completed, to acknowledge that the job has been completed successfully.

Delegation is a means by which pressured key members of staff can reduce their workloads in the certain knowledge that vital tasks will still be performed. It is not always possible to delegate all tasks to other individuals, but delegation can mean greater efficiency, increased motivation, skill development and, above all, a fairer distribution of work throughout a team.

QUESTION TIME
16 minutes

The National Trust's catering department, which is responsible for running around 150 restaurants at Trust-owned properties across the country, has a significant challenge in coordinating the supply and collation of information that can help improve profit margins. Not only are the restaurants widely spread geographically, but each site is encouraged to purchase locally sourced produce and ingredients, in keeping with the culture of the Trust.

Hosted centrally by the National Trust, the Saffron Spice database is accessed through a password-controlled website by both head office and selected personnel at the restaurant sites. Catering managers can record information such as stock usage, purchase invoices and sales data, simply by logging on to the Internet and uploading the data, which is then routed directly back to head office.

Crucially for the National Trust, the move to a centralised structure needed to avoid imposing a rigid process that would conflict with the local sourcing of food products and individual pricing structures. Saffron Spice is designed to enable this flexibility, while also giving area managers and the central catering team information that will aid negotiations with suppliers.

Source: adapted from www.nationaltrust.org.uk

193

1 The National Trust operates a centralised structure. What does this mean? *(2 marks)*

2 Why has the National Trust chosen to centralise in this way? *(6 marks)*

3 The National Trust's centralised structure still enables each of its restaurants to have a degree of autonomy in the sourcing of food products and individual pricing. What does the term 'autonomy' mean? *(2 marks)*

4 Why is there still a level of autonomy for each restaurant, and why is this important to them? *(6 marks)*

Reasons to recruit

Why is recruitment important?

In countries such as Great Britain, with a relatively low unemployment rate compared to other countries, it has become increasingly difficult for businesses and organisations to attract and retain ideal and competent members of staff.

Having experienced and well-motivated managers and other key employees is vital to the short-term and long-term success of the business or organisation. This means that **human resource management** is at the centre of an organisation's planning for the future.

It is important for the organisation to be able to project an attractive image, not only to its customers, but also to individuals who could become key employees in the organisation.

Reasons to recruit

The process of recruiting new employees may be triggered in a number of different ways. The decision to recruit depends on the reasons for the vacancies: some are a direct result of actions by the organisation itself; others are beyond its control and, to some extent, cannot be predicted.

Increasingly, human resource management has to predict probable needs for additional staffing before the vacancy actually arises. If they simply wait for a specific reason to recruit a new employee instantly, then this could cause severe pressure and disruption to the organisation. This means that the Human Resources department has to have a flexible approach to recruitment, with systems in place and contacts with employment agencies already established.

Internal expansion and diversification

Internal expansion and **diversification** revolve around decisions made by the organisation itself.

If a business is expanding its volume of business, then it may find that it no longer has sufficient staff to cope with the work. Before it takes on additional staff to do the work, the organisation needs to be relatively sure that this increased volume will continue.

Or a business may be in the process of diversifying into new areas of work. It will need to employ specialists who have experience in these new areas, and may find that existing employees or managers are

likely to have a working knowledge of the new processes or procedures required.

Employee-related issues

Employee-related issues that could lead to a vacancy can require short-term or long-term planning decisions.

The Human Resources department will become involved in cases when an employee takes maternity leave or replacement staff have to be found to cover long-term sickness. Maternity cover may mean having to take on an employee on a short, **fixed-term contract** for perhaps as long as six months or a year. Providing cover for those on long-term sick leave is more problematic, as there can be no accurate prediction of when the ill employee will return to work, if at all.

Other short-term vacancy planning situations can include:

- employees taking a year out to study or travel the world
- employees being seconded (transferred temporarily) to another part of the organisation (or to another organisation altogether) to receive training and experience.

One of the most difficult situations is replacing experienced employees who have chosen for some reason to leave the organisation. Their skills, abilities and experience can be very hard to replace. Depending on the length of their service and contract conditions, the employee will have to give the organisation a period of notice. This means that they will continue to work for a period of time after they have made it clear

194

to the organisation that they are leaving. Theoretically, this gives the organisation time to recruit or promote another individual, who can then work alongside the existing employee as part of an induction (initial training) process.

Retirement causes a particular problem for any organisation. The person retiring will usually be a highly experienced and well-placed member of staff. Their knowledge of the organisation and its processes will be difficult to replace, no matter how good the candidates are who will eventually be attracted to the vacant position.

> ▶▶ The alternative to recruiting permanent staff is to use what many refer to as a 'sticking plaster' method, to cope with short periods of increased work. This could mean taking on temporary staff, who may have no particular attachment to the work or motivation to do it, or suggesting to employees that they work increased hours and rewarding them for their additional hours.

Taking the decision

An organisation may have created a situation where it needs to recruit additional employees. Equally, it may have been forced into a situation where it needs to either replace existing employees or temporarily cover their posts.

Many organisations are slow to reach the decision to recruit, even when they are aware that additional or replacement employees would be desirable. The recruitment process is potentially long and costly, and they will avoid having to go through it unless the situation is critical.

All too often, organisations wait too long, putting the decision off and placing enormous pressure on remaining employees. This could in turn cause them to leave or to take time off due to sickness.

The decision to recruit usually comes from the direct line manager (the manager to whom an individual would directly report) of the vacant post, who must argue the case. They must show good reason for a recruitment drive and illustrate that additional staff are necessary or that existing staff cannot cover the work of an employee who has left or who is on long-term leave.

QUESTION TIME
20 minutes

1 In a business, who would usually take the decision to authorise recruitment? *(2 marks)*

2 Why might a business need to recruit new employees? *(4 marks)*

3 What is a short fixed-term contract? *(2 marks)*

4 What problems does a business face when it uses internal recruitment to fill a vacancy? *(6 marks)*

5 What problems does a business encounter when a skilled employee leaves or retires? *(6 marks)*

195

KEY TERMS

Human resource management ▶ the increasingly scientific management of employees in a work situation.

Diversification ▶ the process of an organisation moving into new areas of business that they did not formerly deal with.

Fixed-term contract ▶ a signed employment contract that specifically states the maximum period of time that an individual will be working for a business.

The staff recruitment process

The selection process

Once a business has identified that it has a vacancy, it prepares a job description, listing the job's duties and responsibilities. It includes:

*   job title
*   job grade
*   the person to whom the new recruit will report
*   day-to-day tasks
*   job responsibilities.

The business creates a person specification, detailing essential and desirable skills, qualifications or experience. This is useful, as applications can be compared against these essential and desirable lists.

Next, the business chooses how to advertise the post and attract applications from suitable candidates, and sends out the job description, together with details of the business, and gives a date by which applications must be returned.

As the applications arrive, likely candidates are considered for shortlisting, while those without the right qualities are rejected at this stage.

When the deadline for applications has passed, the human resources department meets the direct line manager to discuss the applicants and decide how many should be invited for interview. A day or two is set aside for the interview process.

Not all businesses require applicants to complete application forms. Some ask for direct contact by telephone, email or by calling personally at the office; others ask for a letter of application and **curriculum vitae**, and use these to compare against person specifications.

Application forms

Many businesses use their own standard application forms, which normally ask for:

*   name, address and other contact details
*   date of birth, gender, marital status
*   education
*   work experience
*   qualifications
*   skills, aptitudes and qualities
*   a statement in support of the application
*   names and contact details of two to four referees.

A candidate will usually return an application form without a covering letter. The organisation will have sent a job description and details of its business along with the form, and it is vital for applicants to read this additional information.

The business looks for a number of things on an application form, including:

*   legibility and neatness (application forms that are messy, dog-eared or late will be rejected immediately)
*   relevance of the candidate's skills, experience and qualifications
*   unexplained gaps in education or work experience.

Sometimes a business may judge a candidate on factors that they should not really take into account, such as marital status, gender or location. Strictly speaking, the business would be breaking the law by doing this.

Application forms force every applicant to complete each section, which allows those doing the shortlisting to be able to compare candidates efficiently.

The curriculum vitae

A curriculum vitae (CV) is a condensed history of your life. It should be as short, but as complete, as possible. The main information required is:

*   full name
*   address
*   date of birth
*   education and qualifications
*   employment and work experience
*   hobbies and interests
*   statement about personal qualities and achievements
*   names and contact details of at least two referees.

It is important for CVs to be kept up-to-date. They may need to be adapted for different job applications.

There is no one universal format for CVs – they can be of all kinds of design and length, with different sections, headings or order. This makes it difficult to compare CVs of applicants.

CVs are nearly always typed or word-processed, which makes it difficult for the business to assess the communication skills of the applicant.

Unless instructed otherwise, a CV should always be accompanied by a letter of application.

Application letters

Letters of application should:

*   include an opening paragraph stating where the applicant saw the advertisement
*   state why the job appeals to the applicant
*   state why the applicant is applying for the job
*   include a summary of the applicant's main strengths, stressing their suitability for the job

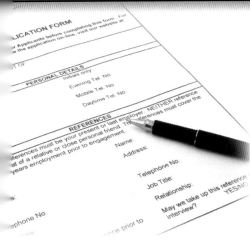

197

- show that the applicant is enthusiastic
- state when the applicant is available for interview and when they could start the job.

For the candidate, the letter of application gives a chance to stress the key points in their CV or on their application form. For the business, it gives an opportunity to see a candidate's real writing skills and, if the letter is handwritten, they may decide to analyse the handwriting.

Interviews

Once the business has made its shortlist, it invites candidates for interview. The interview stage is very important, because it is where the employer and the applicant meet for the first time. Interviews tend to have the following features:

- Interviews are face-to-face. Sometimes they are formal, with a panel of interviewers asking questions, or they can be more informal, giving candidates a chance to explain more about themselves.
- They are designed to assess whether people have the right qualities, attitudes, skills, knowledge and experience.
- The applicant's physical appearance and how they present themselves can be judged.
- Interviewers will see how candidates handle themselves in social situations and whether they have good communication skills.

Curriculum vitae (CV) ▶ a condensed history of your life.

Appointment

After all this, the successful candidate is now offered the job. An order is usually made verbally either face-to-face or on the telephone, and then confirmed in writing. Ideally, the business should wait to see if the successful candidate accepts the job, before sending out rejection letters to the unsuccessful ones.

If the successful candidate confirms that they want the job, a start date is agreed and the business must now prepare a contract of employment. If the successful candidate is already in work elsewhere, they must now resign from their job. The new employer must wait until the successful candidate has worked their period of notice.

The stages of recruitment are aimed at attracting and dealing with a number of potential candidates. Once the applications arrive, the business needs to be careful in sifting through them in order to identify the best possible person for the job. Throughout the process they must offer equal opportunities to all candidates and must make sure that they follow any current laws on pay, discrimination, race and disability.

Interviews are a two-way process. Not only does the employer want to get a feeling about the candidate, but the candidate can also find out whether or not the job would suit them. The candidate can ask questions during the interview. The next natural stage is for the interviewers to choose one of the interviewees and offer them the job.

QUESTION TIME
32 minutes

1 **What is the difference between a job description and a person specification?** *(4 marks)*

2 **How will the business produce a shortlist of applicants for the available vacancy?** *(4 marks)*

3 **Why are application forms useful for a business in the recruitment process?** *(4 marks)*

4 **Why is it hard to assess candidates if CVs are used?** *(4 marks)*

5 **What are the alternatives to application forms and CVs?** *(4 marks)*

6 **Why are job applicants sometimes asked to submit a letter of application as well as a CV or application form?** *(6 marks)*

7 **What is the purpose of the interview?** *(6 marks)*

Appraisal and training

Appraisal interviews

Assessing – or appraising – the work performance of individual employees is usually the role of the human resources department. However, on a day-to-day basis, performance appraisal may be the concern of line managers and supervisors.

Appraisal interviews should be a two-way process of feedback between the manager and employee. The aim is to improve performance through a joint problem-solving approach.

Appraisal interviews are used to:

- identify employee strengths and weaknesses
- determine salary increases in some organisations (however, appraisals are deliberately not linked to salary reviews in other organisations)
- decide who deserves promotion
- aid internal communication processes in the organisation
- work out staff development needs.

Employers should conduct the interview in a pleasant and positive way throughout. The employee should be given notice to allow for preparation, possibly including a self-development review form. A quiet room should be chosen, and enough time allowed for the interview. Interviewer and interviewee should prepare by considering the employee's previous appraisal and subsequent performance. Previous targets should be discussed at the start of the interview. Questions on what has gone well and what has not gone so well should be posed and answered. A summary of what has been achieved should be made at the end of the interview and the employee should be given time to read the appraisal documents.

Employees should make the most of appraisal interviews, by:

- preparing for the interview, making notes of past performance results and anticipating any difficult questions
- not being modest about their strengths or putting too much emphasis on their weaknesses
- being clear about what support is required for future work, such as training, resources or time to reach targets.

After the appraisal, the employee and appraiser draw up an action plan that covers all aspects of the interview. This will form the basis of the next appraisal interview. There will be an opportunity at the next appraisal for the employee to show that issues identified as unsatisfactory in the previous appraisal have been rectified.

Training and personal development

The purpose of appraisal and its related documents is to identify key areas of an employee's qualifications, training and experience that need to be addressed in order to make them more efficient and productive.

A business will be more inclined to approve particular training and development if it meets the business's objectives. Therefore, the training or personal development needs to be relevant to the work carried out by the employee.

Normally, an employee (in consultation with their manager or appraiser) will complete a staff development form, outlining the type of training or personal development recommended as a result of the appraisal.

The employee should identify any areas of knowledge or skills that they feel they need to add to or improve. Certain areas ideal for personal development will be highlighted in appraisals or annual reviews.

The personal development plans that arise from the appraisals will outline the key areas that the employee, supported by

198

their supervisor or manager, and ultimately the human resources department, feel are relevant to the job role.

In the meantime, other opportunities for personal development may arise, such as training courses either within the organisation or arranged by local colleges or training agencies. Human Resources will routinely inform employees of training opportunities, and employees can also look in the local press and libraries for notices announcing training programmes in the area. Many of these external training programmes will either be paid for or subsidised by the employer. If this is not the case, many courses have sliding scales of payment, to help make them affordable.

Transferable personal skills

Employers increasingly look for people with personal skills that they can transfer from job to job. For example:

- a willingness to learn
- good verbal and written communication skills
- self-motivation
- teamwork
- commitment
- energy and enthusiasm
- reliability and honesty
- problem-solving, analytical ability
- organisational skills
- adaptability and flexibility
- ability to meet deadlines
- information technology skills.

Employers are looking for employees who can display the widest possible range of these skills.

QUESTION TIME
29 minutes

1 **What is an appraisal?**
(2 marks)

2 **Identify and explain THREE factors a business should consider in its appraisal procedures.** *(6 marks)*

3 **What is the purpose of an appraisal?** *(6 marks)*

4 **Why are employers looking for employees to have skills that can be transferred to a variety of jobs within the business?** *(6 marks)*

5 **Should a local garage that employs three mechanics and a garage manager implement an appraisal scheme?** *(9 marks)*

199

Because even low-level job roles are becoming more demanding, employees increasingly need to have a wide range of skills and a willingness to learn new skills. This is known as 'multi-skilling'. It provides employees with a broad range of skills that can be transferred from one job role to another.

A prime example would be an individual who has used the Microsoft Office package for an administrative job and has sufficient typing skills to take on secretarial work.

If an employee is multi-skilled and has a wide range of transferable skills, then their future employment prospects are improved. Employers look for flexible, well-trained and highly skilled individuals, who can adapt to various changes in their job roles, as well as accepting and welcoming the need to continually update their bank of skills and knowledge.

Methods of motivation

YOU WILL FIND OUT:

- about induction training
- about the role of training
- about pay
- about styles of management
- about ways of retaining staff

Induction training

A new job means a new start. It also means having to learn about the new business, the policies and practices and how to do the new job. Good employers organise introductory training programmes (induction sessions) to help new employees become familiar with the business and how it operates.

It can take a lot of time and expense to find ideal employees, and if an employee is going to have second thoughts about the new job, then it is likely to happen in the first few days, so the induction programme is important to help ease any doubts. Typical programmes include:

- a first-day welcome meeting
- a guided tour of the organisation
- copies of (or the opportunity to see and read) business documentation, including departmental manuals, health and safety documents and staff handbooks
- an accompanied introduction to new work colleagues
- introductions to and training (or planned training) on any new software, hardware or machinery unfamiliar to the new employee
- an opportunity to sit in on team meetings and to become familiar with the working environment.

Induction programmes can last from a single day to several weeks. It depends on the job itself and the challenges ahead for the new employee. Additional training and a review, to see how well the new employee is fitting into the working environment, will usually follow up the induction programme.

The role of training

An induction programme is just the first of the training and development opportunities that could be offered to new employees. Increasingly, jobs are becoming more complicated and require a broader range of skills. This is particularly true of jobs that involve information technology. It is in the best interests of the business to train its employees to the highest possible standard, in order for them to do their jobs with the highest level of performance.

Untrained or badly trained employees can make mistakes. At worst they can be a danger to themselves and those around them. They can also cause customers and suppliers to become dissatisfied.

It is the responsibility of the human resources department to make sure that all employees attend basic training sessions. After that, specific departments will identify training needs for their employees.

Once the need for training has been identified, the department contacts Human Resources to arrange the necessary details. Human Resources can then decide whether several employees would benefit from this training, or whether this is training specific to one individual employee.

Pay

Pay (also known as 'remuneration') is a key motivator and a way in which a business can retain its best employees. Businesses increasingly use 'reward management' to motivate staff.

Reward management involves creating a pay package (including performance-related pay and bonuses) based on the actual worth or value of the employee to the business. This package tends to be related to the key skills, experience and time that the employee has worked for the business, together with a direct reward system that encourages them to work hard and see their contribution to success rewarded in financial terms.

Pay alone does not mean that employees will remain motivated and happy forever and will not look for a better, more satisfying job elsewhere. Pay needs to be coupled with good working conditions, responsibility and the fact that the business actually demonstrates that it values the employee by giving them training and other opportunities.

Styles of management

Leadership style is the pattern of influence that is used by leaders or managers. A leader must be effective in influencing the behaviour of employees by:

- goal-setting
- planning in advance
- defining timelines and deadlines
- specifying priorities
- establishing ways of evaluating progress and contribution
- defining roles and establishing who has authority to make decisions
- illustrating how outcomes can be accomplished.

A leader also has to create a series of supportive behaviours, on both a group and individual basis, including:

- listening skills
- praise and encouragement
- seeking ideas and input
- sharing information
- assisting others to problem-solve
- providing a reason behind actions.

Ways of retaining staff

Holding on to valuable and effective employees is vital to the continued growth and health of a business. The table below outlines some of the key methods a business uses to achieve this.

METHOD	EXPLANATION
Job previews	The business gives candidates a realistic taste of what the job will involve during the recruitment stage
Accountable managers	The business rewards managers who have a record of keeping good employees and reducing employee turnover
Career development and progression	The business aims to maximise the opportunities for employees to develop their skills and gain experience
Consulting employees	The business encourages employees to express their views, and gives them the chance to air their problems before the situation gets out of hand and they decide to leave
Flexibility	Businesses aim to accommodate individual work preferences, by bringing in flexible working hours
Job security	Employees who feel their jobs are under threat will be looking elsewhere for a more secure post. Security and stability handle this problem
Fairness	Businesses should never discriminate or be seen to be unfair. Rewards should reflect the actual value of the employee to the business
Defending the business	A business should keep internal email addresses confidential. They should not deal with other businesses that have poached employees in the past

It is one thing for an organisation to provide (or to pay for) training and development, but it needs to be assured that this is effective. Once training needs have been identified, processes must be put in place for the business to be informed of the value of the training. The business will want to review the training, usually through feedback from those doing it.

The review and feedback should provide enough information for the business to see whether the training was adequate and positive. It will want to find out whether the employees actually achieved or learnt what they had set out to discover.

There is always competition for the money available for training in a business, as often there is a limited training budget. Managers will want to secure as much of this money as possible for their own staff.

QUESTION TIME
38 minutes

1 What is an induction programme? *(2 marks)*

2 What is the purpose of an induction programme? *(4 marks)*

3 Identify and explain THREE aspects of an induction programme. *(6 marks)*

4 Why does a business provide training to employees? *(4 marks)*

5 What is the role of review and feedback in assessing the effectiveness of training provided? *(6 marks)*

6 Define leadership style. *(2 marks)*

7 How will a leader attempt to influence the behaviour of employees? *(4 marks)*

8 Identify and explain TWO supportive behaviours that a leader may apply in relation to an individual or a group. *(4 marks)*

9 Why is it important for a business to retain its key employees? *(6 marks)*

What have you learnt?

'People in business' is the fourth section of Unit 2 (Growing as a Business). We have considered how important human resources are to large businesses. We have seen that businesses can have different organisational structures and they may use a variety of different methods to recruit, motivate and retain their employees.

We have looked at:

- how businesses may have to reorganise their whole structure
- spans of control, chains of command, centralisation and decentralisation
- recruitment and retention of employees
- the basic recruitment process and how a business selects new employees

- appraisal or performance reviews, and how these are used to help a business identify performance issues and training opportunities
- various types of training, including induction, which happen when an employee first starts in an organisation
- how businesses try to motivate and retain their best employees, including the role of training, pay, and even the style of management used in the business.

Once again, the 'Question time' exercises will have shown you the type of questions you are likely to encounter in the examination for Unit 2. Remember that the mark-a-minute system is a good way to pace yourself. You will know how

much you need to write in order to get those valuable marks.

Your teacher or tutor will be able to give you a copy of the 'Unit Revision Pack' from the *Teacher Support Pack*. It will include plenty of things for you to think about, plus revision ideas. It will also give you a chance to try out a full mock exam paper.

Integrated questions from Sections 1, 2, 3 and 4

Try these exam-style questions. They bring together the topics from Section 1 (The business organisation), Section 2 (Marketing), Section 3 (Finance) and Section 4 (People in business). The only part of Unit 2 that they do not cover here is Section 5 (Operations management). The example below is not a real business situation, but it is typical.

202

PIGOTT PASTRIES LTD

Phyllis Pigott is the managing director of Pigott Pastries Ltd. They supply cafes and petrol stations with a range of savoury pastry products.

The business has grown rapidly over the last three years, from half a dozen employees to nearly 100. To keep up with demand, the factory needs to operate 24 hours a day with three 8-hour shifts.

During the day, Phyllis is assisted by an administration manager, a food purchasing manager, as well as the day shift food production manager. A deputy manager and a shift supervisor assist the day shift food production manager. The same three-level model is also used for the evening shift and the night shift.

But not everything is working as efficiently as Phyllis would hope. There is a high employee turnover, and there are quality issues.

$$\text{Acid test ratio} = \frac{\text{current assets} - \text{stock}}{\text{current liabilities}}$$

QUESTIONS
38 minutes

1 Phyllis is particularly worried about the high employee turnover. Why should this give her concern and what could she do about it? *(4 marks)*

2 How might an appraisal scheme help Phyllis reduce the high employee turnover? *(6 marks)*

3 Should Phyllis review the training programme at Pigott Pastries in order to improve quality? *(8 marks)*

4 Explain the terms 'de-layering', 'delegation' and 'span of control'. *(6 marks)*

5 Pigott Pastries has current assets of £300,000 and stock of £50,000. The business has current liabilities of £100,000. Work out the acid test ratio and comment on what you find. *(4 marks)*

6 As a method of increasing sales and market share, the business has been running a 'buy one, get one half-price' campaign. What sort of marketing activity is this? *(2 marks)*

7 Phyllis is considering offering shares to her key managers, instead of giving them pay increases. Is this a good idea, and what are the advantages and disadvantages? *(8 marks)*

Flow production

What is flow production?

Flow production means switching production methods so that there is a continuous movement of items through the production process. Each item in the production process moves from one stage to the next without interruption. One task is carried out and then the item is moved on to the next task straightaway. Each of the tasks takes the same amount of time, so that the flow of the items in the production process is not held up.

Flow production is often referred to as 'mass production' – the items being made are exactly the same in any production run. A production run means setting up the process so that any number of the same item can be made. For example, food processing factories use flow production. They can set up the production line to cope with different food products each time.

For example Food-processing factory

According to the season, a food processing factory may handle vegetables such as peas. The fresh vegetables enter the production line, are washed and sorted, weighed and frozen, then poured into packaging ready for storage. The production line has to have a continuous supply of vegetables in order to be efficient. At the end of the production run (when all the peas have been processed), the production line is then set up to handle a different vegetable.

Flow production is also used for a number of other high-volume products, such as cars or televisions. At each stage of production, either machines or workers carry out a task which contributes to the completion of the product. The production line itself is continuously moving, allowing a few seconds or minutes at each task stage for the work to be carried out. Flow production is therefore ideal for high-volume products that are in constant demand by customers.

Mass production was created as a production technique in the early twentieth century by Ford, the car manufacturer. They introduced electric motors to make the conveyor belts move along their production line, to keep the cars moving through the factories. Little by little, the cars were made by dropping in the engines, fitting the doors and wheels and so on. In this way, the production could be very efficient. Each worker would carry out a single task, becoming extremely expert at it (and fast). This method is also known as **assembly line production**, where each worker or machine carries out a simple repetitive task, which means that high **throughput** and continuous flow production can be maintained by the business.

Why is it more efficient?

Flow production is considered to be more efficient than job or batch production, because large quantities of products can be created, as long as they are simplified or standardised. The workforce only needs to be semi-skilled rather than highly trained. This cuts down on wage and training costs. Many of the processes can be automated, using robots, simple machines and other mechanical devices.

It does mean that the business needs to have a stock of components and raw materials ready to enter the production line, otherwise the production line will have to be stopped until they are available.

The key advantages are the high use of machinery instead of employees, which means that large numbers of units can be produced at a relatively low cost. The production line can run day and night, only stopping for servicing and checking now and then.

The main disadvantage is that it is costly to change the production process. Machines have to be changed or moved around, so flow production is not as flexible as some other methods of production. Products therefore have to be fairly similar, but certain features can be changed to suit the specific needs of the customer.

KEY TERMS

Assembly line production ▶ a manufacturing process in which parts are added to a product in sequence, usually on a slow but continually moving conveyor belt.

Throughput ▶ the rate at which the production system generates finished products.

For example
Car production line

On a car production line, the business may be making the same model of car, but it can produce them in different colours, with different engines and different numbers of doors, and can switch from estate cars to standard cars without a problem. Optional extras can also be added. Some stages of the production process can be skipped for basic models; other stages can be added for special models.

Mass production is expensive to set up. It is therefore very capital intensive and energy intensive. Capital intensive means that a large investment needs to be made in order to build the production line and the machinery needed to run the flow production. As machines are being run all the time, the energy use is intensive and the costs are high.

Capital intensive also means that machines are more important – and a bigger investment – than the employees working on the production line. Wherever possible, tasks are automated (machines do it). Labour costs are lower, production rates are higher and the cost to make each unit is lower.

Mass production is used only when the business is sure that there will be a long-term high demand for the product. Initial costs are high, and it may take the business some time to cover these costs. But the profits are better in the long term.

QUESTION TIME
22 minutes

The confectionery manufacturer Cadbury runs its production line 24 hours a day, seven days a week. It only stops the line on Christmas Day.

The business uses flow production to efficiently make hundreds of thousands of exactly the same product. Then the production line is set up differently, so that a different product can be made.

A prime example of a product made by Cadbury using automated flow production is the Creme Egg. Melted chocolate is poured into half-egg moulds. The moulds then move down the line and are filled up with the egg white. They are then moved on to the part of the line where the egg yolk is added, then on again to where the tops of the eggs are attached. At the end of the production line, the eggs are wrapped and packed.

1 Cadbury uses flow production. What does this term mean? *(2 marks)*

2 Why might Cadbury use automated flow production to make its Creme Eggs instead of another method of production? *(4 marks)*

3 In each 12-hour shift, 600,000 Creme Eggs are made – a rate of 320 per minute. But there is only enough packaging in the factory for two to three days of production. Why might this be the case? *(4 marks)*

4 What disadvantages may flow production have for Cadbury? *(6 marks)*

5 Batch production is also used in the factory. It is used to make products that are similar, but not quite the same. Different flavours of the same product are an ideal example. Why might batch production also be useful if the business were unsure how big a market might be for a product? *(6 marks)*

205

Efficient production methods

YOU WILL FIND OUT:
- what specialisation is
- what division of labour is
- about improvements in efficiency

What is specialisation?

Specialisation can refer to either a manufacturing organisation or particular elements within the business which aim to deal with a single product or service. Many businesses seek to specialise in a number of different areas.

One of the major ways to achieve specialisation is to create a plant-within-a-plant (PWP). Specialisation can take place in a PWP, while other parts of the manufacturing facility can deal with more standardised products and services. It gives the business the opportunity to begin adapting and providing a manufacturing base for a wider variety of different products or services.

A PWP is often referred to as a 'microfactory'. A microfactory can also be a completely separate facility (not a PWP), located close to customers and set up to fulfil their immediate needs.

What is division of labour?

The term 'division of labour' refers to a strict allocation of work responsibilities.

Before the introduction of automated production lines or flow production methods, skilled employees were given specific job roles. Because of the complexity of their work, it was difficult to give those particular roles to individuals who did not have the same degree of skill. Equally, the skilled individuals were keen to avoid any moves by the management to de-skill their work. This would undermine their position and their pay. Division of labour therefore became a system by which different employees within

a manufacturing business could be identified and paid in different ways.

As the process of multi-skilling has swept manufacturing, coupled with the introduction of more complex technology, many of these former divisions have either disappeared or become blurred. Nonetheless, division of labour can still be seen as an example of specific groups or teams of employees being allocated specific roles that only those individuals carry out.

De-skilling

De-skilling is the process by which division of labour and technological development leads to the reduction of the scope of an employee's specialised tasks. Work becomes broken up and employees lose the skills and knowledge associated with a craftsperson. De-skilling has been seen as a negative impact of technology. It is also seen as a process where a machine can perform a task better than the human hand.

De-skilling involves:

- the maximum breaking up of the labour process as a series of work tasks across the production process
- the minimisation of skill in any work task
- the creation of standardised products
- the use of specialised machine tools (as opposed to general-purpose machine tools)
- the use of the assembly line and methods of continuous production (at a pace set by management and not by the workforce).

Improvements in efficiency

The term 'multi-skilling' relates to the incorporation of a higher level of flexibility into the various job roles across the business. This usually takes place in activities requiring unskilled labour to skilled or technical expertise.

The idea is to create a more flexible workforce and to sweep away any boundaries between different types of work that used to rely on specialised skills. It does require additional training, and can be achieved by the business encouraging job rotation and bringing about other changes to job roles.

The newly multi-skilled employees would also have to be prepared to work at their newly acquired skills and follow training or retraining programmes in order to do so. Commonly, trained employees assist with the retraining of those going through the multi-skilling process.

There are advantages and disadvantages to multi-skilling:

ADVANTAGES

- An organisation can introduce new equipment and working methods quickly
- The employees improve their overall level of skills and knowledge
- All the organisation's resources are used to their full potential
- The employees can contribute more effectively and to their full potential in meeting the organisation's objectives

DISADVANTAGES

- Labour turnover can increase, as employees become more skilled
- The costs of training and retraining programmes can be high
- There could be shortages in particular groups as individuals move around, affecting the way the group might perform in the longer term
- Managers tend not to be involved in the multi-skilling process. The managers often remain rigid in their views of the tasks they should perform
- Employees do not always gain job satisfaction, particularly if they are not involved in tasks they were initially trained to do

The introduction of multi-skilling can affect an employee in more ways than just their work situation. It may spill over into their domestic life, particularly if their extended role involves irregular work hours. However, employees could find that their job satisfaction is increased, because they are no longer so strictly supervised or controlled.

A plant-within-a-plant (PWP) is a manufacturing process concept that sets aside specific areas of the facility for dedicated methods of production or specialisms in the production of parts, components or products.

Each PWP not only has its own location, but may also have its own management and systems.

PWPs also adopt their own strategies, and cooperate with other PWPs, although they are mainly concerned with the continuous improvement of their own facility.

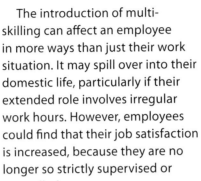

Lloyds TSB

QUESTION TIME
18 minutes

Some businesses, like Lloyds TSB, believe that Britain is being de-skilled. In late 2008, Lloyds TSB announced that two-thirds of all of its ICT work was going to move to India. The main reason given was the lack of skilled ICT graduates in Britain.

In fact, there are fewer ICT graduates in Britain than there were in 1996, the reason being the lack of suitable jobs. Also, if an ICT graduate is out of work for more than 18 months, their skills become out of date.

207

1 Define the term 'specialisation'. *(2 marks)*

2 Identify and explain TWO areas of specialisation for Lloyds TSB. *(4 marks)*

3 Lloyds TSB believes that Britain is being de-skilled. What does this mean? *(4 marks)*

4 Why might a business have to go abroad to find properly skilled workers? *(4 marks)*

5 Why might the skills of an ICT worker in particular become out of date very quickly, if they have not been in work? *(4 marks)*

Lean production techniques

What is lean production?

Lean production aims to reduce waste, while ensuring quality. It is a Japanese management approach that can be applied to all parts of a business – from designing a product, through to its production and distribution.

The idea is that the business can cut out unnecessary costs by making the business as efficient as possible. The process aims to cut out any activity that does not **add value** to the production process. This can involve:

- reducing the amount of stock held by the business
- reducing the unnecessary movement of machinery
- reducing stock and people
- cutting down on other activities.

Using lean production

Probably the most common type of lean production used by businesses is known as 'Just-In-Time' production.

When an order comes in for a particular product, the order itself acts as a signal for the business to begin production of that product. In response to the demand for the product, the business sets in motion the necessary steps to make the exact quantity of that product and to have it ready when the customer expects it to be delivered.

The business keeps its stocks of raw materials, components, part-finished products (work in progress) and finished products to an absolute minimum. This cuts down on costs associated with storing these items and the money tied up in these items, which have not yet been sold.

The business needs to be very efficient at sorting out the production processes needed for all customer orders. Everything has to be planned and scheduled. Often, a business will use computer software to help it plan the production for each period of time and to make sure that it orders in the right levels of raw materials and components from its supplier, exactly when they are needed.

Often, the business uses **Electronic Data Interchange** (EDI) to share information with suppliers and customers, so that everyone is aware of the progress of the order and what to expect (and what to do).

For example Lean production

A bakery buys in sacks of corn. It adds value to the corn (making it worth more), by milling it and transforming it into flour. It adds more value to the corn by combining it with other ingredients and baking loaves of bread. The corn has been transformed by the processes into another product, which is worth significantly more than it was worth when it was purchased by the business as a raw material. The business, through its activities, has added value to the corn. This added value is a vital component of the profit that the business will make.

For example Using lean production

A business receives an order for 1,000 products from a customer. Automatically, the business's software checks the stock levels of finished goods, raw materials and components to find out whether the business has enough finished goods to send out straightaway, or whether it needs to begin production to make them.

If there are insufficient raw materials and components in stock, the suppliers are contacted using EDI to order the necessary stock.

Again through EDI, the supplier confirms whether it has the stock ready to send or whether there will be a delay. After this has been done, the manufacturer can contact the customer and confirm the order and the expected delivery date.

KEY TERMS

Add value ▶ a term that describes any activity carried out by the business that increases the actual value of the products or services that it handles. To increase in value.

Electronic Data Interchange (EDI) ▶ a process that allows the automatic digital sharing of information between companies.

The suppliers will deliver the necessary components or raw materials for the production line as they are needed. In order to keep the production lines going, the suppliers may deliver on a regular basis and only deliver what is immediately needed. The manufacturer does not have to build up stocks of the components or raw materials, instead relying on the supplier to deliver them 'just in time'.

The following tables look at the key advantages and disadvantages of Just-In-Time production:

ADVANTAGES

- Holding less stock means that the manufacturer does not need bigger premises for storage space, so rent, rates and insurance costs are lower
- As the manufacturer only receives stock when it is needed, less money (working capital) is tied up in stock
- Suppliers supply the latest version of the component or raw material. This is particularly important if the materials or components used by the manufacturer might be out of date or perishable stock (such as food materials)
- The manufacturer does not find itself building up a supply of unsold finished products that it cannot sell. It is only making the amount of products that have actually been ordered by customers
- If the manufacturer can ensure that the quality is maintained in production, there is little chance that they will be producing sub-standard or faulty products. As stock is not being held, there is little chance that the products will be damaged in storage

DISADVANTAGES

- There are big problems if mistakes are made in ordering components or raw materials or in the production of the products
- As minimum stocks are held of raw materials, components or part-finished products, if something goes wrong and a whole batch of products is faulty, this could be a major problem. New supplies will have to be ordered in
- The process is only as good as the reliability of the suppliers. If they are unreliable and unwilling to work with the manufacturer, then the system of production is doomed to fail
- If there is a sudden shortage of anything needed for production, the orders will be delayed
- If there is an unexpected order, the business needs to be able to respond straightaway, as all its production is geared up to provide products for actual orders

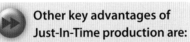 Other key advantages of Just-In-Time production are:

- Set-up times are significantly reduced.
- The flow of goods from suppliers through the manufacturer to the customer are improved.
- Employees gain multiple skills, as they are expected to work on a variety of different products.
- Scheduling of orders and production allows for the better use of employees.
- The relationship with suppliers is more like a partnership.

QUESTION TIME
19 minutes

Autoglym Ltd produces a range of vehicle care products at its factory in Letchworth. In recent years, it has brought in a series of lean manufacturing techniques to improve its production methods.

Its major product, *Life Shine*, is a car-care kit with 20 different components. The right number of components need to be ready for use at the right time, rather than having piles of components stored in the warehouse awaiting retrieval.

Using the new systems, *Life Shine* can be assembled in half the time. The business believes that this has meant a saving of around £100,000 per year. Lead times are shorter and delivery dates are more accurate too.

Source: adapted from www.autoglym.com

1 Define the term 'lean production'. *(2 marks)*

2 What type of system has been introduced by Autoglym Ltd? *(2 marks)*

3 What might be meant by the term 'lead time'? *(2 marks)*

4 Did Autoglym Ltd make the right decision in introducing the system identified in your answer to question 2? *(9 marks)*

5 What are the benefits to customers? *(4 marks)*

209

Is growth a problem?

The challenges of growth

All growing businesses face challenges. New problems arise and new solutions have to be worked out. What may have worked in the past when the business was small may not work now that is larger. Mistakes can be made. This could mean that the business fails, as it has grown too complicated for the owners to manage. They simply do not have the skills to deal with the problems.

If the business is to continue to grow and survive (and to be profitable), it needs to have effective leadership and direction. It needs to make the most of opportunities as they come up, so that it can sustain its growth and survive during difficult times.

To ensure continuous business growth and success, the business needs a stable environment and the confidence of its stakeholders. These stakeholders include customers, investors, employees, suppliers and the wider community.

Stakeholder expectations

The table above summarises a business's responsibilities towards its stakeholders.

Customer confidence

Businesses also need to be aware of changes in consumer spending and confidence. Generally, households respond to fears of higher unemployment and economic slowdowns by spending less, particularly on luxury items such as cars or home improvements. Households save money or find they need to use it for necessities. On the other hand, when the economy is doing well and

STAKEHOLDERS	BUSINESS'S RESPONSIBILITIES
Shareholders	• Being open in all communications • Providing a reasonable return to shareholders, while protecting their original investment
Employees	• Creating employment and development opportunities • Giving confidence to employees • Investing in employees as a vital human resource
Customers	• Developing and maintaining long-term relationships with customers • Offering high-quality services and value for money • Being open and fair towards customers, in terms of standards of behaviour • Fulfilling legal requirements and regulations
Suppliers	• Building mutually beneficial relationships with suppliers and other businesses • Ensuring value for money, increasing efficiency and eliminating waste
The community	• Contributing to and participating in local communities where the business operates • Developing business, local recruitment and the retention of employees • Taking responsibility for the environment in terms of energy use (including costs of distribution), recycling and optimising disposable materials

people are confident about their job security, they are willing to take the risk and borrow more in order to purchase luxury items.

It is not only businesses that are concerned with these changes in consumer confidence and spending. The Bank of England, which sets the interest rates, looks carefully at consumer confidence. From their assessment, they can estimate future demand for products and services and adjust the interest rates accordingly, either to increase confidence (by reducing interest rates) or to reduce overspending (by increasing interest rates).

Consumer confidence, therefore, is affected by:

• **the interest rate and mortgage rates** – increases mean that households have less available income

• **changes in general unemployment and individuals' job security** – worries about jobs cause households to save more and spend less

• **inflation** – prices are increasing, possibly faster than income

• **changes in direct taxation (income tax) and indirect taxation (such as VAT)** – increases mean that households have less available income

• **the availability of lump sums** – such as profits from shares – might encourage households to spend.

Technology

With new technology developing fast, many businesses – particularly smaller ones – are finding it is having an impact on how they run their activities.

In order to take full advantage of technological developments, in addition to keeping up with their larger competitors, businesses have to change their way of working. The business's managers have to realise the potential of the technological changes, particularly in smaller organisations where there may be fewer staff experienced in the use of IT.

Larger businesses, however, are finding that the role of their IT staff is changing. These individuals are required more and more to become involved in other areas and the needs of the business as a whole, such as finance and general management. In addition, many businesses are no longer employing specialist IT staff, but are **outsourcing** these skills.

Why can growth be a problem?

Growth does present major challenges to a business. Many are not geared up to be able to cope with sudden increases in business activity and find it very difficult to cope.

One of the major problems is that smaller businesses have a tendency to respond to increases in activity as an emergency measure. They simply take on new employees, rent bigger premises or place bigger orders, without really thinking about the longer-term implications or planning.

It is not always possible for a business to carefully plan its growth and implement ready-prepared responses to increased business activity. Often they do not know (or cannot predict) the direction of the growth, the overall amount of growth and whether it is likely to continue (it may be a short-term growth period).

Larger businesses certainly have cost advantages over smaller businesses. This can be for a variety of reasons:

*   When buying more products and services from suppliers, businesses can demand better discounts and payment schedules.
*   They can adapt inefficient or costly areas of the business.
*   They can identify areas of business that simply do not work for them financially. They can drop certain products and services, and stop using suppliers that let them down.
*   By producing products and services on a larger scale than before, they can also enjoy cost benefits – they are far more efficient, using better-skilled employees and the latest technology or machinery.

—— **K E Y   T E R M** ——

Outsourcing ▶ using individuals or other businesses to carry out tasks previously undertaken by employees of the business.

QUESTION TIME
31 minutes

1 Identify TWO factors that are required for a business to continue to grow and survive. *(2 marks)*

2 Identify and explain TWO factors that can influence customer confidence with regard to spending on goods and services. *(6 marks)*

3 Why is it vital that businesses are aware of new technological opportunities? *(6 marks)*

4 Why might small businesses find growth more challenging than large ones? *(8 marks)*

5 Explain why stakeholder expectations are important to any size of business and why they may change over time. *(9 marks)*

211

⏩ Without doubt, the changing nature of information technology has had the greatest impact on businesses. The following major technological trends are gradually affecting nearly every business:

*   **the growth of e-commerce** – businesses have to learn the new technologies involved in selling and marketing on the Internet
*   **the trend towards remote working** – which has seen ever-increasing numbers of employees either working from home or in offices connected only to the main business by computer
*   **the trend towards using outsourcing** – this is particularly the case in IT and in customer services, where businesses have established these services abroad.

These trends, and others, mean that businesses need to be fully aware of technological changes in order to remain competitive. Businesses need to appreciate the potential of technological change. Certainly the vast majority of employees now need to be IT literate, in addition to having good writing and numeracy skills.

Growing pains

YOU WILL FIND OUT:

- about coping with growing pains
- about market research and cash-flow management
- about problem-solving
- about new systems, skills and attitudes

Coping with growing pains

Poor planning can be the main downfall for businesses. A business will need to make sure that it has researched the market and that it does not set its objectives too high. Any money spent during the growth phase of the business will need to show a return on that investment. This can take a considerable amount of time.

It is also vital that a business continues to look after its existing customers, while hunting for new ones. Competitors will always be looking for ways to take customers away from the business. If existing customers are ignored, or feel that they are not as valued as they have been in the past, then they may well be lost to the business. The business needs to maintain good levels of customer service, as well as regularly communicating with customers.

Poor control is often a major problem as the business grows. During growth, the relationship between a business's suppliers and customers can be placed under strain and will need to be controlled. A business will become more and more reliant on the ability of suppliers to respond to rapid changes in demand for stock, raw materials and other items. And it must not be preoccupied by the complications of growing, but needs continually to focus on its customers. At all levels, new controls may be necessary, particularly as the number and the value of assets owned by the business increase.

Employees and managers are also vitally important. It is essential that the business takes on the right people to carry out the increasingly complicated jobs. A business will

tend to spend more time and effort in the selection process; it will also invest more in making sure that new employees are fully trained at the earliest opportunity. Generally, management also needs to be aware of the fact that growth will place additional strain on employees. Communication and support are essential for telling employees what the business is trying to achieve and what will be expected of them.

For the owners of the business, the stresses and strains (along with the workload) will increase as the business grows. The business will become more complex, management will take longer. The owners need to look at what can be delegated and what needs their personal attention.

Market research

The conditions in which a business operates are continually changing. Market research is crucial to ensure that the business is not making decisions based on out-of-date information. As the business continues to grow, competitors will be more and more interested in what the business is doing. They will adapt and try to take customers from the business. Even loyal customers cannot be relied on; a competitor with a better deal may be too much of a temptation.

As products pass through their product life cycle, sales growth may slow and profits may drop. It is vital that the business understands where its products and services are in the life cycle in order to work out the best strategies. The business always needs to be thinking about bringing new and profitable products and services to the market.

For market research purposes, a business can use:

- published information, which may give clues about market conditions and trends
- key customers, suppliers and business partners, who may have important market information
- employees, who may have insights about customers and the market.

Cash-flow management

Cash-flow management is very important for any type of business at any stage, but for a growing one it is crucial. The business needs to make the best use of its resources. Each part of working capital needs to be controlled with effective credit management and tighter control over overdue debts.

Good stock control can help, as can better management of relationships with suppliers. Holding old and valueless stock may become a problem. Old stock needs to be sold off as soon as possible to free up funds.

One key decision for a growing business is whether to bring in outside investors to provide additional equity.

Problem-solving

New businesses can often work around problems and challenges by the management focusing in on the issue and **troubleshooting**. This is not really feasible as the business grows, as there are so many calls on the time and skills of the management. As a crisis looms, the management needs to consider whether the crisis is, in fact, more important than other tasks that still need to be done.

For example Handling complaints

One way to handle continual complaints from key customers about service and delivery is by focusing on the customer and smoothing out problems.

A better strategy may be to look at the reasons why there are problems, perhaps changing the recruiting process or bringing in training for employees.

New systems

A key driver in growth is about understanding how to prioritise. Instead of dealing with each problem as a one-off situation, it is better to set up systems and processes that make problems easier to deal with in the future.

Sustained growth cannot be achieved without setting up the right systems (IT systems, paper-based systems or simply the processes) for recording financial information, dealing with customers, handling contracts and employees, and being aware of regulatory requirements.

Without a good management information system nothing will work in the long run. It will be impossible to allocate responsibilities and tasks to anyone. As the business grows, this becomes more and more of problem.

Policies, processes and procedures are vital, so investing in a good information system will bring enormous benefits to the business. It will also ensure that best practice is always adopted.

Changing skills and attitudes

Entrepreneurs may have created and grown the business. They have the abilities to launch a new business, but may not have the abilities to drive the business forward into the future. They may need to learn new skills and attitudes. They will need to delegate, trust others (and their decision-making), and give up personal control of many aspects of the business.

Specialists may need to be brought into the business to help out. It can be useful to take advice from experts, to gain insights and listen to suggestions that may be crucial to the longer-term success of the business.

KEY TERM

Troubleshooting ▶ a form of problem-solving, where a logical, systematic look at the problem aims to reveal how it can be solved.

A business plan that may have made sense a few years ago when the business was launched may not be working now. Business plans need to be constantly updated and strategies need to change to fit the circumstances.

Businesses recognise the fact that more profit and growth can be achieved by developing relationships with existing customers, rather than trying to gain new customers. New customers may increase the turnover of the business, but they may offer lower profit margins. Lower profit margins may not be sustainable over a long period of time.

However, new opportunities should always be sought, as there are risks associated with relying on the same customers. A growing business needs to diversify its customer base to spread out the risks.

Each major change in the business needs careful planning, as new developments bring new risks. It often does not pay to be too adventurous.

QUESTION TIME

26 minutes

Ray is always brimming with ideas. Single-handedly, he created and built up his new business and it now has a turnover of £1.2 million a year.

The trouble is that he never has any time to refine his ideas or to test them out. His days are filled with signing pieces of paper and dealing with suppliers, customers and employees. It's no fun anymore. He wants to get out.

1. **Why might Ray have got into this situation?** *(6 marks)*
2. **How might delegation enable Ray to find more time to focus on his ideas and test them out?** *(6 marks)*
3. **What problems may start to emerge for the business if Ray cannot get the right balance between which areas he should pay most attention to?** *(6 marks)*
4. **Would Ray be right in wanting to sell his business and move on to something new?** *(8 marks)*

Advantages and disadvantages of growth

YOU WILL FIND OUT:

- about keeping or losing control
- about changing how business is done
- about new stakeholders
- about strategic planning
- whether growth is desirable

Keeping or losing control

Adjusting to the challenges of growth can be very difficult. Each time a business grows, additional layers of complexity are added. If the business grows too quickly, everything could collapse – particularly if the owners are not ready for it.

At each stage of growth, the owners move further away from the day-to-day running of the business. Many owners simply have to accept that they will have to take a broader strategic role in order to maintain the general direction of the business. At the same time, they need to develop processes and policies to handle the new demands on the company and its management and employees.

Owners will find it impossible to run the business in the same way as they did when they started it. A larger business is far too complex. Trying to do everything will just mean that they will lose control over the business. So they will have to delegate, by building up a management structure that they trust and can rely on to make decisions on their behalf.

But the owners do not want to create a 'yes mentality', where managers simply make decisions that they think the owners will like. Managers need to be objective, to discuss ideas and look at opportunities as they arise. It is often said that if managers always agree, then it is time to change the management! They should always challenge one another.

It is important for a growing business not to place too much responsibility in the hands of a single manager. If that person were to leave to set up their own business, or to work for a competitor, then the business would have a huge gap in its management.

Changing how business is done

Although a business may not have to change its legal structure as it grows, the bigger it gets, the more important it is that it brings in, or maintains, discipline and professionalism in all its activities.

This may mean adopting:

- clear business terms
- standardised employee contracts
- strict internal guidelines (on issues such as petty cash, expenses, leave entitlements, dealing with customers and suppliers)
- credit-checking of new customers
- health and safety and employment law
- a human resource strategy.

New stakeholders

As a business grows, there will be new internal and external stakeholders in the business. New managers and employees are examples of internal stakeholders. New shareholders, investors or part-owners, new customers and suppliers are examples of external stakeholders.

All stakeholders will expect the business performance levels to continue or improve over time. New budgets and forecasts will be set, and will need to be met or bettered. The different stakeholder groups will want to see regular reports and updates on progress and performance. They will also expect the management to be able to cope with any risks arising, and to take advantage of any new opportunities.

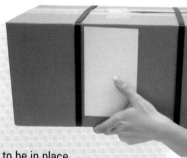

For example Scalability

If a business was dealing with 40–50 orders per day and had to package them up and get them posted, then this may have been easily achievable without a great deal of organisation.

If the business has grown and now sends out 400–500 packages a day, new systems need to be in place to make sure that orders are dealt with efficiently. This may mean new processes, a new invoicing system, checking processes and a host of other considerations.

Above all, the new processes need to be 'scalable' (able to be scaled up). This means that they need to be able to work for 400 orders or 4,000 orders a day, otherwise a new system will have to be created each time the level of sales increases.

Strategic planning

Businesses tend to grow in short, concentrated bursts, stabilising their position in between. Managing this type of growth is essential to ensure that the business is able to take advantage of the next potential growth spurt, having adapted to the new conditions that arose from the last.

Clear strategies and tactics have to be adopted and a growth plan created. Typically, this may mean identifying:

- where the next growth opportunity may come from (through new markets, new customers, new products or services, or by buying a competitor)
- when the next growth period may begin, by carrying out market research and keeping a close eye on trends and developments
- the funding that will be needed and where it will come from to finance the growth period
- whether the growth period will have an impact on the cash flow, the revenues and the profits of the business, and whether these will be good or bad
- whether the business will need to reorganise to take advantage of the growth
- whether there are employees or managers who can be relied upon to take the lead in the growth period and responsibility for steering the business through it
- how the business intends to retain its key employees, so that they are in place to assist (maybe by looking at the pay and benefits of employees)
- whether there are any skills gaps in the business and how these can be filled (through recruitment or training)
- whether the business needs to invest in machinery, equipment or IT before the growth period, to be sure that it is ready.

Is growth desirable?

As a business grows in terms of its turnover, levels of activity and, hopefully, its profits, it will become more difficult to manage and control. Everything will become more complicated – from simple communication with employees and customers to the complexities of the production of products and the range of services, to the implications of any decisions that may have to be made.

For some business owners, growing is not desirable; they are happy to operate at the same level, as they have the opportunity to involve themselves in all aspects of the business and can maintain control over what they have created. Some owners, however, view growth as a new challenge and are happy to bring others in and to delegate, accepting that they will lose some control. Others will decide to walk away, sell their business and start all over again – for them the challenge and excitement is in the creation of a business, not the day-to-day grind of running one.

QUESTION TIME
25 minutes

A business has trebled its income in the last year. It has doubled the number of its employees and has five times as many customers as it had last year. Its costs are four times higher and profits are just a fifth of last year's level.

1 Identify and explain ONE problem of growth. *(2 marks)*

2 Is the business doing well or is it in trouble? Explain your answer. *(8 marks)*

3 Suggest what this particular business is doing right or wrong. *(6 marks)*

4 Would the use of strategic planning be of assistance to this business? *(9 marks)*

215

⏩ Many business owners, as they see their businesses grow, look for a business mentor to give them an independent view of the situation. Usually this means finding someone who has the experience and knowledge to work as a non-executive director. There is always a pool of semi-retired professionals who can act as business mentors – someone who has been through the same processes in the past and may be able to give valuable and objective insights into the situation.

Non-executive directors do not have day-to-day departmental responsibilities. Rather, they operate as advisors, brought in to attend board meetings or to lead a new initiative or development.

Quality initiatives

YOU WILL FIND OUT:

- about quality assurance
- about quality assurance options
- about problems with quality initiatives

Quality assurance

Quality assurance means attempts by a business to assure that agreed quality standards are met throughout the business, primarily to ensure customer satisfaction.

The business will aim to achieve quality, consistency and satisfaction. But this is not always easy as the business grows. There are various quality initiatives that can be put in place to try to deal with this problem.

Quality assurance options

The key quality assurance options are summarised in the table on the right.

216

QUALITY INITIATIVE	EXPLANATION
Total Quality Management (TQM)	In TQM, every part of the business will consider quality issues – from design through to after-sales service. TQM is not just a management tool; the whole business needs to be committed to introducing and managing it. This is perhaps one of the most difficult of all of the quality systems to introduce and manage.
Continuous improvement	This is a Japanese technique, requiring the whole business to be committed to making small, gradual changes to improve the quality of products, employees, processes and services. Again, this needs to be an organisation-wide approach, but it is rather more gradual than TQM.
Benchmarking	Finding a suitable or relevant business to compare with is, perhaps, the first difficult task. The business needs to have a clear understanding of the best practices used by the organisation they are benchmarking themselves against. The business may discover that it is difficult to copy systems and procedures, particularly if the benchmarking business is not operating in the same industry.
Cross-functional improvement groups	These are **ad hoc groups**, which are set up in a business to investigate how the work between departments can be improved. Their main aim is to look at quality issues, improve efficiency and reduce costs. They need to be given the power and authority to investigate, implement and monitor initiatives.
Quality accreditation	To achieve **BSI accreditation**, a business needs to subject itself to an independent inspection and examination. Prior to this, it needs to have a documented quality assurance system. The business will need to ensure that this system extends across the whole business and, if relevant, encompasses the activities carried out on its behalf by subcontractors and suppliers.
Quality circles	Rather like cross-functional improvement groups, quality circles are groups of employees whose role it is to identify problems and recommend improvements to processes. They focus on quality issues and try to identify best practice to improve quality. Quality circles tap into the knowledge and experience of individuals involved in every stage of a production process. The quality circle needs to have the necessary power and authority to press management to incorporate its recommendations.
Training	Businesses can take two different views on training: they can bring in specific job-related training for new and existing employees that should focus on quality issues as a central part of the programme; and on a broader level, specific quality training programmes can be rolled out to the whole workforce. New employees need to be quickly adapted to the quality culture of the business and given a clear explanation of how this matches the key objectives of the organisation.
Zero defects	Like TQM, this requires business-wide commitment. Every employee needs to be part of the quality assurance system. The key aim is to produce products and services that have no faults and that do not present any particular problems. This may mean redesign, a fresh look at the production process or reconsidering any other aspect that could be detrimental to the quality of the products or services delivered.

KEY TERMS

Ad hoc groups ▶ groups set up to deal with a specific problem; they are not usually used to deal with broader issues.

BSI accreditation ▶ this is the British Standards Institution seal of approval for quality standards.

Focus on Quality

Problems with quality initiatives

Undoubtedly, businesses do benefit from the introduction of quality initiatives. However, quality initiatives are not without problems. Cost often inhibits a business in introducing them:

- Before, during and after the quality system has been introduced, inspection costs, either internally or by independent inspectors, could represent a significant cost or could potentially disrupt production.
- Once a quality system has been chosen, there are also training cost implications for both management and other employees.
- The business may also have to consider switching suppliers and purchasing higher-quality raw materials, components or finished goods.

- Many of the systems also need enhanced computer technology or improved production machinery.
- As the business transfers from one way of carrying out the production process to another, production can be interrupted – or at best disrupted – which could cost the business output and profit.

Quality initiatives take time to work. Short-term results may not be immediately apparent. For a time, the whole business will be affected by the introduction of the quality system. The results of training may not be clear until all management and employees have passed through the training programmes.

Businesses, particularly those that have shareholders, will be under pressure to show short-term results from the expenditure in bringing in quality systems. Shareholders are notoriously impatient and often cannot see beyond the short-term, even though quality initiatives require a longer-term view. The investment in the quality systems will mean a cost today, but the benefits may be two, three or even five years down the line. Even when the benefits show themselves in the business's financial performance, they may be difficult to measure, or it may not be possible to state that the quality initiative was responsible.

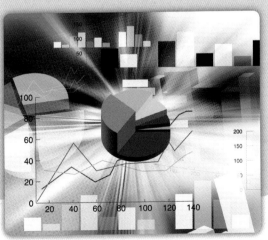

QUESTION TIME
18 minutes

Hannah is a Quality Assurance Manager. She coordinates the activities required to meet quality standards – monitoring and advising on the performance, and measuring it against standards. Hannah works with managers and employees to make sure that the system is working, and advises on changes, training and techniques.

As maintaining quality requires the business to adapt to customer expectations, Hannah uses a wide range of measures to place quality at the centre of the business. These include management systems, approaches such as Total Quality Management, and methodologies such as continuous improvement.

1 What do you understand by the term Total Quality Management? *(4 marks)*

2 What is Continuous Improvement? *(4 marks)*

3 How might the role of a quality assurance manager be difficult at times? *(4 marks)*

4 What problems may a business encounter with the introduction of quality initiatives? *(6 marks)*

217

Identifying quality problems

YOU WILL FIND OUT:

- why quality control is important
- about quality control problems
- about the four stages of quality control

Why is quality control important?

Quality can be a major factor in customers making a purchasing decision in favour of the business. In this respect, quality is an important competitive factor. However, quality levels and the importance of quality depend on how competitive the market is, and to what extent quality plays a part in a purchasing decision.

Having a strong reputation for high-quality products is advantageous for the following reasons:

- It will be easier to establish a new product in the market.
- Customers are more likely to make repeat purchases.
- The product will have a longer **product life cycle**.
- It allows the business to build up a range of products or **brands**.
- It allows the business to charge a higher price for the product, thus generating higher profits.
- Stockists are more likely to want to purchase the product.
- There should be some savings in advertising costs, because the product is instantly recognisable.

If a business, a product or a service is tainted with negative views on quality, then there could be severe implications for the business:

- The business may lose sales and reputation.
- It may have to discount the products.
- The poor-quality image may impact on other products and services offered by the business.
- Retailers may be unwilling to stock the products.

- Customers would be less likely to make repeat purchases.
- If the business has to recall the products, then these will have to be reworked, leading to higher costs in labour and materials.

Quality control problems

Quality control, therefore, means that a minimum quality level needs to be established and maintained by the business.

The first problem, however, is to recognise where quality issues could emerge and to intercept them before the products or services reach the customer:

- The traditional method is to inspect finished goods before they are sent out to customers. It may not be possible to inspect every single product, but a sample of products can be inspected.
- Some businesses use self-inspection by employees who have manufactured the product. This is an important and effective way of carrying out quality control, as it reinforces to all employees the importance of quality.
- Machine checking of quality standards can also be established, particularly in factories where flow production is used. Machinery can be set to measure particular specifications and to alert the operators if a particular product does not meet the specification standards required.

If quality control fails, and products of insufficient quality do reach the market, then it is usually feedback from customers (via complaints

and returned goods) that alerts the business to the quality control problem. It is important that any specific fault or problem with a batch of products is fed back to the manufacturer, so that additional quality control checks can be brought in to prevent it happening again.

Businesses may also use market research to establish whether customers perceive there to be quality problems with a particular product or service. They can also use market research to gauge customers' views of competitors' products and services, and ascertain whether there are any major differences.

The four stages of quality control

For most businesses, quality control is not only about the product itself, but also about any service aspects related to that product. Mechanical fault-checking may pick up faults in products, but it cannot be used to check services.

Most businesses have a broader view of quality control, which falls into four main stages, as can be seen in the table on the opposite page.

KEY TERMS

Product life cycle ▶ the stages through which all products pass, from their development stage to their final decline and withdrawal from sale.

Brand ▶ a recognisable name or logo that is legally protected by the business. A brand name helps customers instantly recognise and identify a product.

218

QUALITY CONTROL STAGE	EXPLANATION
Prevention	This first stage tries to prevent problems from happening in the first place. Even when a product is initially designed, it is checked for its reliability and features, and steps are taken to ensure that the way that it is going to be produced is unlikely to give rise to a high percentage of production errors.
Detection	This means checking that there are no quality problems before the product reaches the customer. Businesses have tended to make detection of quality problems the responsibility of all employees, backed up with computer-aided statistical analysis and other tools to help detect faults.
Correction	A business will want to know why there is a particular problem and what steps need to be taken to ensure that the faults do not recur. This goes beyond simply repairing known faults to products that have already been distributed.
Improvement	Customers have a continually increasing expectation regarding the quality levels of products and services that they purchase. Businesses will at least wish to remain ahead of customer expectations. Often they wish to delight or surprise customers with the level of quality, so that it exceeds customer expectations.

Any business will find it difficult to produce products or services of a consistently high standard if it does not invest in its employees. Employees need a broad range of skills and qualities, which can be achieved through an effective training and development programme. Training also needs to be forward-looking. The workforce will have a level of skills and capabilities, but these may not be sufficient for the business to be able to meet its objectives or maintain and eventually improve its quality standards in the future.

Continuous improvement (or 'Kaizen' as it is also known – see page 107) demands gradual steps to be taken by the business to improve its quality standards. Training can be used to achieve this, particularly if employees are empowered to make their own decisions as members of teams. They can be encouraged to problem-solve and to tackle quality issues.

Clearly, training is not a quick-fix solution to bringing in high-quality standards across the business. It takes time for employees to adapt to their new work roles and to recognise that quality standards can be achieved gradually, by coming up with solutions to each problem as it arises.

QUESTION TIME
24 minutes

1 List SIX possible implications for a business that has a poor product or service quality. *(6 marks)*

2 Why might self-inspection motivate employees? *(2 marks)*

3 Identify and explain the FOUR stages of quality control. *(8 marks)*

4 A business that is not willing to invest in its employees cannot produce goods or services of a consistently high standard. Do you agree with this statement? *(8 marks)*

219

Methods of maintaining consistent quality

YOU WILL FIND OUT:

● about Total Quality Management (TQM)

● about quality circles

● about benchmarking

● about continuous improvement

● about commitment to quality

Total Quality Management

The concept of Total Quality Management (TQM) was introduced by W Edwards Deming in the 1980s. Deming worked with Japanese manufacturers. He developed TQM as a philosophy and a way of dealing with quality issues in Japan and elsewhere.

TQM requires every part of the business and all its employees to have a total commitment to quality control – from design through to after-sales service. TQM describes the idea of 'building quality in', rather than 'inspecting it out'.

Every employee is encouraged to think about how customers need to be satisfied. Major British businesses, such as Tesco, have focused on TQM for many years. The idea is to delight customers with higher than expected levels of quality. One of the hopes is that delighted customers become the best advertisement for the business.

It is not just Japanese businesses that have incorporated Deming's ideas. British car manufacturers use TQM and encourage quality circles.

Quality circles

Quality circles are an integral part of the TQM process. Their focus is on increasing the participation of employees in quality issues.

A quality circle is a group of employees who meet on a regular basis to identify any problems and recommend solutions to the working or production process. The group is involved in continuous development,

quality control and improvement. It aims to contribute to the improvement and development of all projects, and focus on ensuring that human input into quality is as broad as possible.

The effectiveness of quality circles can be measured in three different ways:

- **quality improvements** – a reduction in defects or faults, wastage and customer complaints and returns
- **cost reductions** – a drop in the overall cost of manufacture, failure costs and cost of sales
- **employee attitudes** – a reduction in labour turnover, absentee rates, accidents and employee grievance.

A quality circle selects a problem, analyses it and then suggests a solution. They then present their ideas to relevant managers, who decide whether to implement the solution.

Benchmarking

Benchmarking involves comparing the business against the best practices exhibited by the competitors, or at least against those of leading businesses from other, similar industries. The purpose of benchmarking is to:

- discover how well the business is performing in comparison to other, similar businesses
- set a standard for the business that at least matches, or preferably exceeds, the best identified competitor or other business

- discover new ideas and ways of doing things that can then be put into practice by the business.

For example Xerox

In order to build its reputation in the photocopier market, Xerox pioneered the use of benchmarking in the production of its photocopiers. It looked at each stage of production, as well as the quality of the servicing it offered to customers. This gave Xerox a huge advantage over its competitors in the market.

Benchmarking can bring benefits to the business, as it can identify areas that require improvement and efficiency. It can also save the business money and time, as potential problems can be systematically identified and dealt with. It also allows the business to set itself clear targets.

Not everyone believes that benchmarking is the ideal answer: competitors might be reluctant to release information that could be of value to their rival; benchmarking could merely encourage a business to copy its competitors rather than innovate; or benchmarking could be just a paper exercise as, by identifying a problem, it does not necessarily follow that the business will be able, or willing, to do anything about it.

220

The Japanese vehicle manufacturer Toyota receives nearly three-quarters of a million suggestions from employees on improving quality each year. Around 99% of the ideas are incorporated. Toyota rewards employees who have made suitable suggestions by paying them anything from £2.50 to £1,000.

Continuous improvement

The Japanese call continuous improvement 'Kaizen'. It suggests that all employees should be involved in constant, ongoing improvements. The business needs to give employees the ability to use their talents to identify ways in which to maximise quality, at the lowest possible cost. The idea is to encourage employees to become involved and to create a culture of quality.

Commitment to quality

Quality issues can apply to products, services and processes – from the development of a new product or service through to the after-sales service provided to customers.

Introducing quality systems in a business is not straightforward; nor should it be expected to bring immediate results. It requires the commitment of both management and employees to establish quality control measures, as well as inspection. It may also mean major changes in the culture of the organisation.

Clearly, bringing in quality initiatives costs money and also takes time. The business needs to be assured that these costs and potential disruption to production will bring positive benefits in the future. As we have seen, there are various different ways in which quality systems can be configured. Businesses will adopt one or more initiatives to tackle any quality problems.

> Much of Japan had been levelled by Allied bombing during World War Two. It needed to rebuild its industry. In 1950, W Edwards Deming visited Japan and lectured on quality issues.
> Before Deming, businesses believed that inspection was the key to quality but that quality control cost money. Regardless of quality, businesses would buy from the cheapest supplier and, in order to get the best deals, would play suppliers off against one another.
> Deming suggested that if a business produced defect-free products, then inspection would no longer be necessary. Rather than considering quality control as a cost, it should be seen to increase profits. He also believed that businesses should always work with their suppliers, and only buy from those that were committed to quality. Above all, he did not believe that quality came from quality control; instead it came from the commitment of all of management to quality.

QUESTION TIME
28 minutes

1 Explain TQM, benchmarking and quality circles. (6 marks)

2 What does the term 'Kaizen' mean? (4 marks)

3 Why might a business decide it is necessary to bring in TQM? What are the costs and benefits to the business? (8 marks)

4 What is ONE advantage and ONE disadvantage of benchmarking? (6 marks)

5 Identify and explain TWO ways in which a business can identify whether the use of quality circles has been successful. (4 marks)

What have you learnt?

Operations management is the final part of Unit 2 (Growing as a business). In it we looked at how a business can organise itself to produce products or provide services. We also saw that there are other production methods in addition to the ones we looked at in Unit 1. Of particular importance are the concepts of efficiency and quality assurance, both vital considerations for a growing business.

We have looked at:

- new types of production methods and how a growing business may need to consider specialisation and division of labour and how these affect efficiency
- particular methods used by businesses to improve efficiency, such as lean production techniques

- the challenges facing a business that is enjoying growth. Clearly, there are both advantages and disadvantages to growth. They represent challenges to a business, and the owners and management need to be able to adapt to these changes to ensure continued growth, success and profitability
- the ways in which businesses can try to maintain their levels of quality as they grow. Particular problems are consistency, maintaining the quality of products and services, and how a business can use concepts such as Total Quality Management to achieve this.

The 'Question time' exercises in this section will have shown you the types of questions that you are likely to come across in the examination for Unit 2. We have maintained the mark-a-minute system to help you prepare fully to achieve those marks that you will need for a good grade.

Your teacher or tutor will be able to give you a copy of the 'Unit Revision Pack' from the *Teacher Support Pack*. It has some great revision ideas and also has a complete mock examination paper.

Integrated questions from Sections 1–5

Try these exam-style questions. They now cover all sections of Unit 2. This is not a real business situation, but it is a typical one.

222

MARTIN AND DONALD'S RESPRAY BUSINESS

Martin opened his car respray business five years ago. To begin with, he operated as a sole trader. Then he employed his friend Donald, and they soon had a great reputation, with customers coming to their workshop from an increasingly wide area.

Martin rewarded Donald for his hard work by offering him a partnership, which Donald accepted. Now they need more money to continue to expand. The company has current assets of £22,000, stock is relatively low at just £2,000 but their current liabilities are £18,000.

Martin and Donald took on their first three employees a month ago, but have done no paperwork and are just paying them an hourly rate minus deductions.

Donald wants to change the way the business works. Currently, whoever is available when a job comes in sees it through from start to finish, but this means that other things are building up.

They are about 20% cheaper than their local rivals and Martin thinks this is having an impact on their profits.

They run an advertisement in the local newspaper every week, but they have not bothered to change it for six months. It seems to be working though.

QUESTIONS
58 minutes

1 What problems has the respray business faced as it has grown? *(4 marks)*

2 Calculate the acid test ratio and comment on it accordingly. *(5 marks)*

3 The business has a turnover of £186,000 a year. Advise Martin and Donald whether they should remain as a partnership or form another type of identified legal structure. *(10 marks)*

4 What paperwork and systems should the business have brought in, now that it is employing people? *(4 marks)*

5 Advise Martin and Donald on whether they should continue to have employees skilled in all areas of the respray work, or focus their skills on specific areas of the activity. *(8 marks)*

6 What pricing strategy do Martin and Donald currently use? *(3 marks)*

7 What factors should they take into consideration before deciding whether to alter the price or not? *(6 marks)*

8 Advise Martin and Donald on whether their current promotion strategy should be reviewed or not. *(8 marks)*

9 Recommend to Martin and Donald how the work handled should be reorganised. They want to know the advantages and disadvantages of the solutions proposed, along with why the chosen one(s) should be followed. *(10 marks)*

Written paper

Time allowed: 1 hour

The marks for each question are shown in brackets. The maximum mark for the paper is 60. You need to use good, clear English. Quality of written communication will be assessed in questions 2(c), 3(b) and 4(d).

QUESTION 1

Read Item A, then answer the questions that follow.
Total for this question: *14 marks*

Item A

Variety Produce Plc is a regional chain of medium-sized supermarkets operating within the M25 area. It has grown quickly over the past 10 years, first by buying out Quickshop, a chain of 19 stores, and then by joining forces with Frost Organic Foods. Two years ago the company was floated.

The business prides itself on 'honest quality convenience'. It now has 33 stores, although it is considering closing two of them as they are too close to other stores in the chain. It aims to open five stores a year for the next 10 years.

1 (a) So far, how has the chain managed to grow as fast as it has? Explain your answer. (5 marks)

(b) What is meant by the term 'float'? (2 marks)

(c) (i) Identify what the business's slogan is called in business terms. (2 marks)

(c) (ii) What advantages would the business have enjoyed by becoming a Plc? (5 marks)

QUESTION 2

Read Item B, then answer the questions that follow.
Total for this question: *19 marks*

Item B

At this year's shareholders' meeting of Variety Produce Plc, several major shareholders expressed a concern that the business's name sounds too old-fashioned. The Toure family are still major shareholders and take an active part in the day-to-day running of the business. They promised to look into options to change the name and re-launch as a new brand.

Concerns were also raised that the business does not sell frozen products, only fresh and organic. They believed that this was putting them at a major disadvantage against the competition.

Finally, a suggestion was made to broaden the product range and drop prices to attract more customers, and also, perhaps, to introduce a customer loyalty card.

2 (a) How might the business test out new company names and how might it launch a new name? *(5 marks)*

(b) The business has a limited product portfolio. What might be the advantages and disadvantages of broadening this portfolio? *(5 marks)*

(c) Price-cutting and offering customer incentives have never been used by the business before. Taking the role of a marketing expert, briefly explain to the Board the implications of adopting these marketing initiatives. *(9 marks)*

224

QUESTION 3

Read Item C, then answer the questions that follow.
Total for this question: *11 marks*

Item C

Each of the supermarkets in the Variety Produce Plc chain has a fairly flat organisational structure. Each store manager is responsible for recruiting and selecting their own employees, but job roles across the whole chain, including those based at the Head Office, are handled by the HR director.

The business has a training budget and each store manager has to bid for a part of that budget, explaining why it should be allocated to them.

Each employee, after working for the business for a year, is entitled to a small percentage of the profit of the store. This small percentage increases every two years.

3 (a) Explain what is meant by the term 'a flat organisational structure'. *(2 marks)*

(b) The HR director is unsure whether the current way of allocating money for training and rewarding employees is working because, on average, 10% of the stores' workforce is leaving and having to be replaced every month. Suggest how recruitment, training and retention could be improved in this business. *(9 marks)*

QUESTION 4

Read Item D, then answer the questions that follow.
Total for this question: *16 marks*

Item D

Variety Produce Plc's finance director has selected the Haringey store as the typical store and has extracted the following financial data:

	2010	2009
Sales revenue	£32m	£29m
Gross profit	£14m	£16m
Net profit	£6m	£5m

4 (a) Using the data provided in Item D, calculate the increase in sales revenue between 2009 and 2010 for the Haringey store. *(2 marks)*

(b) Calculate the percentage change in the sales revenue. *(2 marks)*

(c) Using Item D, calculate the net profit margin for the Haringey store for 2010. Show your workings. The formula is:

$$\text{Net profit margin} = \frac{\text{Net profit}}{\text{Sales revenue}} \times 100\%$$

(3 marks)

(d) If the Haringey store is typical, then, using these figures as a basis, discuss whether you think the business is performing better in 2010 than in 2009, and explain why. *(9 marks)*

Introduction to controlled assessments

What is a controlled assessment unit?

Unit 3 (Investigating businesses) is a controlled assessment unit. This means that it is an internally assessed unit. However, AQA (the awarding body for this GCSE) determines the tasks that are set, how you do them (when, where and how you are supervised) and how the work you produce is marked.

The good news is that the controlled assessment is rather like coursework. The big difference is that the work you do for this unit is more supervised and you have a limited amount of time to do it. The Unit 3 controlled assessment is based completely on the topics that you covered in Unit 1 (Setting up a business).

Every year, AQA will release a controlled assessment well ahead of the time when you might be expected to do it, so it will give you plenty of thinking time. You might well do the controlled assessment straight after Unit 1, so that all the information that provides the background for the tasks will still be fresh in your mind.

Each controlled assessment consists of:

*   a very brief scenario, which sets the scene and gives you a focus for the tasks
*   a series of research and planning tasks. Each task details what is expected of you
*   a section that tells you what AQA expects you to include in your final presentation.

The important thing to remember is that you will have a limited amount of time to prepare, research, plan and write up your final presentation. AQA refers to your final presentation as 'your findings'.

What will I have to do?

Basically, you will have to carry out a business investigation of some sort. There is a series of key tasks that require you to collect information, sort that information and then use it for your final presentation. It is very important to evaluate your findings (see below). By studying the relevant sections of Unit 1, you will already have covered the tasks in the research and planning section of the controlled assessment.

You will be given between five and eight hours to research and plan your work. Any help that you receive will be recorded. It is perfectly acceptable for you to work with others during the research and planning stage, but you will not be able to submit group work for your final presentation. You must produce your own presentation. In all probability, the research and planning stage will be split up over several sessions, as you may need time between each session to receive information that you may have requested from a business or organisation.

You will be given at least three hours to write up the final presentation. Again, this might be divided up into more than one session. Your teacher or tutor will collect up anything that you have produced in these sessions and you will not be allowed to take it away with you. They will make sure that your work is kept safe and handed back to you at the beginning of the following session. You cannot expect to receive any help from your teacher or tutor during these sessions, as the sessions are carried out under examination conditions. So you will have to work independently, but under supervision.

Once the final presentation sessions are finished, and you have handed in the final version of your presentation, your school or college will mark your work according to AQA's marking criteria. Later, your work might be re-marked by an AQA examiner, just to make sure that your school or college has followed AQA's marking guidelines.

What are the scenario and tasks?

In the controlled assessment, you will be given a scenario. This sets the scene and explains the focus behind the research and planning tasks that you will have to carry out. You should make sure that in your final presentation, everything is relevant to the scenario.

Each task in the research and planning section tells you precisely what you need to do. This might be:

- carrying out actual research
- making some calculations, or
- thinking about particular aspects of the business and the way it does things.

The final presentation section tells you exactly what needs to be included, such as results of any research and your calculations, a clear conclusion and – most important – an evaluation of your work, which highlights the significance of any key findings that you have discovered.

How should I present my findings?

To achieve the best marks, analyse your findings and evaluate them in your conclusion – do not simply list them without comment. You will also be expected to structure and organise your work so that it is as clear as possible.

You will be able to use ICT, but you must make sure that your spelling, punctuation and grammar are as accurate as possible. You might also want to include a PowerPoint presentation as part of your final presentation. But it is important not to spend too much time focusing on this: content is much more important, as are your analysis and your evaluation.

You will have sufficient time to have carried out all the research and planning that you need. Three hours should be ample to pull all these pieces of information together, organise them properly, make them look presentable and then write up a good conclusion of your findings.

Preparation

YOU WILL FIND OUT:

- what you will need to do before the controlled assessment
- what skills will be assessed
- what Levels 0–4 are

What will I need to do before the controlled assessment?

AQA will release the controlled assessment towards the beginning of the spring term each year.

You will not be expected to do the Unit 3 controlled assessment until you have finished studying Unit 1. Once you have completed Unit 1, you will be in an ideal position to handle the controlled assessment. It really is nothing to panic about – you will be familiar with all the business terms and concepts needed for the controlled assessment.

The idea of the controlled assessment tasks is to make the assessment more valid and reliable than coursework. It actually makes the assessment much more manageable and far less time-consuming and stressful for everyone. It is also clearer that whatever you hand in as your final presentation is all your own work.

The work you will need to do for the controlled assessment means that:

- all the work you do for the controlled assessment will be under direct supervision
- any feedback you receive from your teacher or tutor will have to be noted
- you will have a limited amount of time to complete all your work
- while you can research and plan together, your final presentation has to be your own individual work
- you will have the same access to resources as everyone else in your group, so you will not be disadvantaged if you do not have a computer at home.

By the time you are shown the controlled assessment from AQA, your teacher or tutor will have made sure that you have covered all of the content from Unit 1. You will have had an opportunity to practise an investigation into a business, and all of the resources that you will need to be in place, ready for your research and planning and final presentation sessions.

Your teacher or tutor will explain the range of skills required to produce the best possible quality of work for the controlled assessment.

What skills will be assessed?

The controlled assessment is worth 25% of the overall GCSE, and 40 marks are available for the controlled assessment.

Although 40 marks are available for the controlled assessment, these marks are broken down and allocated to each assessment objective (AO):

AO1 (up to 12 marks)
By simply describing and showing your understanding of the information you have collected, you can only expect to receive a maximum of 12 marks. This shows that you can only recall, select and communicate your knowledge. This is AO1.

AO2 (up to 26 marks)
If you can apply your knowledge and understanding and show that you have been thorough, up to 14 more marks are available. This shows that you can apply your skills, knowledge and understanding in a variety of different ways. It also shows that you can plan and carry out investigations and tasks. This is AO2.

AO3 (up to 40 marks)
To access the other 14 marks available, you need to be able to produce a good conclusion. It must show analysis and include an evaluation that justifies and highlights the significance of your key findings. This demonstrates that you can analyse and evaluate information, then make reasoned judgements and present appropriate conclusions. This is AO3.

Sample answers

For example, suppose you are asked to identify an ideal location in your local area for a grocery convenience store and explain why it is an ideal place for this type of business.

Your answer could be straightforward and without detail, in which case you should not expect a particularly good mark. But if you were to identify the ideal location and explain why you have chosen it, then you are more likely to receive a higher mark.

Below are examples of AO1, AO2 and AO3 answers to this question. As you can see, the AO1 answer is not only brief, but does not have a great deal of detail. It makes no mention of any research that has been done.

The AO2 answer is better, but still not ideal. Very few business terms are used in the response. There are signs that research has been carried out, but the answer does not really make any use of this.

The AO3 answer not only contains business terms, which shows that the person who wrote it understands what they mean, but it also gives a reasoned answer. There is also judgement shown in the answer. The person obviously understands the relevance of what they have discovered.

What are Levels 0–4?

Each of the assessment objectives has different levels, from Level 0 to Level 4. These are used to judge just how good you are at providing evidence of each of the assessment objectives.

If you have not shown any particular evidence (or very little), then you will only receive a small number of marks. If you can show more evidence, then you will leap up the levels and access more marks for each of the assessment objectives.

SAMPLE ANSWERS

AO1

I would choose the housing estate off the A39 because lots of people live there and all the shops in the area have closed.

AO2

I would choose the housing estate off the A39 for the location of the convenience store. This is a highly populated area and there is likely to be a demand for a convenience store, although most families do the majority of their shopping at the larger supermarkets out of town. It would not be possible to compete on price, so customer service and convenience would be important factors in the success or failure of the business. I asked several people on the estate and they agreed with me.

AO3

I would choose the housing estate off the A39. Although there are no shops open in this area there are empty units, which should have relatively cheap rents and rates. Customer service and convenience are unique selling points for the business, rather than price and product range. My market research indicated that 70% of local residents were likely to use a convenience store for some of their shopping needs, particularly if a range of products, such as newspapers, Lottery tickets, top-up cards and fresh milk and bread were available. I have estimated that around 20,000 people live within the catchment area of the estate and that additional sales could be achieved if signs were placed on the A39 exits for passing traffic.

Research and planning

The tasks

In the research and planning section of the controlled assessment, there will be a number of tasks in a bulleted list. The tasks are the information-gathering phase of the controlled assessment, so it is important that you use whatever time you are given to collect as much relevant information as possible. They will tell you precisely what you need to do. They will relate directly to the scenario.

Keywords could include:

- **conduct** – carry out research to identify something about a business or the market
- **develop** – come up with ideas to help you build up a description of something, such as key selling points of a product or service

- **identify** – find out or discover something, such as an ideal location or the type of materials, equipment or services a business might need
- **calculate** – work out the costs of something and therefore the price, or the number of sales that a business might expect to achieve
- **estimate** – make a considered and calculated guess, perhaps on the level of sales or the amount of profit that a business might make.

Each of the tasks is a separate part of the controlled assessment. They are practical activities and are directly related to the subject matter of Unit 1. They will not be beyond your ability and there will be sufficient resources to help you carry them out.

Sample tasks

Below are some examples of research and planning tasks, with some suggestions as to what you could do.

SAMPLE TASKS

Conduct research to identify the service and the market for a business start-up idea to meet local needs.

First, you need to identify what is a local need. What type of service? Why is it needed and is it offered by any other existing businesses in the area? Who would the service be aimed at? In other words, what is the target market? How could you identify the size of that market and whether they would be interested in the service? Who are they buying from at the moment and how likely are they to switch over to a new business offering similar services?

Identify the location of the business.

What type of location does the business need? Where is the ideal location? Is it financially viable to set the business up in this location (cost of rent, rates, etc.)? Would compromises have to be made about the location due to costs and other factors? Does the business rely on passing trade? What are the transport implications? Does the business have to be near customers or suppliers?

Develop a unique selling point

Be clear about what a unique selling point is. In other words, is it a feature of the service or the way in which it is delivered that sets it apart from what is available and offered by competitors? Is it unique enough to make the service sufficiently different and more appealing to the market? Sometimes it is a good idea to ask the market what it would ideally like from a service and then see if that is possible to offer, basing the unique selling point on that feature.

230

Research and planning

You will be given between five and eight hours to carry out the necessary research to bring together all the information you will need for the tasks. It is important to use this time wisely and not to collect and hang onto information just for the sake of it. It needs to be relevant to the tasks, and it needs to be valuable to you when you produce your final presentation.

Your teacher or tutor can give you feedback, but they will record any assistance that they have given you. If there is anything that you do not understand, ask now! It will be too late by the final presentation time, when your teacher or tutor cannot give you any feedback.

In order to speed up the research and planning, you can work as a member of a group, but you will all need to make sure that you have copies of any information you have collected. When it comes to the final presentation, you cannot produce group work – it has to be your own individual work.

The controlled assessment will probably have at least six tasks for you to carry out. Some will take longer than others. Some will rely on the fact that you have collected the information already – and that you understand it – to help you carry out one of the later tasks.

Identify the materials and equipment the business will need.

What basic materials and equipment are needed for the day-to-day running of the business, including capital items and consumables? What products or materials will need to be held in stock for resale? How much will be needed? Where can these be sourced? Above all, how much will they cost?

Calculate the minimum price needed to be charged to cover the costs of the business.

You should now have an idea of the costs involved. Estimate the total cost of providing a particular service on a customer-by-customer basis. This can be calculated by adding up all the costs, estimating the number of customers and arriving at a total cost figure. The minimum price charged should be equal to the total costs.

Estimate the sales and profit for the business.

You need to assume that the business will not be interested in just covering its costs, but will want to make a profit. You therefore need to work out how many sales the business is likely to make. This needs to be realistic. You should then give reasons why you are adding a particular amount over and above the costs of the business as the final price that you will charge customers. You could apply a flat percentage (such as 20% on every sale), or you could decide that each transaction you make should produce a specific amount of profit for the business (such as £10 or £20).

For example

Unless you know what type of materials and equipment a business will need and their costs, you will be unable to work out the costs to the business. Nor will you be able to work out how much profit that business might make from a certain level of sales. You will not be able to estimate the level of sales unless you have identified the potential demand for that product or service.

The final presentation

YOU WILL FIND OUT:

● about making the best use of your time

● what you need to check before you hand in your work

Making the best use of your time

In the research and planning stage of the controlled assessment you will hopefully have collected sufficient information – and understood it – to be able to use the final presentation time wisely. You will already have seen what is required of you in the final presentation, and you may already have had the chance to produce a rough draft.

You will be given up to three hours to write up your findings. If you have special assessment requirements, you will be given extra time. Your school or college will decide whether you will be given a single three-hour period, or whether there will be more than one session.

You will not be allowed to take away with you anything that you produce during the final presentation. Your teacher or tutor will collect it in at the end of each session and look after it for you until the next session. Your teacher or tutor cannot give you any feedback

during the final presentation time. So if there is anything that you do not understand in the research and planning time, ask then – or it will be too late!

You must work independently. If you worked as part of a group during the research and planning stage, you need to make sure that that you have copies of everything that you prepared together.

The final presentation is carried out under exam conditions. You will be supervised all the time, but you will have access to any resources you need, such as a computer.

It is important to remember that the controlled assessment tests your decision-making skills. The examiner wants to see how you use data and information, and how you solve problems. They are also interested in how you analyse and evaluate what you have found out.

What you need to check before handing in your work

The final presentation section of the controlled assessment paper will tell you exactly what your presentation should contain. You must make absolutely sure that everything you have been asked to do is included in the work that you hand in at the end of the three hours. If anything is missing, you will not have provided sufficient evidence that you have organised your research, planning and presentation properly.

Sample contents

In the box on the right is an example of what might be needed in a final presentation and suggests what needs to be contained in it. It follows on from the sample tasks that we looked at on pages 230–1.

232

SAMPLE CONTENTS

The name of the business and the service you will be offering

Fairly straightforward, but you should probably indicate what type of business it is (its legal structure) and provide a brief list of the type of products or services that will be sold.

The results of your market research and how your service will meet a local need.

Briefly, how you identified a local need and how your market research proved or disproved that the local need did in fact exist. How will the service meet that need?

The expected income, expenditure and profit.

How did you work out the expected income of the business? What assumptions did you make and how did you work out the prices that you intend to charge? Likewise with the expenditure, what did you decide that the business needed to buy? How did you discover the costs? How did you arrive at the ideal profit margin? How was this calculated and what assumptions have you made when you have compared costs and income?

Unique selling point of the business.

How was this identified? Is it significant? Does it make the business sufficiently different from the competitors? Why might it be an attractive feature of the business, as far as customers are concerned?

A conclusion explaining why your business idea is a good one.

This is where the analysis and evaluation come in. You need to justify everything that you have said and any conclusions or assumptions you have made. What has been particularly relevant in your findings? Why are they so significant? How have these findings channelled your thinking? You may also identify areas of research that would have been more appropriate or conclusive, if the time had been available to you. Remember, it is not an evaluation of how you worked, but an evaluation of what you have found out. You could suggest recommendations or ways forward based on data or information that you have discovered.

You will also need to ensure that you include relevant business concepts, issues and terminology and show that you understand them. Do not fall into the trap of just dropping business terms into a sentence and thinking that this will do. You should use specialist terms frequently, but effectively. In the example above, say what a unique selling point is and do not assume that the examiner understands – explain it. You should also show that you understand the differences and the relationships between income, expenditure and profit.

Make sure that you have spelt everything correctly. Check your punctuation and grammar. They need to be as accurate as possible, because marks are awarded for these.

Headings are a good idea and so are bullet points. Page numbering is advisable. Use cross-references if you need to. For example, you can write in your presentation that your market research information can be found in a different section of your work. Above all, make sure that your work is well structured and well organised.

Evaluating your own findings

What is evaluation?

Assessment Objective 3 (AO3) requires you to analyse and **evaluate** evidence. It also requires you to make reasoned judgements and present appropriate conclusions. Overall, AO3 accounts for 35% of the GCSE; 8.75% of those marks are available in Unit 3, the controlled assessment.

So what is evaluation? It is showing that you understand the relative importance of the findings and ideas included in your answer. It is not sufficient just to list your findings. You need to comment on them, suggesting why some are more important or more fundamental than others. You need to explain how you have drawn conclusions on the basis of the findings. You can only do this by identifying those findings that suggest to you why a particular course of action or a particular set of circumstances, advantages or disadvantages – or even a figure that you have calculated – are of the greatest importance.

Good evaluation begins by making sure that you have all the key findings at your fingertips. You are required to structure your ideas and organise them in a clear and straightforward way. You then need to look at them carefully, analysing each one and deciding which of them is important and why. Explain why you have identified these as key findings:

- How have you ranked them in importance?
- What are their implications?
- Do the findings suggest a particular course of action? Why is that so?
- What might be the implications if that particular course of action were ignored?
- Could the business afford to ignore this?

Always use business terms in your evaluation. It shows that you have understood where the key findings fit into the overall picture and what they refer to, as well as what they may affect.

If you were asked to look at a business that produces luxury goods and decide whether there would be a demand for them in your local area, it would be a good idea to look at issues beyond taste and fashion.

You may want to look at the level of employment in the area and the average income. Home ownership might also be important. In order for customers to be able to afford to buy luxury goods, they need to have sufficient disposable income. This issue might be more important than how successful the business might be in marketing its luxury products, or how experienced its sales staff are.

A good evaluation would suggest that demand would be driven primarily by customers who have sufficient disposable income to afford the luxury products. If there are sufficient potential customers, then other issues (such as the marketing, sales staff, fashion, tastes, trends, local competitors, access and convenience, delivery and a host of other issues) might then also be relevant.

234

The five levels for Assessment Objective 3

AQA has identified five levels of response in AO3, which focus on the evaluation side of your answers:

THE FIVE LEVELS FOR AO3

Level 0

At Level 0, no marks are given because you have not made any conclusions. You have not analysed, nor have you evaluated.

Level 1

At Level 1, you have included some conclusions based on the information that you have collected. You have made some judgements, but have not really explained them. The examiner understands what you have said, but you have not developed your ideas. Also, you have hardly used any business terms. Your spelling, punctuation and grammar are a bit hit and miss, and you have not checked your work. The examiner would give you between 1 and 3 marks only for AO3.

Level 2

At Level 2, you have reached some simple conclusions based on the information you have collected. You have also made some judgements based on limited evidence and you have not highlighted the significance of the results of your investigations. Your work is reasonably well organised and structured. Spelling, punctuation and grammar are better, but there are still some mistakes. You have used some business terms but not very often. The examiner is likely to give you between 4 and 6 marks for AO3.

Level 3

At Level 3, you have made some appropriate conclusions based on a fair analysis of the information that you have collected. You have made a judgement about your findings and identified the significance of some of them. Your ideas are pretty well organised. Your spelling, punctuation and grammar are quite accurate, and you have used appropriate business terms where necessary. The examiner will probably give you between 7 and 10 marks for AO3.

Level 4

At Level 4, you have provided a range of good conclusions based on an analysis of your key findings. You have evaluated the information, and you have given a good justification for its significance. Your work is well structured and organised, clear and appropriate. Your spelling, punctuation and grammar are accurate. You have used business terms quite often and in the right place at the right time. The examiner would be able to give you between 11 and 14 marks for AO3.

Practice really does help. It is important to remember that all three units of this GCSE have AO3 marks available. The controlled assessment itself does not break down the marks available for each part of your presentation, so it is difficult to be precise about where you should evaluate. However, the big clue is in the fact that you will always be expected to present a conclusion. This is where you can make a judgement on the importance of your findings.

Understanding the marking criteria

YOU WILL FIND OUT:

- how the marking works
- about the five levels for AO1
- about the five levels for AO2
- about the AQA checklist

How the marking works

AQA will release a mark scheme that will be used by your teachers or tutors to identify acceptable answers and levels of response to tasks. This will ensure that everyone's work is marked in exactly the same way.

Teachers and tutors are trained by AQA to mark the tasks, but AQA will take a sample of the marking and double-check it. Your teacher or tutor will confirm to AQA that it is your own work. They will also double-mark, to make sure that the grades that you have been given are absolutely fair.

There are 40 marks available for Unit 3:

- By providing just a basic AO1 answer, you will only net a maximum of 30% of the available marks. For an AO1 answer, you are unlikely to get anything more than about an F grade for Unit 3.
- Another 14 marks are available if your answers are of AO2 standard. This now means that you are moving towards a C grade for Unit 3.
- In order to get a better grade than a C, you must include some analysis and evaluation. Another 14 marks are available if your answers are of AO3 standard.

Let's look in a little more detail at what is required for AO1 and AO2. (See page 235 for the five levels for AO3.)

The five levels for Assessment Objective 1

THE FIVE LEVELS FOR AO1

Level 0

If you have provided very little information and have not shown any understanding of business concepts, issues and terminology, then you will not be awarded any marks at all. This is Level 0.

Level 1

You have shown that you have collected some information but it is quite limited, and you have not really made an attempt to organise it. The examiner will not have seen that you really understand business concepts and issues, so the maximum they can award you is 3 marks.

Level 2

Your information collection is fairly limited, but you have made an attempt to organise your work. The examiner will be able to credit you for a limited understanding of business concepts, issues and terminology, so you can expect to get **4–6 marks**. At this point you are still only halfway towards getting the 12 marks available for AO1, so more effort is necessary.

Level 3

You have used a range of different sources and your information is relevant. Your work is far more organised, and the examiner can see that you have a good knowledge and understanding of business concepts, issues and terminology. As a result, you could get **7–9 marks**.

Level 4

Your work is much more relevant and detailed. You have used a wide range of sources. Your work is well organised and understandable. Above all, you have shown that you really do understand business concepts, issues and terminology. The examiner is likely to award you **10–12 marks**.

At AO1, you have simply shown that you can recall, select and communicate your knowledge and understanding. But you have not really applied anything yet, or shown that you understand the relevance of what you are saying in relation to the scenario of the controlled assessment. To do this, you need to be working at AO2 standard at least.

236

The five levels for Assessment Objective 2

AO2 is all about being able to apply your skills, knowledge and understanding. It also means showing that you can plan and carry out investigations and tasks.

Remember there are up to 14 marks available for AO2, in addition to the 12 marks that will automatically be awarded to you at AO1 Level 4, because by providing at AO2 level, the assumption is that you have already recalled, selected and communicated your knowledge and understanding.

THE FIVE LEVELS FOR AO2

Level 0

You have not applied your knowledge and understanding to your investigation, so you will not receive any additional AO2 marks.

Level 1

If you have made some attempt to apply your knowledge and understanding to your investigation, so you can receive up to another **3 marks**.

Level 2

You have really got to show that you can apply your skills, knowledge and understanding when you carry out the investigation and bring all of your pieces of work together. This can give you an extra **4–6 marks**.

Level 3

Plenty of marks are available at Level 3. You will have to show that you can really apply your skills, knowledge and understanding in your planning and the completion of the tasks. The examiner can then award you an extra **7–10 marks**.

Level 4

At Level 4 – the top end of AO2 – there are **11–14 marks** available. You will have to have effectively applied your skills, knowledge and understanding across all of the work you have handed in.

So you may have secured the 26 available marks for AO1 and AO2, but you really need to produce a decent conclusion, which includes analysis and evaluation, to get you those valuable AO3 marks (see page 235).

The AQA checklist

The guidelines above are general. For each of the controlled assessments, AQA will produce a checklist of everything they expect to see in your final presentation.

The checklist will include:

*   key business terms that AQA will expect you to use
*   acceptable and unacceptable ways of carrying out research
*   correct ways to calculate business figures, such as income, expenditure or profit
*   the kind of issues that AQA will expect you to highlight in your analysis and evaluation in the conclusion.

Don't forget that the examiner will also be looking at your use of English, including your spelling, punctuation and grammar.

Mock controlled assessment 1

Scenario

Your local area has been awarded a government grant of £50,000 to set up a social enterprise.

The social enterprise must provide a service that meets a local need and ideally offers work to the unemployed people.

Research and planning

You will need to:
- conduct research to identify the service and the market
- develop a way to recruit employees
- identify the ideal location of the social enterprise
- identify the materials and equipment the social enterprise will need
- calculate the minimum price you will need to charge to cover the costs of the social enterprise
- estimate the sales and the amount needed to break even.

Final presentation

Your presentation must be produced under controlled conditions. You will have up to **THREE** hours to complete this work. This can be split over a number of sessions supervised by your teacher.

Your presentation should contain:

- the name of the social enterprise and the service you will be offering
- the results of your market research and how your service will meet a local need
- an explanation of how you will recruit your employees
- your expected income and expenditure and whether you will break even
- a conclusion explaining why your social enterprise idea deserves to be awarded the grant.

You may use PowerPoint, but this should only be **a small part** of the presentation.

On the page opposite we will look at how you could begin to carry out the research and planning for this controlled assessment. It is important to remember that you can work together in this phase of the controlled assessment. This might be particularly useful if you have several different sources of information to investigate.

You should use your time wisely to organise your group properly, allocating tasks to each individual and agreeing when and how the information will be fed back to the rest of the group.

If you are working as a member of a group, it is vital that everyone has copies of information that each individual has collected, so that you all have a full picture. You need to make sure that this is done before the final presentation sessions, as by then it will be too late to share information.

You will be given 5–8 hours for the research and planning part of the controlled assessment. Every minute counts. There will be time to search the Internet, to contact local businesses or organisations and, perhaps, for your teacher or tutor to arrange for speakers to come in to give brief presentations to you.

Whatever is collected during the research and planning phase of the controlled assessment can be shared group work. But you must produce your own work when it comes to the final presentation. It is not simply a question of putting your name at the top of material that you have collected as a group and expecting this to be sufficient for your own presentation.

You might want to think about how you would go about collecting the necessary information you would need for this mock controlled assessment before you turn the page to see our suggestions for researching and planning it.

238

Research and planning

1 Conduct research to identify the service and the market

Every area has a local need that is not already being addressed by commercial businesses, charities or local government. It must be a service that you can make a charge for, to cover your costs. Remember that a social enterprise is not necessarily interested in profit, but it needs to generate enough funds to cover its costs and, perhaps, make a modest profit. They would reinvest this to ensure that new services can be offered and the social enterprise can continue to operate.

Ideally, a social enterprise would offer a service to a disadvantaged group, or perhaps a group that has been largely ignored. Sports and after-school activities, or services for the elderly or those who live alone are ideal examples. Local charities, community groups, local government and local newspapers will probably have a good idea as to what service is missing and could be offered by a social enterprise.

You may not have time to send out questionnaires to different groups. But you could design a questionnaire and ask people directly, either face-to-face or over the telephone. Work out what you need to know and only ask questions related to that. Focus on figuring out what type of service would be ideal for the local area, and the type of person who would use that service. You will also need to know if they would be prepared to make a small payment towards the costs of that service.

Using simple 'yes' or 'no' questions will not provide you with enough information. Ask more open questions to get opinions. To make sure that you get down all of the information, either record the answers on a tape recorder or make sure that at least two of you are writing down the responses to your questions.

2 Develop a way to recruit employees

One of the conditions of the grant is that you should provide work to unemployed people, so this may actually determine the type of service that you offer. You will need to know what type of skills unemployed people in the area are likely to have, so that you can use these skills. A good place to start would be Jobcentre Plus or the local authority, which will have an idea of how many people are unemployed and what kind of skills they might have. It will be perfectly possible to retrain people, but this will add to the costs. So avoid offering a service that requires highly skilled employees, as it may be impossible to find local unemployed people who have the necessary skills and experience.

You could recruit people through Jobcentre Plus. Jobcentre Plus will match unemployed people with job descriptions and identify whether or not they have the kind of skills that you are looking for. They can even screen some of the candidates for interview and then recommend the best ones to you, leaving you to make a final decision.

There are, of course, other ways of recruiting, such as placing advertisements in local newspapers or using the media to encourage people to contact you direct.

3 Identify the ideal location of the social enterprise

The location of the social enterprise will very much depend on whether the customers will be coming to you or whether you will be going to the customers. If the customers come to you, then you need to be in a convenient location that is easy to get to by foot or by public transport. If you go out to the customers, then the location is not so important, but it may mean buying vehicles or somehow arranging for your employees to get to the customers.

The type of service you are offering will affect the amount of space you need in a building. Larger buildings in prominent positions are expensive; smaller ones in more out-of-the-way places tend to be far cheaper. Local estate agents and local newspapers will have lists of available commercial properties, and will be able to tell you whether they are for sale, lease or rent, and the costs involved.

4 Identify the materials and equipment the social enterprise will need

As you will be offering a service, you will not need to buy in a great deal of stock – just materials and equipment to run the operation. You may, however, need vehicles and equipment to provide the service. Use local newspapers to work out the cost of vehicles, and remember that everything has a running cost – vans need to be serviced and they need fuel, as well as road tax, MOTs and insurance.

5 Calculate the minimum price you will need to charge to cover the costs of the social enterprise

A social enterprise is not concerned with making a large profit; it needs to make enough to cover its costs and a little bit extra. Your target market is not likely to be able to afford high prices. So you need to set your prices according to what your market can afford and to enable you to just cover your costs. Charging too high a price will mean that your target market will not be able to afford to use your services. No matter how valuable that service may be, the social enterprise could fail.

Calculate your total costs, estimate the number of customers, divide your total costs by the number of customers and this will give you a cost per customer that you will need to cover.

6 Estimate the sales and the amount needed to break even

The sales and the amount needed to break even must be realistic. Very few new businesses, even social enterprises, attract all of a market – or even a large part of it – at the beginning. It is a slow growth period. As news of the service spreads around the local area, more potential customers will contact the social enterprise or will be interested if the social enterprise contacts them.

Remember that your sales are equal to the total number of customers multiplied by the price charged. In order to break even, the social enterprise needs to cover its total costs by this sales figure. In other words, break-even is when the income of the social enterprise is equal to its expenditure.

239

Mock controlled assessment 2

Scenario

Your local council is offering a number of rent-free and rate-free (for two years) shop units in your area, to encourage new businesses to set up.

They are also offering a £10,000 grant (repayable after two years) to each of these new businesses.

They require you to produce a business plan to qualify for the scheme.

Research and planning

You will need to:

- conduct market research to identify products or services and the market
- develop a draft business plan, including business aims and objectives
- identify the ideal location for the business
- identify the materials and equipment the business will need
- estimate the sales and profit for the business
- calculate whether the business will be in a position to repay the £10,000 after two years.

Final presentation

Your presentation must be produced under controlled conditions. You will have up to **THREE** hours to complete this work. This can be split over a number of sessions supervised by your teacher.

Your presentation should contain:

- the name of the business and the products and services you will be offering
- an outline business plan, including the business aims and objectives
- the expected income, expenditure and profit
- whether the business will have generated enough profit after two years to pay back the £10,000
- a conclusion, explaining why your business deserves to be part of the scheme.

You may use PowerPoint, but this should only be a small part of the presentation.

On the opposite page we will look at how you could begin to carry out the research and planning for this controlled assessment. It is important to remember that you can work together in this phase of the controlled assessment. This might be particularly useful if you have several different sources of information to investigate.

You should use your time wisely to organise your group properly, allocating tasks to each individual and agreeing when and how the information will be fed back to the rest of the group.

If you are working as a member of a group, it is vital that everyone has copies of information that each individual has collected, so that you all have a full picture. You need to make sure that this is done before the final presentation sessions, as by then it will be too late to share information.

You will be given 5–8 hours for the research and planning part of the controlled assessment. Every minute counts. There will be time to search the Internet, to contact local businesses or organisations and, perhaps, for your teacher or tutor to arrange for speakers to come in to give brief presentations to you.

Whatever is collected during the research and planning phase of the controlled assessment can be shared group work. But you must produce your own work when it comes to the final presentation. It is not simply a question of putting your name at the top of material that you have collected as a group and expecting this to be sufficient for your own presentation.

You might want to think about how you would go about collecting the necessary information you would need for this mock controlled assessment before you turn the page to see our suggestions for researching and planning it.

Research and planning

1 Conduct market research to identify products or services and the market

In order to be successful, the business needs to offer either products or services for which there is a local demand. It could include products or services that cater for a niche market. This is probably more likely, as existing businesses will already be providing products and services for mass markets.

Try to profile your ideal customer, and estimate how many exist in your local area. One good way to identify a potential demand is to create a brief questionnaire and use it to ask a number of people what sorts of products and services they would like to buy but find difficult to locate in the local area. You can then choose the range of products and services that are in greatest demand.

2 Develop a draft business plan, including business aims and objectives

You do not have to create a complete business plan. You just need to be aware of the content of a business plan. Think about the areas of information that the local council would expect to see in a business plan. This will help you focus on:

- how you will market your products
- how you have identified a demand
- how you will sell your products and services
- your pricing structure
- what kind of premises you will need
- the costs involved.

Most important are the business aims and objectives. You will have seen typical aims and objectives in Unit 1, such as survival, profit, market share and customer satisfaction. Make a brief statement of the business aims and objectives. These need to fit the type of business that you are intending to set up.

3 Identify the ideal location for the business

The location will depend on the type of business. If you were setting up a small convenience store, for example, then a shop unit nowhere near housing would be inappropriate. It would also be inappropriate for you to have a remote shop if the bulk of your customers did not have transport or you were not near a transport route. If you are relying on customers coming into the shop unit, there needs to be considerable passing trade.

There may be reasons why the shop units are empty. For example:

- they may be in too remote a position and not easily seen by potential customers
- there may be no parking nearby
- there may be no bus stops near them
- many of the other shops in the area may have closed down.

Choosing the location is very important and can mean the difference between success and failure of a new business.

4 Identify the materials and equipment the business will need

This will depend on the type of business. If you are offering products and services, you will need to buy in stock. Identify where you will get this from. If you are offering a service, then materials and equipment will be more limited, but you still need to identify and source them.

Make sure that you include costs. This will be important when you have to estimate your expenditure and, ultimately, your profit and whether or not you will be able to pay back the £10,000 at the end of the two years.

5 Estimate the sales and profit for the business

You will not have to create a cash-flow forecast, but you should try to estimate how many products and services you will sell, certainly over the first two years.

You will already know your costs. To work out the value of your sales, you will need to have added a margin to those costs to contribute to your profits. Your profits each year are equal to the difference between your expenditure and your income. If your income is greater than your expenditure, then this is profit. If your expenditure exceeds your income, then you will need to adjust your prices to create a realistic profit. A business cannot afford to operate at a loss.

Remember, you will need to have generated at least £10,000 of profit by the end of the second year in order to pay back the grant.

6 Calculate whether the business will be in a position to repay the £10,000 after two years

This can be calculated fairly easily. Calculate your profit for the first year and then assume (justifying your assumptions) that your sales will go up in the second year, so your profit should be higher. You need to make sure that your total profit over the two years is at least £10,000.

It is important to remember that you will need to pay yourself. You cannot be expected to run a business for any length of time without some form of reward. You will also need to reinvest in the business some of the profit that you have made, to help it grow. You will have to replace stock, equipment and materials.

Any figures that you suggest should be realistic. It is unlikely that the examiner would accept that you would make tens of thousands of pounds profit, but if you can justify your figures, no matter what they are, then the examiner will accept the fact that you have thought it all through.

Although you do not have to produce a business plan, you could use the headings from a business plan to help you structure your final presentation. This will give you a helpful checklist.

The name of the business and the products and services offered are important. Remember to identify the business aims and objectives. Be realistic about your income, expenditure and profit. Ridiculous figures that show you will make a fortune will alert the examiner to the fact that you have not done a thorough job and that you are being over-optimistic. A highly optimistic business plan is as unlikely to impress as a pessimistic one.

And last but not least, don't forget to include a conclusion. Explain why your business idea deserves to be part of the scheme. Highlight your key findings and show why they are so significant. Also stress that you will be in a position to pay back the £10,000. It is worthwhile mentioning that you will also be in a position to pay rent and rates after two years, as this part of the offer ends at the end of that period as well. This would be an additional expenditure.

Picture credits

The publishers would like to thank the following for permission to reproduce images in this book.

Index

Bold page numbers refer to key term definitions.

247